125 YEARS of BAR none
WOMEN LAWYERS in ILLINOIS

Edited and compiled by
Gwen Hoerr McNamee

Published by the
Chicago Bar Association
Alliance for Women
321 South Plymouth Court
Chicago, Illinois 60604-3997

Copy Editors:
Karen Clanton,
Julie Melvin,
Patricia R. McMillen
and Gwen Hoerr McNamee

Sponsorship Development:
Jennifer Fischer

Advertising Representative:
Joseph Tarin

Organized by the
Chicago Bar Association
Alliance for Women

Co-Chairs, Alliance for Women:
Elizabeth Turley
and Janet Koran

Co-Chairs, 125th Anniversary Project:
Honorable Elaine Bucklo
and Gwen Hoerr McNamee

Designed and Printed by
ABS Graphics

Sponsored by
Lexis-Nexis

CONTENTS

PREFACE

This book, and the Chicago Public Library exhibit which it accompanies, began in 1994 as a labor of love to celebrate from a historical perspective the 125th anniversary of women lawyers in Illinois. Acting on a suggestion from Laurel Bellows, founder and Chair of the Alliance for Women, and from the Honorable Elaine Bucklo, United States District Court Judge and Alliance Member, I began an inquiry into women's history by trying to establish a definitive list of the first one hundred women to join the bar in the state of Illinois.

When Judge Bucklo first requested such a list from the Illinois Attorney Registration and Disciplinary Committee, the ARDC reported that in the nineteenth century, the clerk of the Supreme Court recorded the names of women who were admitted to the Illinois bar on pink cards. The list of the first one hundred lawyers so recorded, however, included two men and omitted over half a dozen women noted elsewhere as having earned their Illinois license. It took the next year to produce an accurate list, which now appears in the center pages of this book. Along the way, it became clear that the history of women lawyers in Illinois had yet to be written. Further exploration soon revealed a rich and compelling story of courage, creativity, and perseverance that had a transformative effect on the legal profession.

In 1995, Judge Bucklo and I formed the 125th Anniversary Project Committee to celebrate the lives and work of the early women lawyers. Mary Dempsey, Commissioner of the Chicago Public Library Center (and herself an attorney), enthusiastically agreed to hold and facilitate an exhibit at the Harold Washington Library. An appeal to the Chicago Bar Association's Alliance for Women yielded the other principal volunteers on the dual projects.

The individual authors of each biography contained in this volume are for the most part, law students, professors, and practicing attorneys who were asked to volunteer their time to make both the exhibit and the book a reality. Lawyers accustomed to drafting contracts and arguing cases entered archives, visited historical societies and became census researchers. One of these lawyers, Patricia McMillen, after an initial assignment—the biography of Catharine van Valkenburg Waite which appears herein—completed many additional assignments related to both the exhibit and the book and made a substantial contribution to the structure of both. Slowly, through the work of Patricia and many others, the book and exhibit took form.

The reader will quickly note that not all of the first one hundred Illinois women lawyers have been treated at length in this book. In one sense, of course, this is not unusual: history has always accorded more attention to some lives than to others. Sadly, however, during research, it became inescapably clear that only the barest records of many women's lives would be found in time for this book. Still, I hope that through continued, creative, and persistent effort, some of the remnants of these lives will yet be uncovered.

The book is organized around the key subject areas which form the backbone of the Chicago Public Library exhibit. Following an introductory chapter, the first section of the book sets forth the historical struggle of women to gain the right to practice law in Illinois; this section is followed by biographies of Myra Colby Bradwell, Alta May Hulett, and Ada Miser Kepley, each of whom played a primary role in that struggle.

Each following chapter introduces a subject area—from making a living in the law to political and social reform activities—followed by biographies of women whose activities exemplify that subject area while also representing diverse approaches to the subject. Of course, none of the women studied was easily or strictly categorizable. As is the case for women lawyers today, each of our forebears engaged in a full spectrum of activities. Nevertheless, this book outlines the biographies of our predecessors within the subject areas in which they made substantial strides for women lawyers.

In addition to the authors whose by-lines appear in this book, countless archivists, librarians, living descendants of Illinois' early women lawyers, and other individuals, throughout the state of Illinois and beyond have been essential to the preparation of both this book and of the Chicago Public Library exhibit.

While it is, of course, impossible to name each such individual contributor, I particularly would like to note with appreciation the contributions of the following:

Charlotte Adelman, Marion Atarod, Amy Brock, Helen Burke, Christine Clark, Fay Clayton, Jennifer Fischer, Wendy Grossman, the Honorable Helen Gunnarrson, the Honorable Sophia H. Hall, Susan Horn, Mia Jiganti, the Honorable Joan Humphrey Lefkow, Mary von Mandel, Terrence Murphy, Patricia Nikolitch, Bridget O'Keefe, Ellen Partridge, the Honorable Aurelia Pucinski, Mary Hutchings Reed, Amalia Rioja, Esther R. Rothstein, Jemi Sager-Millen, Susan Salita, Kaarina Salovaara, Patricia Costello Slovak, Professor Julie Spanbauer, Professor Rebecca Tannenbaum, Elizabeth Turley, the Honorable Ann C. Williams, Zeophus Williams, Lexis Nexis, ABS Graphics, Mary Ann Bamberger and Patricia Bakunas of the University of Illinois at Chicago Library Special Collections Department, Archivist Archie Motley of the Chicago Historical Society, Assistant Dean Susan O'Brien of Chicago Kent Law School, John Molyneaux of the Rockford Public Library, the LaSalle County Historical Society, the Reddick Library, Laurel Quaid of the McLean County Historical Society, Phil Germann of the Historical Society of Quincy and Adams County, Phil Lewis of the Effingham Regional Historical Society, Lloyd Patton of the Historical Society of Washington County, the Carroll County Genealogical Society, Mel Schroeder of the Joliet Area Historical Society and Museum, the St. Clair County Historical Society, the Greene County Historical and Genealogical Society, Alan Walker of the McDonough County Historical Society, Anne Chandler of the Kankakee County Historical Society Museum, Robert S. Jordan of the LaSalle County Genealogy Guild, Nancy Huntley of the Lincoln Library, the John Marshall Law School Library, the Illinois State Historical Library, the Illinois State Archives, Keith Letcshe, Marielen Martin, the American Bar Association Commission on Women in the Profession, the Benton Historical Society, the Lombard Historical Society, Caroline Sexauer, the Sophia Smith Collection at Smith College, the Schlesinger Library at Radcliffe College, the Cook County Law Library, the Northwestern University School of Law, the National Association of Women Lawyers, the Women's Bar Association of Illinois, the University of Illinois Law Library, Calumet High School, Titus M. Karlowicz of the Western Illinois University Library, the Wilmette Historical Museum, William Broom and the Mabel M. Broom Collection, the Bentley Historical Library University of Michigan, the Third District of the Illinois Appellate Court in Ottawa, Illinois, the State Historical Society of Iowa, the United States Supreme Court Curator's Office, and the University of Illinois at Chicago Women in History Group.

I extend special gratitude to Drs. Rima Lunin Schultz, Katrin Schultheiss and Leo Schelbert for their insight and guidance, which significantly enhanced the content of this book. I am deeply indebted to the assistance of the staff of the Special Collections Division of the Harold Washington Library, and particularly to Andrea Telli and Elizabeth Holland. I am also grateful for the significant contributions of Karen Clanton and Julie Melvin. Above all I thank Patricia McMillen for her insight, vision, attention to detail, dedication to this project and personal support.

Finally, I thank Dennis, for his colossal support that enabled the culmination of this project and Jack and Sadie for the joy they add to my life.

To the memory of the early women lawyers, and in hopes that their accomplishments may be remembered for generations to come, I dedicate this book.

Gwen Hoerr McNamee
March 1998

INTRODUCTION

by Gwen Hoerr McNamee

American women first organized in 1848 in Seneca Falls, New York to protest the legal restrictions that denied them their rights to vote, have access to education, and participate in most occupations. Married women, who faced even more restrictions than single women, demanded the rights to own property, sign contracts, control their wages, and have custody rights to their children. Though church and state told women to stay home, those who needed to work for wages worked as domestic servants or in factories. After the Civil War, when the federal government passed amendments that deemed formerly enslaved men to be citizens and ensured equal protection and the right to vote to citizens regardless of race, women asked whether these rights applied to them.

In the twenty years after Seneca Falls, women gained some limited rights. A few colleges were opened to middle and upper class women, and some of these women read law in the offices of sympathetic male lawyers. Finally, in 1869 women's rights advocates challenged the laws that barred them from the legal profession. Due to the efforts of Myra Bradwell, Ada Kepley, and Alta Hulett, women in Illinois triumphed in 1873 when Alta Hulett was admitted as the first woman lawyer in the state. There were one hundred Illinois women lawyers by 1901.

The ensuing first generation of women lawyers in Illinois, though a small percentage of all Illinois lawyers, influenced the legal profession as they used their training to advance the cause of all women. They formed partnerships, served clients and used their legal expertise to shape social and political policy. These women were neither uniform in their methods nor in their goals. Most did practice law. Some established law offices and sought a living practicing law for paying clients. Some gave advice on business and real estate transactions while others prosecuted and defended criminals. Some women also formed associations to provide the professional, practical, and emotional support they needed to participate in this predominantly male profession.

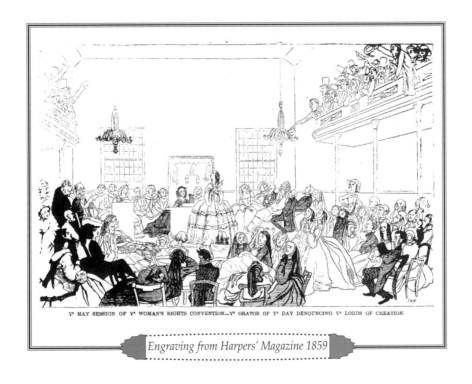

Yᵉ MAY SESSION OF Yᵉ WOMAN'S RIGHTS CONVENTION—Yᵉ ORATOR OF Yᵉ DAY DENOUNCING Yᵉ LORDS OF CREATION.

Engraving from Harpers' Magazine 1859

Perhaps most significantly, however, women used their legal knowledge and skills to advance reforms that specifically assisted women and children. Working closely with other social reformers in Illinois, early women lawyers offered legal representation for women and children, drafted and enforced protective labor legislation, established the nation's first juvenile court, and created innovative placement options for young girls who were brought before the court.

Women lawyers also used their legal expertise to obtain the vote for all women. At a time when woman suffragists were challenging definitions of citizenship, women lawyers were allowed direct participation in a system that restricted their freedom in explicit and ancillary ways.

In 1900, as now, lawyers were prominent in political life, too; thus women lawyers sought election to political office and the judiciary. With women lawyers in the legislature, the mayor's office and on the bench, women changed not only the face of politics but its focus.

In Illinois, as elsewhere, there were women who chose a different path. Some who earned their law degree and were admitted to the bar pursued alternative careers. In some cases, their legal training and professional status allowed them to advance within their alternative careers: women educators became principals, women in business more effectively managed their affairs, and women writers came to edit their own legal journals. At least one of the first one hundred women lawyers in Illinois abandoned the law altogether and established a successful career practicing medicine instead. The various paths of women trained in law highlights the breadth of impact they were able to make.

Needless to say, the first women lawyers in Illinois needed and received the support of sympathetic men and institutions. Chicago was unique in having prior to 1900 four law schools that opened their doors to women students. The day-to-day lives of this first generation of women lawyers in Illinois were also filled with smaller, more mundane issues: deciding what to wear, finding a place to eat lunch, and finding a bathroom to use. Through their solutions, women lawyers changed the physical space as well as the procedural and intellectual landscape of the profession.

The pages that follow tell the stories of some of the women who accomplished these feats and made these changes. While it is true that many achieved great victories, perhaps, as Julia Lathrop remarked when Mary Bartelme was sworn in as the first woman judge in Illinois, it was their day-to-day service that is the most important. Lathrop quoted Justice Oliver Wendell Holmes who once remarked,

> My keenest interest is excited not by what are called great questions and great cases, but by little decisions which the common run of selectors would pass by because they do not deal with the constitution or a telephone company, yet which have in them the germ of some wider theory, and therefore some profound interstitial change in the very tissue of law. (Lathrop Speech, [1923] Mary Bartelme Papers)

The history of the first generation of women lawyers in Illinois is full of triumphs and defeats, but it was their perseverance, their day-to-day dedication to the fight, that opened the profession to women and changed many of the laws that govern our lives.

THE FIGHT TO GAIN ENTRANCE

In June 1869, after graduating as valedictorian from Iowa Wesleyan and studying law in her brother's office, Arabella Mansfield was admitted to the Iowa bar without objection, the first licensed woman lawyer in the United States. Two months later, Myra Bradwell - the founder and editor of the *Chicago Legal News* - was denied admission to the Illinois bar on the grounds that she was a woman. The court initially sent Bradwell a letter stating that she could not be a lawyer because she was a married woman. Bradwell published the note in her paper along with a legal brief challenging the ruling. The court then issued a formal opinion that, married or not, Bradwell was denied admission because she was a woman. The court ruled that because the statute controlling bar admissions used the male pronoun "he", women were to be excluded. In 1870, Bradwell appealed her case to the United States Supreme Court. While her case was pending, two other women sought admission to the Illinois bar, Alta Hulett from Rockford and Ada Kepley from Effingham. Kepley had graduated in 1870 from the University of Chicago Law School, the first woman law school graduate in the country. Both were refused admission because of their sex.

After her application was denied, and while Bradwell's case was on appeal, Alta Hulett decided to try a different approach to gain entrance to

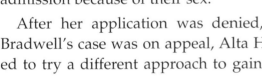

Arabella Babb Mansfield
State Historical Society of Iowa

the bar. Inspired by the recent advances in legislation that allowed women in Illinois to own their wages, Hulett resolved to change the law. With the assistance of Bradwell and Kepley, Hulett drafted a bill that prohibited sex as a bar to any occupation or profession and delivered her speech "Justice versus the Supreme Court" throughout the state, winning support for her cause. On March 22, 1872, the Illinois legislature passed her bill enacting the first anti-sex-discrimination law in the country.

In 1873, the Supreme Court finally ruled in Bradwell's case, upholding the denial of her license by reasoning that the standards for admission to the bar were for each state to decide. Justice Bradley wrote a concurring opinion agreeing with the decision that denied Bradwell her license, and arguing that divine law supported the ruling. He wrote that women by their nature were to be wives and mothers and were unfit to practice in the professions. Chief Justice Salmon P. Chase, appointed to the court by President Abraham Lincoln, was the sole dissenting justice.

Revealed in the following biographies of Bradwell, Hulett and Kepley is the final chapter in the fight to gain entrance and the beginning of the story of what happened after these harbingers opened the legal profession to women.

MYRA COLBY BRADWELL

By Caroline Goddard and Gwen Hoerr McNamee

A tireless advocate of women's rights, Myra Colby Bradwell was well known for her outstanding abilities in both legal and social reform circles. Her progressive stance on such issues as married women's property rights, suffrage, political reform, and the legal profession served to make her one of the most influential women of the nineteenth century.

Myra Colby was born in Manchester, Vermont on February 12, 1831, the youngest of five children born to Eben and

Abigail Hurd (Willey) Colby. Shortly after Myra's birth, the Colbys moved to Portage, New York, and in 1843, settled in the township of Schaumburg, Illinois. Active abolitionists, the Colbys taught Myra early the responsibility to fight against injustice.

Intelligent and ambitious, Myra Colby took advantage of the new opportunities opening for women to receive higher education. Female seminaries began appearing in the 1830s in the eastern and midwestern United States and increased in number after the Civil War. The seminaries principally prepared women to teach, as the demand for schoolteachers was increasing sharply. Thus, after studying first in Kenosha, Wisconsin, and then at the ladies' seminary in Elgin, Illinois, in 1851 Colby began her career as a schoolteacher.

On May 18, 1852, Myra Colby married James Bolesworth Bradwell of Palatine, Illinois. James Bradwell had been born in Loughborough, Leicester, England on April 6, 1828, and emigrated with his family in 1829, settling in Jacksonville, Illinois, where James was educated in the public schools. James Bradwell had furthered his education by studying law and taking a partial course at Knox College. He began practicing law while he was still a student.

Shortly after their marriage, Myra and James Bradwell moved to Memphis, Tennessee, where they opened a private school and worked as instructors. In 1854, they returned to Illinois, settling in Chicago, where they would reside until their deaths. Their first child was born that year, and although three more followed, only two survived: Thomas (b. 1856) and Bessie (b. 1858). James Bradwell continued his legal education in Chicago and in 1855, he was admitted to the Illinois bar. He entered into a partnership with a brother-in-law, built up a practice, and in 1861 was elected a Cook County judge. He was re-elected in 1865.

Myra Colby Bradwell

From F.B. Wilke *The Chicago Bar* (1872) Chicago Historical Society

Since the early years of their marriage, Myra Bradwell had been reading law under her husband's guidance, but her study was now interrupted by the Civil War. She was active in relief work for wounded soldiers and their families and was prominent in the Chicago branch of the Sanitary Commission, formed in 1861 to assist the Union Army. In addition to donating food, clothing , and medical supplies, women throughout the North and West held bazaars and fairs to raise money to support the Union hospitals; the 1863 Sanitary Fair held in Chicago raised $86,000, and the Fair held in 1865 raised $250,000.

After the war, Bradwell resumed her legal studies. In 1868, after securing the special permit then necessary for a woman to open a business in the state of Illinois, Bradwell established Chicago's only weekly legal newspaper, the *Chicago Legal News*. The Bradwells also set up a printing, binding, and publishing company that worked in tandem with the newspaper. From the first issue, dated October 3, 1868, Bradwell used her paper to report court decisions, advocate reforms to the legal profession, and support women's rights, paying special attention to women's growing participation in the legal profession. On February 27, 1869, Bradwell reported that Mary E. Magoon

was a practicing jury lawyer in North English, Iowa. The following year, she noted the admission of Arabella Mansfield, a married woman, to the Iowa Bar.

When Chicago was incorporated in 1837, a white man desiring licensure as an attorney only needed to show that he had studied law under a reputable attorney and then pass an informal oral examination in front of a presiding county judge. In May of 1869, new standards for admission to the bar were instituted, requiring in addition to the oral examination that the applicant submit either a law degree from a recognized law school or a certificate from a practicing attorney stating the applicant had studied law for two consecutive years, at least six months of which were spent in Illinois. These new admission requirements, which would be further revised and strengthened over the next decade, were lauded by the *American Law Review* as an example of the positive movement to professionalize the field.

On August 2, 1869, Myra Bradwell satisfied the new requirements and received her certificate of oral examination, qualifying her to enter the practice of law in Illinois. She thereupon applied to the Illinois Supreme Court for admission to the bar. Wary that her sex might be viewed as a barrier to her admittance, Bradwell accompanied her application with a brief supporting her admission. Bradwell explained that the governing statute did not specify being male as a requirement to be an attorney in Illinois. She acknowledged that the statute did use the male pronoun "he," but argued that Chapter 90, section 28 of the *Illinois Revised Statutes* specified that "when any party or person is described or referred to by words importing the masculine gender, females as well as males shall be deemed to be included."

The court, however, summarily denied Bradwell's license, ordering the clerk of the court to send a letter so informing Bradwell, without rendering a formal opinion in the case. Bradwell published the court's letter in the *Chicago Legal News*. The letter indicated that Bradwell's application was denied because she was a married woman. The court was referring to the law of coverture, a principle under which the husband and wife's legal existence are merged into one, and a married woman needed her husband's signature to make any legal transaction binding. Since she would not be bound by contractual obligations made only between herself and her clients, a married woman thus could not, logically, practice law.

Bradwell countered the court's argument by re-petitioning, filing a second brief arguing that most married women's legal disabilities had been removed by recently enacted laws. While awaiting the court's decision, on January 2, 1870, Bradwell — anticipating an adverse decision from the Illinois court — submitted an additional brief setting forth two federal constitutional claims: first, that the denial of her application on the basis of her marital status violated the Equal Protection Clause of the Fourteenth Amendment (which had been ratified on July 9, 1868, just a year before Bradwell's initial application for an Illinois law license) and, second, that the state had violated the Privileges and Immunities Clause of the Fourth Article of the U.S. Constitution. These two claims would later allow Bradwell to appeal to the United States Supreme Court.

The Illinois Supreme Court again denied Bradwell's application, this time in a formal opinion arguing that, married or not, she could not practice law because she was a woman. Bradwell published the court's decision in the *Chicago Legal News*. Justice

The Waite Court, c. 1873 — 1877

Photographer S. M. Fassett, Collection of the Supreme Court of the United States

Lawrence's majority opinion reasoned that the legislature never intended women to be admitted to the bar. If Bradwell were to be admitted, Lawrence wrote, there could be disastrous repercussions: "every civil office in this state may be filled with women." The court, said Lawrence, was not prepared to open the office of governor, judge or sheriff to women.

Bradwell appealed the Illinois decision to the United States Supreme Court, retaining Wisconsin Senator Matthew H. Carpenter as her attorney. Carpenter based his argument on the Privileges and Immunities Clause of the Fourteenth Amendment arguing that Illinois could not abridge the right of citizens to practice their chosen profession. The Court considered Bradwell's case as a test of the breadth of the new Fourteenth Amendment and withheld ruling on Bradwell's case for three years while they considered the Louisiana Slaughterhouse cases, which required an interpretation of the same amendment.

While Bradwell's case was pending, she and her husband James offered their assistance to Alta Hulett, an aspiring attorney from Rockford, Illinois. Hulett, who had also been denied a law license by the Illinois Supreme Court, decided to draft legislation enabling women to be admitted to the Illinois bar.

On April 15, 1873, the Court affirmed Illinois' decision denying Bradwell a law license, ruling that the right to practice law was not a privilege covered under the Fourteenth Amendment. Although Hulett's anti-discrimination provision had, meanwhile, become Illinois law on March 22, 1872, Bradwell refused to reapply to the bar under the new law. As James Bradwell recounted after his wife's death, "[Myra Bradwell] felt that if the court could not take the matter up again, she would not ask them to do it." (*Chicago Legal News* vol. 26 [1895] p. 208, 210). (In 1890, when Bradwell was fifty-nine and travelling in Mexico, the Illinois Supreme Court, at the urging of James Bradwell, would at last act on his wife's original motion of 1869 and admit Bradwell to the Illinois bar. Two years later she was also admitted to practice before the Supreme Court of the United States.)

As a result of the denial of her law license, the *Chicago Legal News* became the focal point of Bradwell's legal career. A brilliant success from the start, the *Chicago Legal News* quickly became the most prominent legal newspaper in the Midwest, known for its broad and judicious coverage of the legal news of the entire country. For twenty-five years, Bradwell discussed and evaluated opinions of lawyers and the courts, as well as new legislation. She advocated such reforms as regulation of railroads, local zoning ordinances, improved court procedures and courtrooms, and implementation of new and better standards in the legal profession. Bradwell also addressed such issues as temperance, prison reform, and the rights of women.

As the debate over women's rights unfolded, Bradwell's *Chicago Legal News* became an arena in which vying concepts of women's place and powers were argued and developed. The traditions of domesticity and motherhood led many people to argue for women's participation in the political world as an extension of their role within the household. Still others argued for women's increased power in society based upon the belief that there were no intellectual differences between men and women; they argued for a public role for women based upon citizenship and equality.

Drawing from these two views, Bradwell proposed that although men and women were different, relegation of women to the household sphere should not be the end result of this difference. She insisted that women deserved a greater role in the public arena, arguing that to think otherwise constituted immoral and irresponsible behavior on men's part in particular, and society's in general. As rational and honorable citizens, men had a duty to recognize their fellow female citizens' capabilities.

THE FIGHT TO GAIN ENTRANCE

As the drive for women's rights increased, gaining the franchise became of increasing importance to Bradwell. Chicago's first two woman suffrage conventions were held simultaneously in February, 1869; both conventions sought the vote for women, but they differed on issues of strategy. Myra and James Bradwell attended the convention arranged by Mary Livermore and featuring Elizabeth Cady Stanton and Susan B. Anthony, who took the position that woman suffrage and black suffrage should be made inseparable. Bradwell, while supporting both black and female enfranchisement, believed woman suffrage would be delayed if the two campaigns were united. Nevertheless, when the Illinois Woman Suffrage Association (IWSA) was established at the end of the Stanton/Anthony convention, Mary Livermore was its first president and Myra Bradwell the corresponding secretary. Bradwell would continue to serve on the IWSA's executive committee for many years, and at its initial convention, was selected (along with Livermore and Kate Doggett) to be a representative to the Equal Rights Association convention scheduled for May.

Immediately after the February convention, the IWSA began its work. Both Myra and James Bradwell served on the legislative committee, which first lobbied for a bill giving married women the right to control their own wages. The bill passed the Illinois legislature in a month's time, becoming law on March 24, 1869. This was the second of the Illinois Married Women's Property Acts, the first passed in 1861 to allow married women the right to ownership of their separate property brought to a marriage. In Bradwell's view, these advances in married women's property rights provided a foundation for the promotion of woman suffrage. As ownership of property expanded women's legal independence, Bradwell was certain that women's concerns would start to cross the boundaries of the household into the need for full recognition and participation in politics.

Bradwell's paper recorded women's progress in other states and territories, praising Wyoming and its politicians, for example, for giving women the vote. In 1891, Illinois finally passed a "school suffrage" statute allowing women to vote on local school issues. Bradwell lobbied hard for its passage through the *Chicago Legal News*. The law was immediately contested in the courts, but for the first time, the Illinois Supreme Court decided a woman's rights case in favor of women. In 1893, a year before her death, Bradwell voted for the first time, casting a ballot in a Chicago school board election.

Chief Justice Salmon Portland Chase (1864-1873)

Engraver Alonzo Chappel, Collection of the Supreme Court of the United States

Bradwell also used the *Chicago Legal News* as a forum for discussions of social reform. For example, Bradwell developed a keen interest in the running of asylums from her first-hand knowledge of the sufferings of Mary Todd Lincoln, a long-time friend of the Bradwells. Concerned about Lincoln's overspending and the consequent effect on her estate, her son Robert Lincoln had initiated proceedings that ended in his mother's committal to the Bellevue Place asylum in 1875. Bradwell was successful in getting Mary Todd Lincoln released, but only after a protracted battle with Robert Lincoln and the asylum's resident physician.

Myra Bradwell continued to edit and publish the *Chicago Legal News* until the end of her life. Throughout her long career, she advocated the advancement of women in many public forums, believing that there was no occupation from which women should be barred on account of either their gender or their marital status. Herself the first woman member of both the Illinois Press Association and the Illinois State Bar Association, Bradwell was successful in opening many professional doors for future generations of women.

One of Bradwell's last undertakings was as an advocate for women's representation in the 1893 World's Columbian Exposition. Bradwell joined forces with Chicago reform activist Emma Wallace to form the Woman's Department. In October 1889, the two organized a mass meeting in Chicago. Two thousand women demonstrated their support for women's involvement in the planning and mounting of the exposition. The woman's board that resulted assisted the all-male committee that was lobbying Congress to have the exposition held in Chicago. As a member of the executive committee of the Woman's Department, Bradwell went to Washington, D.C. and helped to establish a lobbying headquarters there.

On April 25, 1890, Congress decided that the Exposition would be held in Chicago. After further lobbying and controversy, the national commission organizing the Exposition appointed a Board of Lady Managers to establish a Woman's Building as part of the upcoming Exposition. The Board of Lady Managers comprised two women from each state and territory, two from the District of Columbia, eight members at large, and nine delegates from Chicago. Myra Bradwell, one of these delegates, was also on the committee of ten women that determined the structure and operation of the Board, and chaired the Women's Congress Committee of the World's Congress Auxiliary on Jurisprudence and Law Reform, an organization formed to hold presentations and discussions of intellectual import during the Exposition.

In 1891, Bradwell discovered that she had cancer. Bradwell continued her work on the Exposition and on the *Chicago Legal News*, as always assisted (in both endeavors) by her daughter, Bessie Bradwell Helmer, and (in the management of the *Chicago Legal News*) by her husband James. As the Exposition drew near, Bradwell's condition worsened dramatically. Determined to see the Exposition after it opened in May of 1893, Bradwell moved to a hotel near the grounds for one week. She attended the fair in a wheelchair for an hour or two each day, then, at the end of the week, returned home never to leave her bed again. She died on February 14, 1894, at the age of sixty-two, and was buried in Rosehill Cemetery in Chicago.

A diplomat from the start, Bradwell was often cited as a shining example of her sex's limitless potential and capabilities. Throughout her career, she strove to bridge the gap between the legal profession and women's social advancement, creating a powerful force in the struggle for women's equality.

ALTA MAY HULETT

By Gwen Hoerr McNamee

A woman of exceptional ability and resolve, Alta Hulett authored and secured passage of the law that allowed women to enter the legal profession in Illinois. At the age of nineteen, Hulett became the first woman lawyer admitted to the Illinois bar.

Alta May Hulett was born on June 4, 1854, in Rockton, Winnebago County, Illinois. She descended from a line of accomplished lawyers, beginning with Hulett's paternal grandfather, Guy Hulett, Sr., a judge, physician, and editor in the LaSalle area. The senior Hulett exhibited an enthusiastic and independent character that would also appear in his granddaughter. Hulett's father, "Dr." Guy G. Hulett, was also multitalented. In addition to his work as a well-respected member of the LaSalle County bar, he earned the title "Doctor" for his medical abilities. Hulett's uncle, McAllister Hulett, was also a respected lawyer in LaSalle. All three men were described as brilliant.

Despite his ability, Hulett's father did not attain great wealth. When he died in 1860, Guy Hulett left his wife and two daughters with only limited means. Hulett's mother, Altie, took in boarders to support the family, enabling Hulett to begin her education in the public schools. Though she was an excellent student, Hulett was forced to interrupt her education in 1864 for employment in the Rockton tele-

graph office to help support the family. Hulett became so proficient at the telegraph that she was promoted to operator at the tender age of ten. Fortunately, the family finances soon improved allowing Hulett to resume her schooling. She graduated from Rockford High School in 1870 at the age of sixteen.

Hulett began her career as a schoolteacher in 1870, but was also determined to fulfill her family's legacy in the law. In the evenings after a day of teaching, Hulett engaged in a self-taught course of reading law. After a few months, she entered the law office of prominent, forty-five-year-old Rockford attorney William Lathrop to continue her legal studies. Most assuredly Hulett was aware of the obstacles she faced in entering the legal profession in Illinois, since by the time Hulett began studying law, the Illinois Supreme Court had already denied Myra Bradwell's application for admission to the bar and Bradwell's case was on appeal to the United States Supreme Court.

Undeterred, Hulett focused her energy and intellect on her legal studies. She passed the bar examination in 1871 and applied for admission to the Illinois bar. The Illinois Supreme Court quickly denied Hulett's petition because she was a woman. Hulett was bolstered in her professional ambition, however, by the tremendous support she received from her hometown. A local newspaper, the *Rockford Register*, sharply criticized the Illinois Supreme Court for its unequal treatment of the sexes.

With Bradwell's case still pending on appeal, Hulett decided to try to enter the bar by changing the law. She sought the aid of several individuals knowledgeable in the law and sympathetic to her cause, including her mentor, William Lathrop, and Myra and James Bradwell. Hulett also received assistance from Ada Kepley, a recent graduate of the University of Chicago Law School and the first woman law school graduate in the country, whose application to the Illinois bar had also been denied, and from Kepley's husband Henry, a lawyer and former judge.

Using broad language which would ultimately benefit women in fields other than the law, Hulett wrote a bill that prohibited the use of gender as a barrier to any profession or occupation in Illinois. After first winning the support of Representative Thomas Turner of Freeport, who agreed to introduce the bill in the Illinois House of Representatives, Hulett began a strenuous campaign to ensure the bill's passage. Myra Bradwell filled her newspaper, the *Chicago Legal News*, with articles supporting women's entrance to the legal profession; James Bradwell lobbied his contacts in the legislature. Hulett wrote a persuasive

Alta May Hulett

THE FIGHT TO GAIN ENTRANCE

lecture in support of the measure entitled "Justice versus the Supreme Court." Halfway through her seventeenth year, she delivered the address on November 25, 1871, in Rockford's Brown Hall to a capacity crowd. All three of the Rockford newspapers reported on the event, noting that approximately 400 people were turned away because the hall was overflowing.

In her address, in a candid but respectful manner, Hulett criticized the Illinois Supreme Court for their decision in Bradwell's case, arguing that Illinois law in fact supported women's entrance to the legal profession. Making a persuasive case for the equality of the sexes, Hulett called for an end to discrimination based on sex. The crowd, hesitant at first, cheered Hulett by the end of her address. She was described by the *Rockford Journal* as a new star on the lecture field. From Rockford, Hulett took her lecture to other venues in Illinois, winning additional support for her bill. She also argued her case to the Joint Judiciary Committee of the Illinois House and Senate.

Hulett's bill had undergone minor revisions during the Legislative process. Legislators had inserted the military and road construction as exceptions to women's open access to occupations. The amended bill was called for a final vote on March 22, 1872. The tally showed that while the bill received approval from the majority of the votes cast, the approval was short of the required majority. After Representative Haines called for a reconsideration of the vote, Representative Turner, who had introduced the bill, argued persuasively for its passage, and on the second vote, the bill passed by the required majority. Governor Palmer promptly signed the bill into law. Upon learning of the Governor's approval, Hulett was later reported to have remarked, "I shall never again know such happiness." (*Chicago Inter-Ocean* [March 31, 1877])

While the new law opened the legal profession to women, the same Illinois legislature passed new measures, requiring all aspiring lawyers henceforth to complete an additional year of legal studies. Hulett moved to Chicago to fulfill this new requirement, studying for her additional year in the law offices of Sleeper & Whiton under the tutelage of Chicago lawyer Joseph Sleeper.

In 1873, Hulett re-applied for admission to the bar. She was required to take a second bar examination which she passed with high honors, receiving the highest score of all twenty-eight applicants. On June 6, 1873, two days after her nineteenth birthday, Alta May Hulett became the first woman in Illinois admitted to the bar.

Hulett immediately engaged in the practice of law. She opened an office on LaSalle Street, in the heart of the Chicago legal district, and quickly earned the respect of the bar as a strong advocate for her clients, comprised mainly of business men and women. Lawyer Charles Mosher, in the *Centennial Historical Album of Biographies of the Chicago Bar*, described her thus:

> Alert, studious and energetic, she has met with almost uniform success in her legal practice... She is an easy and fluent lecturer, concise and spirited in argument and forcible in delivery. Miss Hulett is a genial and talented lady... ([1876] p. 49)

Hulett's career was characterized by her colleagues as exceptional. It was recorded that she never lost a jury trial. In addition to her law practice, Hulett was one of the first women in Illinois to hold the office of Notary Public and one of the first women admitted to the United States District Court for the Northern District of Illinois. A keen intellect, she served as corresponding secretary for the Chicago Philosophical Society, an organization composed of some of Chicago's brilliant and radical minds, including lawyers Charles Waite, Ellen Martin, and Mary Fredrika Perry. Though still very young, Hulett was reported to have often said that she "was not made to be married." *Chicago Tribune* (March 28, 1877). Instead, throughout her practice she lived with her mother in Chicago.

Tragically, however, Hulett had inherited the disease of pulmonary consumption. Forced to retire from practice in November of 1876, she moved to California with her mother, stepfather, and sister in the hope that the milder climate would help her health. Hulett was heartbroken that she could no longer practice law and feared that her case would be used by men opposed to women lawyers as proof that women were too weak to practice law. Alta May Hulett died in San Diego on March 26, 1877, just short of her twenty-third birthday.

Hulett's achievements, however, live on. Hulett's friend, lawyer Ellen Martin, noted that Hulett's life did much to cultivate public support for women lawyers. After Hulett's death, the Chicago Bar Association demonstrated its regard for Hulett by holding a memorial in her honor. Distinguished members of the bar praised Hulett for her intellect, her acumen, and her good nature. The Association passed a resolution in Hulett's honor, creating another first when they placed a copy of the resolution in the four courthouses located in Chicago. The women lawyers of San Diego also remembered Hulett in 1957 when they held a ceremony to mark Hulett's grave at Mt. Hope Cemetery.

Hulett overcame social and legal obstacles to achieve success in her chosen profession. Her talents were so strong that, according to her obituary in the *Chicago Tribune*, even those who believed women did not belong in the legal profession respected Hulett's "earnestness, ability and worth." With unblemished integrity Hulett opened the legal profession to women, argued steadfastly for women's equality and lived her life with true passion.

ADA MISER KEPLEY

By Jennifer T. Nijman and Margaret Brady

Ada Miser Kepley was the first woman law school graduate in the United States. She assisted in drafting a bill banning sex discrimination in professional occupations which, upon its passage in the Illinois legislature in 1872, finally allowed women admittance to the Illinois bar. Kepley obtained her license to practice law in 1881, was active in suffrage, temperance and equal rights work, and ran for the position of Illinois Attorney General on the Prohibition Party ticket.

Ada Harriet Miser was born on February 11, 1847, in Somerset, Ohio to Henry and Ann Miser. She had two sisters and one brother. When Ada was thirteen years old, the family moved to St. Louis, Missouri, where she attended grammar school and two years of high school. In 1866, the Miser family moved to Effingham, Illinois, where Ada met Henry B. Kepley, a local lawyer who had joined the Effingham County bar in 1862. They were married in November 1867.

In 1868, Ada Miser Kepley began studying law in her husband's office. Shortly after this introduction to the field, she applied to Dean Henry Booth for admission to the University of Chicago Law School. Kepley was accepted into the one-year law course. In June 1870, Ada Kepley received her LL.B. degree in a ceremony where, according to the *Chicago Legal News*, "When Mr. North in his valedictory announced that the robes of the legal profession were, for the first time in the State, to be placed upon a woman, the men and women of that vast audience manifested their approval by round after round of applause." (*Chicago Legal News*, vol. 2 [1870] p. 320). The bachelor of laws degree was conferred upon Kepley by a unanimous vote of the trustees of the college.

After Kepley's graduation from law school, she was presented, along with other members of her class, to Charles Reed, State's Attorney of Cook County, to obtain her license to practice law. Reed refused to issue Kepley the license, explaining that Illinois law did not permit women to enter the learned professions. After this refusal to allow Kepley into the Illinois bar, the Kepleys assisted Alta Hulett and Myra Bradwell in formulating a bill banning sex discrimination in professional occupations. This bill became law on March 22, 1872. Despite passage of the bill, Kepley did not apply to the bar until 1881. Her license to practice law was issued on January 27, 1881.

Although Kepley did not receive her license until January 1881, on November 16, 1870, she was admitted to practice law in the court of Judge Decius in the Circuit Court of Effingham County. Judge Decius believed that the motion to allow Kepley to practice in his court was proper and in accord with the spirit of the age, which allowed women to earn a living by honest business or profession. Because of the standing Illinois statute at that time, Kepley was not allowed to recover any money for her services at the bar, and could be fined three dollars for every one dollar that she received in fees.

During the 1870s, Kepley worked at her husband's practice while she became involved in many reform issues, most importantly, suffrage, equal rights, and temperance. In 1881, Kepley joined the Prohibition Party and ran for Illinois Attorney General. Although there was little chance of Kepley's gaining the position, her campaign was important for the reform issues she espoused and publicized, especially women's right to vote, women's right to hold public office, and temperance.

Kepley was a strong supporter of the belief that women should be allowed to vote and became an active suffragette. She withdrew from the Prohibition Party when obtaining the vote for women was dropped from the Party's agenda and only returned to the Party when it was replaced. At one point, Kepley worked with the Woman's Christian Temperance Union (WCTU) to obtain 40,000 signatures on a petition to the Illinois legislature to create an amendment to the Illinois state constitution allowing women the right to vote. Unfortunately, no amendment was submitted to the legislature as a result of the petition.

Kepley is also noted for her temperance work. A common cause supported by nineteenth century women lawyers, the temperance movement was an attempt to aid women and children who suffered from the physical and emotional abuse of an often intoxicated husband or father. Encumbered by restrictive property and divorce laws, many women hoped to improve their situation by limiting a man's access to alcohol. Ada Kepley fought for the cause. She held national, state, county, and local offices in the WCTU. In 1884, the officials of Effingham refused to allow the WCTU access to local buildings for their meetings. Kepley and her husband purchased a Methodist church, which they converted to a meetinghouse, and named the Temple. For twenty years, the Temple was the Effingham headquarters of the WCTU. It was used for a meeting place for various temperance groups and was used by many church groups. At the Temple, children were instructed in the teachings of the WCTU. Kepley formed a youth group, the Band of Hope, which stressed the dangers of alcohol. The

Ada Miser Kepley

Mabel Broom Collection

THE FIGHT TO GAIN ENTRANCE

Band of Hope was present at all public temperance events and all public events sponsored by the WCTU.

In December 1885, Kepley began the publication of *The Friend of Home*, a monthly temperance paper of which she was editor from 1885 to 1896. In *The Friend of Home*, Kepley published the names of those who patronized the local saloons, causing much uproar in Effingham. This publishing of names often caused conflict between families, church groups, those in the liquor trade, and upholders of temperance beliefs. Kepley herself was often ridiculed for her temperance efforts, and was once shot at by the son of a well-known Effingham liquor dealer who was angry because she had published his name for being drunk.

Kepley was a strong advocate for laws restricting the passage of obscene materials through the mail system. Through her efforts, the Illinois legislature passed a stringent bill regulating the sale of obscene material. In 1883, Kepley founded the High Cult Emerson Club, a women's reading circle. Kepley held the position of president in the club for thirteen years. She was a member of the Illinois Federation of Woman's Clubs and in 1895 she represented the Effingham Club at the Federation's annual meeting. In 1885, Kepley joined the Equity Club, a correspondence club for women lawyers. In 1886, she was elected as an Effingham school official, a position that she held for six years. In 1892, Kepley was ordained a minister in the Unitarian Society. Kepley was a notary public, a member of the Daughters of the American Revolution, and a member of the Illinois State Bar Association. She was also a lecturer and traveled extensively around the country and world, speaking on her experiences on reform issues.

After Henry Kepley's death in 1906, Kepley was alone as the couple never had any children. She went into seclusion on their farm outside Effingham, and became a broken woman, poor and reportedly somewhat eccentric. In 1912, she published a temperance book entitled *A Farm Philosopher: A Love Story*. She also wrote a World War I song titled "My Sweetheart Over the Sea Who Fought for Liberty." Kepley peddled the song on street corners and published pleas to friends and associates to buy her writings. She was frequently seen on Effingham streets in outdated clothes, handing out candy for children and food for dogs. On June 13, 1925, Kepley died, a charity case at St. Anthony's Hospital, Effingham, Illinois.

Ada Kepley was a groundbreaker for the education of women lawyers in the United States. She was a champion of equal rights and woman suffrage and strongly supported the role of women in the professions.

THE LAW SCHOOLS THAT DID ADMIT WOMEN

By Gwen Hoerr McNamee

The modern construction of the legal profession emerged after the Civil War with the development of legal education. The growing popular emphasis on science in the late nineteenth century was embraced by lawyers and applied to the legal profession. Believing that science separated an amateur from a professional, many lawyers adopted the view that a formal education was required to enter the profession, rather than the previous apprenticeship system of reading law in the office of a practicing attorney. Reversing the philosophy advanced by President Andrew Jackson in the 1830s - that the learned professions did not require any special qualifications and should be available to ordinary men – some elite lawyers sought to reclaim the profession by adding the requirement of a law school education to enter their ranks.

The curriculum within law schools was also changing. Christopher Langdell, the new dean of Harvard Law School in the 1870s, developed and instituted the case method approach to legal education, under which a student discerns legal principles from written judicial opinions of court cases. At Harvard, Langdell also instituted the Socratic method of teaching, wherein professors ask students a series of questions leading to a truth, rather than disseminating legal knowledge through a lecture. Through these innovations, the status and appeal of law school education began to rise.

Ironically, although professional elites intended law schools to be a means of narrowing the field to certain candidates (Harvard University Law School did not admit women until 1950), the growing number of these schools also opened new opportunities for women to study law. (As Jerold S. Auerbach argues in *Unequal Justice: Lawyers and Social Change in Modern America*, (London: Oxford University Press, 1976) aspiring Jewish and southeastern European immigrant lawyers also benefited from the increased professionalism of the law.) Some law schools admitted women from their beginning, while others decided to admit women to increase their enrollment in order to remain solvent.

It was in the Midwest that women found the most opportunities to obtain a legal education. Michigan University, later the University of Michigan Law School, was among the first schools to openly admit women into its law department, and Illinois, in particular, boasted four law schools that admitted women before the turn of the century.

The University of Chicago Law School was established in 1859. In his history of that institution, Frank L. Ellsworth asserts that due to the pressure of Myra Bradwell, the law department agreed to admit women. In 1870, Ada Kepley was the law school's first woman graduate and the first woman to graduate from any law school in the country.

The building housing the University of Chicago Law School was destroyed by fire in 1871. The following year, classes resumed, but the law school began negotiations with Northwestern University to merge the two law schools. This occurred in 1873 and the following year the law department took the name "The Union College of Law of the Chicago University and the Northwestern University." The law school continued to admit women and became well known for its support of women in the profession.

In 1891, the merger between the two universities ended and the Union College of Law became Northwestern University School of Law. The University of Chicago did not open its own law school again until 1902. Two women were admitted in its first class.

The Chicago College of Law was established in 1889 as part of Lake Forest University. In its catalogue, the College stated clearly that "No distinction will be made in the admission of students on account of sex or color." The catalogue for the years 1890-91 lists one woman in the third year class. The Chicago College of Law became the Chicago-Kent College of Law in 1900 through a merger with the (formerly all-male) Kent College of Law. The post-merger school continued to admit women students.

Illinois Wesleyan University had a College of Law, known informally as the Bloomington Law School, from approximately 1873 to 1927. The first woman graduated from this law school in 1879.

John Marshall Law School in Chicago has admitted women since its founding in 1899.

Undoubtedly, the ready availability of legal education for women in and near Chicago provides one reason for women's meteoric success in entering the Illinois bar during the nineteenth century. As Massachusetts lawyer Lelia Robinson noted in 1890 in her article on women in the law, "The palm of seniority in this new departure of conferring a degree for a regular course of legal study upon a woman must be awarded to the Union Law College of Chicago and Chicago is altogether the banner city in the number of its women lawyers." (Robinson, "Women Lawyers" *The Green Bag* vol. 2 p. 13 [1890])

THE PRACTICE OF LAW

With the elimination of legal restrictions to the profession, women immediately began to practice law in Illinois. They entered every facet of legal work and were diverse in their approaches as well as their goals. In 1876 the second and third women admitted, Mary Fredrika Perry and Ellen Martin, formed what was most likely the first all-women law partnership in the country and opened an office on LaSalle Street.

Women admitted to the Illinois bar went to work intent on proving that they could successfully practice law, maintain their womanhood, and break through additional legal restrictions. Though women were not yet full citizens, still unable to vote or sit on juries, these first women lawyers continued to break barriers within the profession. They represented state and local governments, prosecuted and defended criminals, advised corporations and litigated civil suits.

But women still faced cultural mandates telling them to stay home, labeling those who ventured into the public realm as unladylike, and excluding them from the power structure within the profession. Women of color faced even greater cultural prejudices and restrictions. These additional barriers resulted in a slow rise of women entering the law, and only one African-American woman, Ida Platt, was admitted to the Illinois bar in the nineteenth century.

The stories that follow reflect the diverse careers of many of the first women lawyers in Illinois, spanning the years from the 1870s to the 1950s. The biographies in this section are arranged chronologically by date of admission to the Illinois bar. Following the stories of Perry and Martin is the story of Cora Benneson, admitted to the Illinois bar

LaSalle Street north from Monroe Street, Chicago, Illinois, circa 1880s

Chicago Historical Society (negative number ICHi-21118)

in 1880. Benneson was also admitted to the Michigan and Massachusetts bars and, in addition to numerous other accomplishments, maintained a lucrative law practice for twenty-four years. Kate Kane Rossi, who specialized in criminal defense, developed a reputation during her forty years of practicing law as a tenacious advocate for her clients and women's rights. Mary Merrill Schwenn, the twenty-first woman, was a successful attorney who mysteriously ended her life as a recluse in Kirkwood, Missouri. In contrast, Cora Hirtzel, admitted to the Illinois bar in 1890 and the first woman Assistant Corporation Counsel in Chicago, maintained a career that won the respect of the top lawyers in the city. Effie Henderson, who began her career in Bloomington, Illinois, moved to Long Beach, California, in 1903 where she continued to practice real estate law.

By 1894, the Illinois bar was comprised of forty-four women lawyers and a number of African-American men. The first African-American woman lawyer, Ida Platt, was admitted in June of that year. Platt successfully practiced law in Chicago for over thirty years.

As opportunities for all women continued to expand, the Illinois bar continued to admit women lawyers who practiced law in a variety of areas with a diverse set of goals. Loise Foskette, also admitted in 1894, was a well-respected criminal defense attorney in Chicago. Mary Eva Miller practiced both civil and criminal law and earned public attention for receiving $42000 in fees for probating the estate of a millionaire client, the highest fee paid to a woman attorney to that time. Mae Isabelle Reed, who opened a law office first in Ottawa, Illinois, and then in Columbus, Ohio, maintained a practice in probate law. Marion Garmory began practicing business law in Rockford, Illinois in 1898 and maintained her private practice into the 1950s. Ellen Roberts, originally from Kansas, came to Chicago and, in just eleven years, was a member of several of the elite professional organizations in the city. Isabel Quinlan, admitted to the Illinois bar in 1901, established a permanent law office in Benton, Wisconsin, in 1916 where she practiced law for nearly half a century.

These women, while all practicing lawyers, were diverse in their areas of practice and their professional goals. Though all these women spent some time in Illinois, they were also diverse in their place of origin and the places they ultimately settled. Some were married with children, others never married. Some earned a prosperous living through their practices; others attained only modest financial success. Yet each found a way to forge a career in the law when women lawyers were considered a rarity and, in every way, the profession was characteristically male.

MARY FREDRIKA PERRY

By Elizabeth M. Streit

Mary Fredrika Perry the second woman to be admitted to the Illinois bar, established a law partnership with fellow University of Michigan Law School classmate Ellen Martin, most likely the first law partnership in the country owned by women. Although Perry suffered an untimely death at the age of thirty-two and practiced only eight years, she became a well-respected and admired member of the Chicago legal community and her passing was greatly mourned, not only by her partner, Ellen Martin, but by many male judges and lawyers of the era.

Mary Fredrika Perry was born to Dr. Frederich and Caroline Latham Perry on January 12, 1851, in Mendham, New Jersey. When Dr. Perry died in 1868, the remaining family moved to Coldwater, Michigan. In 1870, Mary Fredrika Perry began

Mary Fredrika Perry

studying law with the firm Shipman & Loveridge. She remained with this firm until the fall of 1873, when she entered the law department of what was then called Michigan University. Perry chose to attend Michigan University (later the University of Michigan Law School) after she and her friend Ellen Martin were denied admission to Harvard Law School because they were women.

Perry was admitted to practice law in Michigan in March 1875, and in the fall of that year came to Illinois. Her examination for admission to the Illinois bar was spectacular, prompting an examiner opposed to the admission of women to the profession to remark to Myra Bradwell that Perry had surprised the court, the examiners, and the entire bar by passing with by far the best examination of any member of the class.

After obtaining her license to practice law on September 17, 1875, Perry practiced alone for a short time and then established a partnership with Ellen Martin in Chicago. Martin and Perry lived in Lombard, Illinois, with Perry's family, and commuted to the city. The firm Perry & Martin specialized in real estate law, but was also known for its pro bono work for poor women. Perry and Martin also conducted business as loan brokers to supplement their income.

Mary Fredrika Perry quickly developed a reputation as a hard-working, well-prepared lawyer. An 1880 article in a daily newspaper of the time the *Chicago Inter-Ocean* (reprinted in the *Chicago Legal News*) described her as "a fair little woman" and "a worthy example of the successful Western woman, quiet but 'almightily in earnest.'" In an interview for the article, Perry observed that she was continually asked the same two questions about Perry & Martin's practice: first, whether it was concentrated in divorce and criminal work, and second, whether its clients were mainly women. Perry continued:

> I do not now recall. . .a single instance of inquiry into the business of a woman lawyer (and these are frequent) in which one or both of these questions were not asked. The theory seems to be that because a woman has chosen a field in which women do not usually work, her line of duty in that occupation must tend to an extreme. (*Chicago Legal News* vol. 12 [1880] p. 434)

The *Inter-Ocean* noted that Perry had very little criminal or divorce work and that she had about the same proportion of female clients as any other lawyer.

In addition to her legal work, Perry devoted substantial time to intellectual and reform societies such as the Chicago Philosophical Society and the Illinois Social Science Association. A colleague of hers, John W. Ela, remarked that in her work for these societies, as in her legal work, Perry was always thoroughly prepared and gave a clearly expressed and thoughtful analysis in all her papers and discussions.

Mary Fredrika Perry paid a price for excelling in the many activities in which she was involved. The winter of 1883 was particularly harsh and, on one very cold day, Perry purchased several dozen woolen mittens and braved the weather to distribute them to gloveless poor people on the street. Shortly after that incident, she fell ill with pneumonia and never fully recovered. Mary Fredrika died at home in Lombard on June 3, 1883, and was buried in Prospect Park. Perry never married and had no children.

The members of the Chicago bar met Perry's death with great sorrow. At an extraordinary session held shortly after her death, a large group of judges and lawyers gathered to give stirring eulogies to Perry's memory. All of the eulogies were recorded in the *Chicago Legal News*. Judge Tuley, before whom Perry had tried her last case, remarked:

> I feel that in the death of Miss Perry, not only the legal profession, but the women of the country, have suffered a great loss. She was known to many of them as a woman of very considerable literary attainments. As a lawyer, she was a rising young lawyer, and a representative woman, who bid fair to confer much honor upon her sex in the pursuit of the most arduous and difficult of all professions. (*Chicago Legal News* vol. 15 [1883] p. 347)

At the end of the eulogies, the gathered group adopted the following resolution, which was sent to Perry's mother and a sister and to the United States Court and the circuit and superior courts in Chicago:

> Having heard with feelings of regret and of profound sorrow of the premature death of Miss Mary Fredrika Perry, of this city, an honoured member of this bar, we do most earnestly testify to her many virtues and accomplishments as a woman, and to her ability and brilliant prospects as a lawyer, as well as the respect and admiration with which she was regarded personally and professionally by the bench and the bar. We lament her early departure the more because she was one of the few pioneers of her sex who had entered our profession, and was fast demonstrating to the world the great success which a woman can achieve in a pursuit calling for the highest qualities to secure distinction. (*Chicago Legal News* vol. 15 [1883] p. 347)

Mary Fredrika Perry was an outstanding lawyer with a stellar reputation among her fellow lawyers of the Chicago bar. Despite the great prejudice with which women lawyers were still viewed at the time, Perry's conscientious devotion to the law, and to causes for the poor, gained her the respect and admiration of even the most traditional male judges and lawyers. Had her life not been cut short after only eight years of practice, she undoubtedly would have become one of the most prominent members of Chicago's legal community.

ELLEN MARTIN

By Gwen Hoerr McNamee

Ellen Martin was a tough lawyer and a courageous women's rights advocate. The third woman lawyer in Illinois, Martin practiced law in Chicago for forty years; but she is perhaps best remembered as an ardent suffragist that "did all in her power to advance the cause." (*Chicago Legal News* vol. 48 [1916] p. 333)

Ellen Annette Martin was born on January 16, 1847, in Kiatone, New York, to Mary Eliza Burnham Martin and Abraham Martin, a notable attorney. In her youth, Martin's father would tell Ellen and her two brothers, Willis and George, the details of his cases and explain his legal arguments. Martin, inspired by her father, eventually followed his example by entering the legal profession.

Ellen Martin began her education in the New York public schools, first at Jamestown Academy, then Randolph Academy, finally graduating from Clinton Liberal Institution in 1865 at the age of eighteen. At some point during her schooling, Martin met Mary Fredrika Perry, a bright, compassionate young woman who

Ellen Martin

was also interested in the law. Perry and Martin developed a friendship that lasted until Perry's premature death.

In 1871, Ellen Martin began studying law in Jamestown, New York at the prestigious firm of Cook and Lockwood, where Governor Fenton maintained his law office. Years later, when asked to give advice to women attorneys young in their careers, Martin would respond by describing her experiences as a student in the New York law firm. Martin explained that the office was open in the evenings, when prominent businessmen and legislators would often come by to discuss their private and public affairs. Martin would listen and learn. She also benefited from her discussion with the other two law students in the office, and she was active in the local young lawyers' club that met weekly in town to discuss the law and current issues in the community. Martin believed early that her success was dependent on her business and legal acumen as well as hard work.

After studying law for two years, Martin, along with her friend Mary Fredrika Perry, applied for admission to the Harvard University Law School. Harvard, which had not yet admitted any women to its law department, rejected their applications. Martin recounted their response in an article she wrote for the *Chicago Law Times* years later,

> [We] were refused admission to Harvard Law School, the reason privately assigned being that it was not considered practicable to admit young men and young women to the Law Library at the same time, and it was not considered fair to admit to the Law School without giving privileges of the library. I believe the authorities have not yet found any way to get around or over this mountain of difficulty. (*Chicago Law Times*, vol. 1 [1886] p. 83)

Undaunted, Martin and Perry applied to the University of Michigan Law School, which had already admitted women. In 1873, Martin and Perry began law school in Ann Arbor. They quickly earned the respect of their classmates. Another woman law student described them as

> bringing with them a love and devotion for the profession of law not to be distinguished; and they soon gave evidence of the talents and power of labor that in a few years made them leaders in this new field for women. (Virginia Drachman, *Women Lawyers and the Origins of Professional Identity in America: The Letters of the Equity Club, 1887-1890* [Ann Arbor: The University of Michigan Press, 1993] quoting Jane Slocum [1887])

Ellen Martin graduated from law school and was admitted to the Michigan bar in 1875. On January 7, 1876, after passing an examination in Illinois, Martin was admitted as the third woman to the Illinois bar, following Alta Hulett in 1873 and Mary Fredrika Perry in 1875. Perry and Martin then opened a law office on LaSalle Street.

Tragically, Perry died in 1883 after braving a winter storm to hand out gloves to those on the streets. Perry's death devastated Martin. At Perry's memorial service Martin revealed the depth of her feeling for her partner:

> She had rare intellectual power which seemed more wonderful the more one knew her... She had a kindness of heart and was a true and faithful

friend. Life with her was a continual joy, full of brightness and full of comfort. (*Chicago Legal News* vol. 15 p. 348 [1883])

Martin remained so devoted to Perry that she maintained the firm name Perry & Martin throughout her forty-year career.

After Perry's death, Martin devoted herself to her work. She expressed her philosophy in her letter to the Equity Club, a national women lawyers' correspondence group, writing "law is a severe task master and demands undivided allegiance." While the seeds for this perspective were planted early in Martin's legal career, it was Perry's death that caused Martin to speak out against women lawyers donating their services to the needy. She explained,

> Up to the time of Miss Perry's sickness we did a great deal of work for women for little or nothing. Miss Perry's death was caused by overwork – in doing a great deal of work for women for nothing and then enough more to make a living... When Miss Perry died I said, and have followed the rule since, when I have anything to give away I will give it in money and not in legal services... (Drachman, *Women Lawyers* pp. 114-5)

The cause Martin did support was the advancement of women's rights, both in the legal profession and in society. In 1887, Martin wrote an article on the status of women within the legal profession for the first volume of the *Chicago Law Times*. She gathered information on women lawyers across the country and included stories passed on by women lawyers on the circumstances of their admissions. Martin also assisted women starting out in the profession when she could. In 1890, Martin took in Zetta Strawn as a law student in her office.

Martin's main passion, however, was winning women's suffrage. She gained public attention for her successful effort to vote in a Lombard municipal election in 1891. Martin noted that the town charter did not specify that a voter must be male. Meeting the qualifications listed, Martin took her legal support with her to the polls. She approached the three election judges and demanded to cast her ballot. When they refused, Martin indicated that she had prepared a brief on the issue that she would read to them, though it would require that they postpone the election for a day or two. Two of the judges reportedly remarked that "they had rather she cast her vote than read her brief." (*Inter-Ocean* [April 11, 1891]) Martin promptly voted, went into town, and collected fourteen

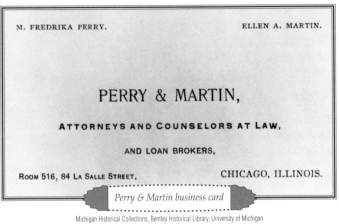

M. FREDRIKA PERRY.   ELLEN A. MARTIN.

PERRY & MARTIN,

ATTORNEYS AND COUNSELORS AT LAW,

AND LOAN BROKERS,

ROOM 516, 84 LA SALLE STREET,   CHICAGO, ILLINOIS.

Perry & Martin business card

Michigan Historical Collections, Bentley Historical Library, University of Michigan additional women, including Perry's mother and sister, who also cast their ballots. Though the town magistrates moved swiftly after the election to change the law assuring that only men could vote in the future, Martin's efforts did continue the movement toward full suffrage.

Martin turned her suffrage activities to a more formalized venture during the 1893 World's Columbian Exposition, designed to celebrate the 400th anniversary of Columbus's encounter with the Americas. In the year prior to the fair, women in Chicago and throughout the country began lobbying to ensure women's achievements would be included at the Exposition. Though a Woman's Department was established, some women professionals were concerned that only women's charitable work would be highlighted. Martin joined with other leading women lawyers and doctors, devoted to issues of women's suffrage and the advancement of women in the profession, to form the Queen Isabella Society in August 1889.

As chair of the Isabella Society's law department, Martin organized a three-day meeting of women lawyers at the Isabella Clubhouse on August 3-5, 1893. Thirty women lawyers from across the country attended the conference, where fourteen prominent women practitioners discussed legal issues affecting women. Martin discussed the Myra Bradwell case in detail. After the conference, the women lawyers, intent on continuing their efforts, organized the National League of Women Lawyers, with Ellen Martin as the secretary.

Inspired by this success, the following year Martin constructed another collective effort to win the vote for women through one of the most progressive women's organizations in the city, the Chicago Woman's Club (CWC). Organized in 1876 as a philanthropic venture, the CWC consistently dedicated itself to understanding and improving the lives of women and children in Chicago. As a member, Martin proposed that the club establish a Political Equality League modeled after other such organizations in the East. The Chicago league was founded on October 24, 1894, with the stated purpose "to promote the study of political science and government and foster and extend the political rights and privileges of women." (*Chicago Political Equality League Annual 1895-1991* [Chicago: Chicago Woman's Club, 1911] Chicago Historical Society) Martin immediately took a leadership role and served twelve years on the board of directors, four years as corresponding secretary, and seven years as the chair of the suffrage committee. Martin continued with committee work for the Chicago Political Equality League for twenty years, until she retired in 1914 at the age of sixty-seven, one year after women in Illinois won Presidential suffrage.

After practicing law for forty years, Ellen Martin closed the law firm of Perry & Martin in 1915 and retired to her home town of Jamestown, New York. She died a year later, on April 27, 1916, at the age of sixty-nine. Martin's long and courageous career served as an inspiration for women lawyers in Chicago and across the country. Her friends and colleagues remembered her for her love of the law and her enduring struggle to establish true equality for women.

CORA AGNES BENNESON

By Karen Clanton

Cora Benneson was a scholar who, among her numerous accomplishments, practiced law. Admitted to the state bars of Illinois, Michigan, and Massachusetts, Benneson traveled around the world to study legal procedures and the status of women in the legal profession in other countries. She held a fellowship in history at Bryn Mawr College and became a respected expert on the role and authority of the federal government, publishing and presenting many papers on the subject. Finally, she was a leader who inspired the organization and incorporation of groups ranging from literary clubs to women's political groups.

Cora Benneson was born to Robert and Electa Park Benneson on June 10, 1851 in Quincy, Illinois. Robert Benneson, a native of Delaware, came from Philadelphia to Quincy in 1837. In Quincy, he became a very successful businessman by first establishing a lumber business and then starting a company that bought and improved real estate. He was twice the president of the Quincy Board of Education and was partly responsible for the passage of the original act levying taxes for Illinois schools. Elected Mayor of Quincy in 1857, he preserved the credit of the city during the Civil War by giving his personal notes for its debts. He served as a director for various corporations and endeavors and as a trustee for the Unitarian church he and his wife helped establish. Mr. Benneson is said to have valued his wife's judgment and advice above all others concerning business matters.

Electa Park Benneson, originally from Massachusetts, was involved in civic and community efforts in Quincy. She was deeply involved with the Woodland Home, an asylum for orphans and the indigent. Mrs. Benneson, who tutored her children at home, constantly took up new studies and is said to have had scholarly instincts and rare literary taste. The family regularly entertained people of note at their home, including authors Louisa May Alcott and Ralph Waldo Emerson.

Cora Benneson, the youngest of four girls, excelled academically at an early age. During home tutoring, she and her sisters edited a weekly magazine called *The Experiment*, which contains Benneson's first writings. At age eight she won a prize offered by her mother for contributing a satirical piece on a fashionable woman's social call, entitled "A Visit." Young Cora was an avid reader who at the age of nine requested that she be allowed to help keep her father's books. By the age of twelve, she was reading Latin at sight and had an acquaintance with history and the best literature. She finished the course at the Quincy Academy, the equivalent of high school, at fifteen and graduated from the Quincy Seminary by age eighteen.

Early on, her mother noted Benneson's ability to get to the core of an argument and to summarize a conversation in a few words. Her analytical approach was not confined to home or school. Permitted to take a pencil and paper to church, Benneson often drew trees as she listened to the sermon, with the trunk representing the main thought and the branches representing the ideas leading out from it. In her judgment, the merits of a sermon depended upon whether or not it could be "treed." (Mary Esther Trueblood, *Representative Women of New England* [1904])

Cora Benneson attended the University of Michigan only five years after women students were first admitted. She completed the four-year course there in three years, graduating June 27, 1878 with an A. B. degree. Her first public appearance at the university took place during her freshman year, at a debate in which she argued that Homer wrote the Iliad, proving her argument by using the internal evidence of the book. She gave an extemporaneous speech — unexpected and uncommon for women at the time — and won the debate. By her senior year she was elected editor of *The Chronicle*, the leading college newspaper, becoming the first woman to fill the position.

Benneson applied to Harvard University Law School upon graduating from college. Her application was signed by five Harvard alumni, yet was refused on the grounds that the facilities at the university were too limited to make suitable provision for women. On October 1, 1878, she became instead, one of two women in the 175-student class entering the University of Michigan Law School. She soon joined the Illinois Club Court where she researched and argued legal issues, often defeating her opponents. By January of 1879, Benneson was elected associate judge of the Illinois Club Court. Benneson's graduate thesis — "What is due process of law as applied to judgment rendered upon notice, without personal service?" — was approved by Judge Cooley on January 15, 1880.

Never confining herself to the law, while on vacation in Illinois, Benneson founded the Young People Club, later called the Unity Club, in Quincy where men and women gathered to discuss the leading topics of the day. She became a presiding officer in the Webster Society, the leading debating society on campus, and one year after entering law school, was elected secretary of the senior law class. Benneson also served as secretary for a joint meeting of the senior and junior law classes.

Cora Benneson did not embark upon the practice of law until fourteen years after graduating from law school. Instead, she earned her master's degrees in jurisprudence and German from the University of Michigan in 1881. She would later apply to study for the degree of Doctor of Philosophy at Harvard University in 1894. Again, Harvard would reject her because of its strong stand against coeducation, but she would receive graduate status at Radcliffe.

Shortly after completing her studies at the University of Michigan, Benneson set out to travel around the world to study legal procedures in other countries and the status of women in the legal profession. Her tour started in San Francisco and led westward to Hawaii, Japan, China, Burma, India, Arabia, Abyssinia (Ethiopia), Egypt, Palestine, Turkey, and the principal countries of Europe. She observed that the best opportunities for women desiring to study jurisprudence abroad were offered at Zurich, where degrees were conferred irrespective of sex. She also commented on the question of the admission of Italian women to the bar in a letter to the Equity Club recounting the story of Lydia Poet, who passed the equivalent of the bar examination but whose admission was objected to on the ground of sex. During her travels in December 1883, Benneson also commented that "while the position of the American woman is not yet exactly what it should be and what I hope it may sometime be, still in traveling in Oriental countries one realizes that in our own we have much to be very, very thankful for." (Helen Warning, "Pioneer Women of Quincy" The *Quincy Herald-Whig* [February 20, 1977] p. 60) Upon her return, she traveled first to Quincy and then to Minneapolis, St. Paul, Cincinnati, Philadelphia, Boston and other cities to speak to well-attended gatherings about her travels.

In 1886, Benneson worked briefly for West Publishing as the law editor for the *Atlantic Reporter*. She accepted a history fellowship from Bryn Mawr College a year later. At Bryn Mawr, she studied administration with future President Woodrow Wilson, then a young professor, and continued her studies in jurisprudence and political history.

Cora Agnes Benneson

Michigan Historical Collections, Bentley Historical Library, University of Michigan

Although Benneson was admitted to the Michigan bar on March 24, 1880 and to the Illinois bar on June 5, 1880, her legal practice did not begin in earnest until 1894 when she was admitted to the Massachusetts bar. She is said to have gradually acquired a large and successful practice in Boston. She was a justice of the peace and the trustee of the Edward Everett estate. Her colleagues attributed her success in part to her philosophy and demeanor, which was never dogmatic or aggressive. Her code of conduct was portrayed as follows: "to study hard, think quietly, talk gently, act frankly, await occasions, hurry never." (Trueblood, *Representative Women of New England* [1904]) Calmness and deliberation were the words often used to characterize her. Her motto, adopted when eighteen and posted on her office walls, was "Verite Sans Peur", meaning "truth without fear."

On January 30, 1895, Benneson became qualified as Special Commissioner in the Council Chamber of Governor Greenhalge at the Massachusetts State House at Boston. Her appointment was renewed in 1905 and held until her death. In 1899, already a recognized authority on government, her papers "Executive Discretion in the United States" (1898) and "Federal Guarantees for Maintaining Republican Government in the States" (1899) were read before the American Association for the Advancement of Science and resulted in her election as a fellow in that society. A year later she was elected secretary of the association's social and economics sections.

Benneson was also active with women's issues, particularly those involving education. At the First International Council of Women, held at Washington, D.C. in 1888, she read a paper on college fellowships for women which was said to have had influence in increasing the organization's opportunities for original research. She was also said to be ready to support any movement that would provide women a fuller, richer, and more productive life.

Benneson's involvement with women's organizations began before her career as a lawyer. On February 14, 1870, she had joined Quincy's Friends in Council, the oldest women's study club in the city. In 1879 she became an honorary member of the group and was re-elected as an honorary member in 1880. She became corporation counsel of the Woman's Club House Corporation on February 10, 1896, and a director in January 1897.

Benneson was also very active in the College Club in Boston. She persuaded the stockholders to incorporate and handled the incorporation herself after presenting the articles of a new constitution for the club. She spoke at the club in 1896 concerning opportunities for women in the practice of law. A month later she drew up the by-laws of the Political Equality Club in Cambridge, Massachusetts. During this time Benneson also became an honorary member of the Illinois Historical Society.

A persistent theme in Benneson's work and life was that reforms cannot be forced upon society, but must come through a natural evolution. Regarding the role of women in the future, she stated:

> The coming woman will not hesitate to do whatever she feels will benefit humanity and she will develop her own faculties to the utmost because by so doing she can best serve. She will have a home, of course. She will not marry, however, for the sake of a home, because she will be self-supporting. The home she will help to found will not be for the selfish gratification of two individuals but a center of light and harmony to all that come within the sphere of its radiance. Many so called duties that drain the nerve force of the modern woman, the coming woman will omit or delegate. One duty she will not delegate — the character moulding of her children. The woman of the future comes not to destroy, but to fulfill the law. She will not confine her influence to a limited circle. It will be felt in the nation's housekeeping. Wherever she is needed, there she will be found. (Warning, "Pioneer Women")

Cora Benneson did not marry or have children, but she maintained close ties to her sisters, to whom she often wrote, and remained close to many of the alumni of the University of Michigan.

In 1918, Benneson gave up the active practice of law and worked to become a teacher of civics at the Massachusetts Board of Education's school in Boston for the Americanization of immigrants. While preparing for that position, she suffered a breakdown in health and died on June 8, 1919, in Boston.

Cora Benneson was a person of uncommon talents whose achievements were extraordinary for a woman of her time: attainment of three degrees from the University of Michigan, travel around the world, and admittance to the bar in three states. She was first and foremost a well-respected scholar whose work in the areas of literature, history, and the law were renowned. She was also a leader whose vision and expertise inspired many organizations.

KATE KANE ROSSI

By Gwen Hoerr McNamee

Kate Kane Rossi was a lawyer, first and foremost. She dedicated her life to the practice of law and fought for the rights of the underdog. Rossi specialized in criminal defense work and was an aggressive advocate, overcoming staunch gender discrimination.

Kate Kane Rossi was born in Wheeling, West Virginia in 1854. She moved to Wisconsin with her family during her childhood. Little else is known of Rossi's early years.

Rossi began her formal legal education in 1877 at the University of Michigan Law School. After a year of legal study in Ann Arbor, she returned to Wisconsin to study law in the office of Janesville attorney A. A. Jackson. In Wisconsin, she developed a close relationship with Lavina Goodell, the first woman admitted to the Wisconsin bar. Goodell had studied law in the law office of A. A. Jackson and Pliny Norcross in 1873, been admitted to the Janesville bar in 1874, and immediately begun practicing law.

In July of 1875, the Wisconsin Supreme Court had questioned Goodell's authority to bring an appeal to their court, asserting that a lawyer needed to be admitted to its bar in addition to admission to the circuit court bar. Goodell had presented a strong argument supporting her petition for admission, but in 1876, the Wisconsin Supreme Court had denied Goodell's petition for admission to its bar on the basis of her sex. Despite the supreme court's decision, Goodell had continued to practice law in the lower courts of Wisconsin.

In addition to the setbacks in Goodell's career, she also had family pressures. Goodell's mother was institutionalized and her father needed his daughter's financial and emotional support. Rossi visited Goodell's home and office nearly every day during the 1870s, becoming an important friend to Goodell, who in turn served as a mentor for Rossi. (Catherine B. Cleary, "Lavina Goodell, First Woman Lawyer in Wisconsin" *Wisconsin Magazine of History* vol. 74 [Summer 1991] pp. 243-271.

On September 6, 1878, Rossi was admitted to the circuit court bar in Janesville, becoming the second woman lawyer in Wisconsin. Rossi worked with Goodell and her law partner, Angie King, who in 1879 became the third woman admitted to the Janesville bar. Goodell, meanwhile, was finally admitted to the bar of the Wisconsin Supreme Court in April 1879. According to historian Catherine Cleary, Goodell's reaction to her victory was bittersweet. While she was thrilled at her own success, she was distressed that Rossi was not included.

Kate Kane Rossi

From James Bradwell, *Portraits of Twenty-Seven Illinois Women Lawyers* (1900), University of Illinois at Chicago The University Library Department of Special Collections

Both Rossi and Goodell left Janesville in 1879. Goodell moved to Madison, but, tragically, died within a year. Rossi went to Milwaukee, set up a law practice and began to work. Later in her career, Rossi would reflect on these first years in practice, remarking,

> I soon learned after my admission to the bar, that the only way to demonstrate a woman's ability to practice law, was for her to drop all collateral lines of work and side agitations and devote herself wholly and entirely to her profession. (Alice L. O'Donnell, "A Long Way Baby: Women and Other Strangers Before the Bar," *Yearbook 1977* [Washington D.C. Supreme Court Historical Society, 1977] p.62)

Rossi loved practicing law and engaged in her profession with passion, specializing in criminal defense. Lawyer Catharine Waugh McCulloch explained that Rossi had sympathies for the underdog, zealously defending those who lived in unfortunate circumstances. "[Rossi] was a vivid, colorful personality," McCulloch wrote, "outspoken and somewhat pugnacious in her attitude toward her opponents; but tender and warm-hearted to those she defended from prosecution." (Catharine Waugh McCulloch "Kate Kane Rossi" in the Grace Harte Papers, Schlesinger Library, Radcliffe College)

Rossi's spirited tactics in her criminal practice resulted in more than just a reputation for pugnaciousness. In April 1883, after practicing law in Milwaukee for four years, she herself became a defendant, spending time in jail for her response to a judge's decision in a municipal court case. The event made national news. The *New York Times* published seven stories on Rossi during the thirty days it took to resolve the incident. The series of events began when Judge Mallory refused to appoint Rossi defense counsel in a pending case. Rossi had represented the defendant in a previous matter and the defendant specifically requested that Rossi be his appointed attorney. Judge Mallory denied the request and appointed a male lawyer, P. J. Somers, as defense counsel. Rossi explained to the press that this was not the first time that Judge Mallory had demeaned her in court:

> I have been conscious for some time that Judge Mallory has been trying to drive me out of his court. He has continually insulted and misused me, but I bore it because I thought no one else

noticed it but myself, although clients, whose business I have solicited refused to employ me, stating that cases would suffer because I did not receive fair treatment. (*New York Times* [April 22, 1883] p.1)

This time, after Rossi was denied the case, she left the courtroom and went to her office. That afternoon, Rossi returned to the courtroom and, in full view of the whole court, picked up the judge's water glass from his bench and dashed it in his face. Judge Mallory shouted "Arrest this woman," and Rossi was dragged to jail. Mallory then fined Rossi fifty dollars for contempt of court and ordered that she remain in jail until the fine was paid. Rossi refused to pay the fine.

Rossi was released from jail the next day after bringing a habeas corpus proceeding arguing that Mallory had failed to comply with proper procedure in finding a person in contempt of court. Rossi had her liberty while Judge Hamilton of the County Circuit Court reviewed the case. Six days later, on April 30, 1883, Rossi lost her appeal, was remanded to custody, and ordered to serve ninety days in jail or pay the fifty dollar fine. Rossi, still refusing to pay any money, went peaceably back to jail. On May 21, 1883, after serving twenty-three days, the *New York Times* reported that Rossi was released from jail.

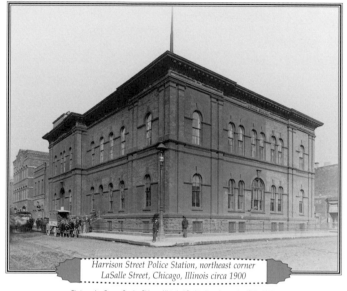

Harrison Street Police Station, northeast corner LaSalle Street, Chicago, Illinois circa 1900

Photographer Barnes-Crosby, Chicago Historical Society (negative number ICHi-19067)

Within a year after her release, Rossi moved to Chicago. She was admitted to the Illinois bar in March 1884 and resumed her law practice in her new home, continuing to specialize in criminal defense. Shortly after the World's Columbian Exposition in 1893, Rossi won public attention for defending women charged with prostitution, labeled by the press as "white slaves." According to the *Chicago Tribune*, the police would arrest women nightly "by the hundreds" and take them to the Harrison Street Police Station. Rossi would defend as many as fifty to one hundred of these arrestees daily.

During her first years in Chicago, Kate Kane married Vincenzo Rossi. Vincenzo Rossi was a notary who worked in his wife's office and, at one time, was an unsuccessful candidate for alderman for the first ward. The couple had one child, a son, Alessandro.

Over the years Rossi, too, sought several judicial and government appointments. She was a candidate for judge in the probate and, later, superior courts and ran for state's attorney

on the "Abolition of female slavery" ticket. In February 1908, Rossi applied for appointment to the city prosecutor's office. When her application was denied, Rossi demanded that her husband be given a city position. Rossi tried to arrange a meeting with Mayor Busse to discuss this possibility. When she was refused the opportunity to see the mayor, Rossi tried to physically force her way into the mayor's office. The *Chicago Tribune* reported that it took two police officers to contain Rossi. She was charged with disorderly conduct and taken to the Harrison Street Police Station. Rossi took her case to trial and was found not guilty by a jury.

Controversy continued to color Rossi's career. Two years after the Busse incident, the *Chicago Daily Herald* reported that Rossi had slapped a police officer at the Harrison Street Police Station after he insulted her. Rossi had offered to represent Officer August Zimmerman in a case where the officer was involved in a dispute with his neighbor. The officer declined to press charges against Rossi for assault.

In 1911, Rossi applied to Chicago Mayor-elect Carter H. Harrison II to be appointed Chief of Police. Rossi spelled out her qualifications in an open letter to the Mayor after he failed to respond to her request. Rossi explained that she would work to protect the citizens of Chicago, particularly women and children as well as working men who were subject to dangerous work conditions.

Despite her assessment that her career focused only on her practice, Rossi did engage in some reform work. She participated in women's rights activities, though her activist goals were related to her legal work. Rossi's main reform effort was directed toward improving conditions in the jails, an interest which may have originated in Janesville, where Lavina Goodell had begun a campaign to improve conditions in the jails in 1875. In 1900, James Bradwell reported in the *Chicago Legal News* that Rossi devoted much of her energy to this cause. Particularly, Rossi argued for the appointment of matrons in police stations to protect women defendants brought to city jails.

Rossi was also a strong supporter of other women in the legal profession, supporting African-American women lawyers as well. Rossi developed a respect for Charlotte E. Ray, the first black woman lawyer admitted to the bar in the United States, in Washington, D.C. in 1872. (Again, this relationship may have begun in Janesville, Goodell had met Ray in New York in 1876.) When the *Chicago Legal News* ran a column in 1897 inquiring as to the first woman lawyer of color, Rossi responded, explaining that Charlotte Ray was the first to open a law office. Rossi remarked correctly that despite Ray's ability, she was forced to give up her practice because of the popular prejudice she experienced.

Rossi practiced law until 1920 when she was required to retire because of her health. Though she died in her home in Palos Park, Illinois on November 21, 1928, her reputation as a fierce advocate lived on. In 1934, Chicago lawyer Nellie Carlin described Rossi's reputation as a criminal defense attorney, explaining that because Rossi would engage in the same tactics and language as the male attorneys, men held her up as an example of why women should not practice law. Carlin expressed the sentiment of many women lawyers when she celebrated Rossi's career, remarking

> All honor to Kate Kane... she was one of the pioneer lawyers who brooked insult and ridicule from the unthinking crowd and who made possible, today [in 1934], the presence of the woman lawyer on our Circuit, Municipal and Appellate Benches of the United States. (Charlotte Adelman *WBAI 75: The First 75 Years* [Paducah, KY: Turner Publishing Company, 1992], quoting Nellie Carlin 1934)

During her forty-year career Rossi vigorously fought injustice against working men, women, and children as well as barriers and prejudice against women in the legal profession. Rossi was not inhibited by social convention. She neither restrained her ambition or her method. Rossi, true to her cause, bravely demanded her own rights, the rights of women, and those of her clients.

MARY MERRILL SCHWENN

By Gerald S. Schur and Leisa Brunson-Braband

Upon Mary Merrill's death, a local newspaper headline read, "The Strange Case of Mary (Merrill) Schwenn — Law Graduate, Kansas Lawyer, Kirkwood Recluse." The newspaper headline accurately summarizes the unusual life of this early woman lawyer and women's rights activist.

A native of Astoria, Illinois, Mary Merrill was born in 1862, and was one of two children. Merrill's only brother, William Sherman Merrill, pursued a career in farming in Ontario, California. Mary Merrill attended law school at the University of Michigan, Ann Arbor. In one commentary, Lettie Lavilla Burlingame, a classmate, remarked of Mary Merrill that "[she had a] generous nature."

Merrill served as secretary of her law school class during 1885 and was one of two women in the graduation class of 1886. Her fellow female classmate, Burlingame, served as class poet during that same year. Both women were elected to their posts by the predominantly male student body.

The year after her graduation, Mary Merrill was admitted to the Michigan and Illinois bars, but opted to practice law in Wichita, Kansas. Merrill remained in Wichita for the early part of her law career.

Reports indicate that Merrill was an acclaimed leader in the women's movement. It may have been through her activities for women's rights that Merrill met Kansas lawyer and political activist Mary Elizabeth Lease. Lease earned a national reputation for her passionate lectures supporting the Populist Party. In 1892, Lease enjoyed support of women's rights activists from every political party in Kansas during her unsuccessful campaign for the United States Senate.

Shortly after Mary Merrill began practicing law in Witchita, she formed a law partnership with Lease. They opened law offices in Topeka and Kansas City. A year later, however, Lease moved to New York after the 1896 defeat of William Jennings Bryan, the Populist and Democratic candidate for President.

At some point in time, believed to be still early in her career, Mary Merrill moved to Kirkwood, Missouri. She bought property in Kirkwood that was valued, at her death in 1937, at nine thousand dollars. The Kirkwood property included a large house that Merrill rented to others.

On October 23, 1937, Mary Merrill was discovered dead in a humble one-room shack located on her property. Her body was found on an old mattress in a corner of a bare room. The premises' only other occupants were a pair of black cats. The only items of note in the shack were fourteen cents, some potted plants, and Merrill's law diploma from the University of Michigan. She had died without a will at age seventy-five. Although her obituary lists her name at death as "Mary [Merrill] Schwenn," indicating she had a husband at some point in her life, she died alone.

Despite beginning a promising career as a pioneering woman lawyer, Mary Merrill lived the last years of her life in poverty. As the local newspaper observed in its publication of Mary Merrill's death notice, "[it is hard to fathom]...why a woman intelligent enough to win a law degree and with character enough to practice law far ahead of the women's movement should have chosen this life as a recluse." (*St. Louis County Leader* [Oct. 29, 1937])

Note: Gwen Hoerr McNamee contributed to this article.

CORA B. HIRTZEL

*By Patricia R. McMillen
and Professor Julie Spanbauer*

Widely respected for her skills as a brief writer, Cora B. Hirtzel earned the distinction of becoming Chicago's first female Assistant Corporation Counsel and conducted a long and successful private law career.

Cora Hirtzel was born in December 1860 in Ottawa, Illinois, then a thriving Illinois city with large populations of Irish and other Northern European immigrants and the only German-language newspaper between Chicago and Peoria. Hirtzel's father was born in Switzerland, her mother in Germany. It appears that the family— including at least one older sibling, a sister, Louise (b.1857)—left the Ottawa area soon after Cora's birth, since there is no record of them in the 1870 census for Ottawa.

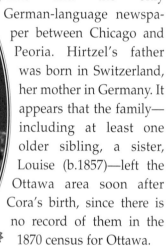

Cora B. Hirtzel

From James Bradwell, *Portraits of Twenty-Seven Illinois Women Lawyers* (1900), University of Illinois at Chicago The University Library Department of Special Collections

After reading law in the office of Jackson & Thompson in Oakland, Wisconsin and with one Judge George Gary, in 1887 Hirtzel moved to Chicago, where she worked for lawyer W. C. Goudy while completing her formal law studies at the Chicago College of Law. She finished law school in 1890 and was admitted to practice in October of that year. Two years later, in 1892, she left Goudy's office to open her own practice. Although "some probate and other practice came to her without her really seeking it," she specialized in writing trial and appellate briefs, as "she rather preferred the study and working out of legal propositions to actual practice in court." ("A Woman As Corporation Counsel" *Chicago Legal News* vol. 29 [1896] p. 341) Purchasers of her briefing services included, among many other respected attorneys, Clarence Darrow. It is, perhaps, some measure of her ambition, as well as success, that she obtained her first telephone listing in 1892, less than twenty years after the gadget had been introduced at the 1876 Philadelphia Centennial, and the same year long-distance service was introduced between New York and Chicago.

In 1897, one of her clients, Chicago Corporation Counsel Charles S. Thornton, lured her from private practice to become Chicago's first female assistant Corporation Counsel. Her duties, again, centered on briefing legal propositions.

Hirtzel joined the Illinois State Bar Association in 1898 and remained in the city office until 1900, when she left to form a law partnership with Nellie Carlin, a former associate in Darrow's firm Darrow, Thomas & Thompson. The firm of Hirtzel & Carlin was located at room 437 of the Chicago Stock Exchange Building and specialized in probate matters. An item in the January 20, 1900 *Chicago Legal News* enthused that either Carlin or Hirtzel "would make an excellent master in chancery."

Cora Hirtzel remained in private practice in Chicago until 1938. She never married, but lived for at least some time with her sister, Louise, also a professional, who at one point rose to the position of head bookkeeper with a large iron firm. The places and dates of death of both sisters are unknown.

EFFIE HENDERSON

By Kristen Fligel and Deanne Fortna Jones

Effie Henderson, the thirty-seventh woman admitted to the Illinois bar, was "a woman of ability and her legal work since her admission [was] such as to gain the respect of her professional brethren." (*Chicago Legal News* vol. 32 [1900] p. 341)

Henderson was born on October 29, 1859, in Towanda, Illinois. She was the eldest child of Franklin and Sarah (Metcalf) Henderson. She had four brothers who survived to adulthood: Frank, George, Edwin, and Harry. Their father, Franklin, a farmer and grain dealer, was for ten years supervisor to the township of Towanda, and Chairman of the Committee on Railroad Assessments for McLean County. During his tenure, he became involved in litigation involving railroad assessments in which the people were hugely successful against the railroads and which established by court decision, and subsequent legislation, the concept of equal taxation. Her observation of these events, or hearing of stories about them, presumably was at least partially responsible for Henderson's eventual interest in the law.

Henderson spent her early life in Towanda, and in 1877 attended prep school at Illinois Wesleyan in Bloomington. Ill health forced her to give up her studies her senior year. She completed law school, however, receiving her L.L.B. in 1892. Henderson was the only female graduate of her law class of thirteen. She spoke at her graduation, entitling her address "The Star that Rose in the West." The Bloomington *Daily Pantagraph* reported that her class, the eighteenth of the University, was considered a strong one.

Henderson was admitted to the Illinois bar on June 14, 1892, and thereafter was a sole practitioner for approximately eleven years in Bloomington, Illinois, practicing mainly in the area of real estate law. Although a fire in the Bloomington courthouse in 1900 destroyed the local court records from

Henderson's era, there are three reported Illinois Supreme Court cases in which she represented the appellant regarding a real estate matter. Henderson's brother Frank also studied law at Illinois Wesleyan and was admitted to practice in 1881. He became a prominent lawyer in Bloomington; however, the two did not combine their practices.

Effie Henderson never married and had no children. She was a lifelong member of the Methodist Episcopal Church and lived with her mother in Bloomington. After her mother's death in 1903, Henderson moved to Long Beach, California, where she continued to practice law in the area of real estate. She died in her home on February 5, 1938 after a short illness, and her body was returned for burial in the family plot in Bloomington, Illinois.

IDA PLATT

By Denise R. Jackson

The forty-eighth woman — and first African-American woman — admitted to the Illinois bar, Ida Platt successfully practiced law in Chicago for over thirty years. Though she avoided public attention, Platt was a woman of courage and determination who opened the Illinois legal profession to women of color.

Ida Platt was born in Chicago on September 29, 1863. City census takers classified Platt's parents as "mulatto", indicating they were of biracial heritage. Her father, Jacob E. Platt, was a lumber merchant born in New York. Her mother, Amelia Platt, a native of Pennsylvania, was a homemaker. The couple had seven children: Jacob, Ellen, Amelia, Maria, Mary, Alice, and their youngest, Ida.

Platt was educated in the Chicago public schools. She graduated from Chicago High School, also known as Central High School, in 1884 at the age of sixteen. During Platt's years in the Chicago public schools, several important events took place. One such event, the Great Chicago Fire of 1871, resulted in the destruction of one-third of all schools. Many of the remaining schools were initially used as shelters for the homeless. Platt's high school was used as a makeshift court for one year, and burned school buildings were not replaced for at least three years.

Attitudes toward racial integration also shifted sharply during Ida Platt's childhood and school career. In 1863, the city council adopted an ordinance requiring all African-American children to attend segregated schools. The council, however, also ruled that children with only one-eighth "Negro" blood be allowed to attend the regular schools. This

Ida Platt

From James Bradwell, *Portraits of Twenty-Seven Illinois Women Lawyers* (1900), University of Illinois at Chicago The University Library Department of Special Collections

measure was later repealed. After the repeal of the ordinance, it was said that "Negro citizens of Chicago actually suffered less discrimination in education than those in the rest of the State." (Mary Herrick, *The Chicago Schools: A Social Political History* [Chicago: Sage Publications, 1971] p.53)

Finally, curriculum and conditions of education were changing. In 1865, German organizations demanded that German be taught in the public schools. In 1867, small pox vaccinations were required for all children attending school. In addition, music was added to the curriculum during Ida Platt's lifetime.

Ida Platt's secondary education thus took place in an integrated classroom, and included music and languages. According to several articles, Ida Platt became proficient in French and German. In addition, she studied music with Madame Eugenie de Roode Rice and was an accomplished pianist.

A year before graduating from high school, Platt began working in the insurance office of Mr. Holger de Roode. For approximately nine years, she worked as de Roode's private secretary and stenographer. She also managed the office's claims department.

In 1892, Ida Platt also took on an even bigger challenge, as she began working in the law firm of Jesse Cox and entered law school as an evening student at the Chicago College of Law. The school had been organized in January 1888, and was initially called the Chicago Evening College of Law. The following year, the school was renamed the Chicago College of Law, and thereafter became the Law Department of the Lake Forest University.

In 1894, after successfully completing this coursework, Ida Platt graduated with honors in the school's sixth graduating class, consisting of 122 students. Upon Platt's graduation, the *Chicago Legal News* noted:

What changes 25 years have wrought for the colored race, now a colored person, and that colored person a woman, is allowed to study law in the same classes with white men and white women, graduate with them from the same law college with honor and upon an equality. ("Miss Ida Platt" *Chicago Legal News* vol. 26 [1894] p. 352)

The year after Platt graduated, the *Precedent* also acknowledged her completion of the law program, noting that "Among the students in the Law School last year was a young Negro girl who graduated at the head of her class, and who was also an accomplished musician and linguist." Although the article failed to mention her by name, it is clear that the statement referred to Platt, as she was the only African-American woman to have graduated from the school.

Shortly after she earned her law degree, Platt in 1895 became the first African-American woman admitted to the Illinois bar. (The first African-American man, Lloyd G. Wheeler, had been admitted twenty-five years earlier, in 1869.) The *Chicago Legal News* quoted a Supreme Court justice as he signed Ida Platt's license: "We have done today what we have never before — admitted a colored woman to the bar; and it may now truly be said that persons are admitted to the Illinois Bar without regard to race, sex or color." ("Miss Ida Platt," *Chicago Legal News* vol. 26 [1894] p. 352)

Despite these gracious words, Platt's trail would contain many obstacles. Only one woman of color had been admitted to practice law in the United States before Platt. Charlotte E. Ray, a graduate of Howard University, was admitted to the Supreme Court of the District of Columbia in 1872. Ray was held in high regard by the other women of the bar and did open a law office, but because of the prejudice she faced, she was forced to give up her active practice of law.

After graduation, Platt began working in the law offices of her former schoolmate, Joseph Errant, by then a well-known lawyer and a member of the Chicago Board of Education. Errant's interests included the political, social, educational, and economic reform movements. He promoted the Protective Agency for Women and Children and founded the Bureau of Justice. Errant also spoke out on behalf of the poor and disadvantaged. In a speech to the Illinois State Bar Association in January 1888, Errant encouraged his listeners to create a court system available to all people regardless of differences, where everyone would be treated fairly, and where legal cases of the "poor and friendless" would be as zealously fought as the cases of others.

Despite her intellect and ability, the support of Errant and others like him was crucial to Platt's success. In 1890, a mere four years before Ida Platt graduated from law school, there were only thirty African-American women who had college degrees. Twenty years later, women still accounted for only about one percent of the legal profession. Being a woman and African-American was a "double impairment" for life in general and particularly in the white-male-dominated legal profession.

By hard work and clever strategy, however, Platt was able to overcome many of the obstacles she faced to establish a prosperous law practice. Utilizing her linguistic and business skills, she developed a large client base of foreign immigrants. In 1906, Platt established her own law office on Van Buren Street. In 1912, she moved her office to the prestigious location of 36 South State Street, where she maintained her practice until 1928. Late in her career, she joined the Women's Bar Association of Illinois and maintained her membership through 1928.

Ida Platt disappears from the historical record in 1928. Though she had, by then, practiced law successfully in Chicago for over 30 years, much of her life still remains a mystery. The little that is known of Platt's personal life is that after her father died in the 1880s, Platt lived with her mother and sisters on the southeast side of Chicago. After their mother died in 1902, Ida continued to live with her sister Amelia, a librarian at the Chicago Public Library.

Though she was the first African-American woman to engage in a successful law practice, Platt's accomplishments were sometimes overlooked. In 1920, while Platt was still practicing, *Chicago Legal News* editor Bessie Bradwell Helmer innocently reported that Violette Anderson of Chicago was the first colored woman to be admitted to the bar in Illinois. Apparently unaware of Platt's efforts and achievements, Anderson said, "It was a hard uphill struggle, but I persevered. I hope to be able to do much for the uplifting of my people, for I realize that my work is only begun." ("Miss Violette N. Anderson," *Chicago Legal News* vol. 52 [1920] p. 405) Anderson then engaged in a successful career upholding her ideals.

But Platt had not been completely forgotten. In 1927, a bright, young, ambitious black woman lawyer, Edith Sampson, acknowledged Platt's standing as the first woman lawyer of color in Illinois and praised both her ambition and her courage in this endeavor. Sampson followed Platt's tradition and achieved tremendous success of her own: first in private practice, then as assistant Corporation Counsel for the City of Chicago, and finally as a Circuit Court judge in Cook County.

Ida Platt blazed a new trail for women as she overcame prejudice against her sex and her race. She succeeded not only in her own endeavors but also as an example of excellence that countless women have followed.

Note: Gwen Hoerr McNamee contributed to this article.

LOISE FOSKETTE

By Professor Ralph L. Brill

Although cut short by her premature death, the career of Loise Foskette as both educator and criminal defense attorney was, by all accounts, one of distinctive success.

Loise Foskette was born on December 8, 1866, the daughter of Mr. and Mrs. Andrew Foskette of Palatine, Illinois. Her grandfather, Lyman Staples, was an early settler of that town (then known as Salt Creek Precinct) and according to a story in Myra Bradwell's *Chicago Legal News*, "a friend of the Bradwell family for nearly half a century...one of James B. Bradwell's earliest clients and lifelong friends." Although not a lawyer, during his lifetime, Staples was also a loyal subscriber to the *Chicago Legal News*, which would later report that "when she got so she could read, [Foskette] used to pull down the copies of the *Legal News* from [her grandfather's] writing desk and hunt for a "versus", saying, "versus means a row; two people have had a row and I want to read about it." (*Chicago Legal News* vol. 26 [June 30, 1894] p.352)

Despite this precocious start, however, Foskette's first career objective appears to have been, not law, but education. After completing the Chicago public schools, Foskette took teacher training at Cook County Normal School, graduating in 1886. She then taught first at the Central Park School and later at Talcott School.

In 1892, Foskette began the study of law at the Chicago College of Law. She received her diploma in 1894, graduating near the top of her class with an average grade of 96, eleven points ahead of the required passing grade of 85. Studying law in the evening, Foskette continued to teach school during the day, yet she was said never to have missed a recitation of her law school class.

Following graduation and receipt of her law license on June 15, 1894, Foskette opened a law practice with an office in the Ashland block. While continuing to teach evening classes — again at Central Park School, and then at Ellen Mitchell School — she built a successful practice, becoming known primarily as a criminal defense lawyer. In 1895, the *Chicago Legal News* wrote of the then twenty-eight-year-old Foskette:

> She is a good speaker, treats the court and opposing counsel with politeness, selects a jury with excellent judgment, examines a witness with skill, and presents the prisoner's defense with great strength to the jury. (*Chicago Legal News* vol. 27 [August 3, 1895] p. 418)

The same article reported Foskette's successful defense, that week, of one Bernard McQuillan, accused of robbery:

> Judge Baker appointed Miss Foskette to defend [McQuillan]. He was prosecuted with vigor by that eloquent criminal lawyer, James Todd, who presented Prendergast to the gallows, for killing Mayor [Carter] Harrison [I]. [Todd's prosecution had been successful, obtaining a verdict of guilty after only an hour's deliberation by the jury.] The trial lasted nearly half the day. The jury was out about twenty minutes and brought in a verdict of not guilty, and the prisoner left the courthouse with words of praise for the woman lawyer who

had snatched him from the grasp of one of our ablest prosecutors. (Quoted in the *Chicago Legal News* vol. 27 [1895] p. 418)

Foskette was outspoken in her support of suffrage for women. In a letter to the *Chicago Tribune* in May 1895, while arguing that woman's desire to vote was "based upon a natural right, not a special privilege," she nonetheless noted the special claims of working women:

> The woman who works for her bread wants the ballot because she knows its power... She knows that without it she will continue to dwell in a state of wage-slavery. Employers almost invariably assume a woman will work for a wage that will support but one individual. How many men, even among the humblest laborers, would consent to work for $5.22 a week? And yet that is the average weekly wage paid to the working women of the United States. (Quoted in the *Chicago Legal News* vol. 27 [1895] p. 321).

Tragically, Foskette's life ended shortly after her thirtieth birthday. Although accounts of her physical fortitude prior to 1896 vary— she was described by some as "physically weak, with a frail, delicate body" and by others as "in excellent health"—in the spring of 1896, she developed "the grip", which worsened, becoming consumption. With her mother, Foskette moved South in late 1896 in hopes of improved health, but she never recovered. She died at Citronelle, near Mobile, Alabama, on March 6, 1897.

Foskette's many friends mourned her at a funeral held March 9, 1897 at the Methodist church in Palatine. There, Universalist pastor Reverend T. B. Gregory movingly summed up the feelings of all:

> Life is not merely so many days and months and years; it is so much activity, so much earnest, honest toil in the cause of God and humanity. Measured in days and years, our friend's existence was a brief one, but she lived while she lived...She died with her face set toward the mark and with her hand outstretched to grasp the prize. (*Chicago Legal News* vol. 29 [1897] p. 243).

Note: Patricia R. McMillen contributed to this article.

Loise Foskette

From James Bradwell, *Portraits of Twenty-Seven Illinois Women Lawyers* (1900), University of Illinois at Chicago The University Library Department of Special Collections

MARY EVA MILLER

By Donna M. Lach

Mary Eva Miller, the fifty-eighth woman admitted to the Illinois bar, is remembered both for her achievements in a varied law practice and for her active role in social welfare, particularly with respect to the advancement of women.

Mary Eva Miller was born to Charles and Ellen Miller on a farm in Calhoun County, Michigan in the mid-1860s. Although Mary Eva Miller never married nor had any children, her two brothers, Charles and Louis, and three sisters, Myra Wells, Nellie, and Carrie Ott, blessed her with a number of nieces and nephews.

Proficient in her early education through the country school district, Mary Eva studied Latin and French at Marshall High School. She earned her college degree in teaching at Michigan State Normal School in Ypsilanti. Following her graduation in 1886, she taught school in Portland, Michigan, for one year. Then Mary Eva changed career paths and went to work for the office of the Calhoun County Clerk. There, she learned to operate a typewriter.

The winter of 1888 found Mary Eva Miller attending a stenography school in Chicago, the city in which she would spend the rest of her life. In the fall of 1889, she took a position as a typist and stenographer for the publisher, A. C. McClurg & Co., where she remained until the spring of 1890. Thereafter and until 1894, Mary Eva Miller used her stenography skills to work for prominent Chicago lawyers, including Charles H. Aldrich, the Solicitor General of the United States. There lay the seed of her ultimate career choice.

In October 1893, she began her legal studies at the Chicago College of Law. Being only one of two women in a graduating class of ninety-two students, she graduated from law school with honor in 1895, and was admitted to the Illinois bar on June 12, 1895. Later, she served as the secretary of the Chicago College of Law Alumni Association. An inveterate student, Mary Eva Miller took post-graduate studies in law and received a bachelor of laws from Lake Forest University.

Mary Eva Miller's legal career took off with a gallop. After graduating from law school, she set herself up her office in the Monadnock Building with both a civil and a criminal law practice. During the course of her legal career, she was also associated in business with W. E. Makeel and Elmer E. Rogers in the Unity Building.

Early in her legal practice, she made a reputation for herself by representing a criminal defendant charged with

Mary Eva Miller

From James Bradwell, *Portraits of Twenty-Seven Illinois Women Lawyers* (1900), University of Illinois at Chicago The University Library Department of Special Collections

burglary. It was through happenstance that Mary Eva Miller made her mark in her first jury trial. While she was sitting in Judge Frank Baker's courtroom, a criminal defendant, whose attorney did not appear, was brought for trial. Judge Baker, who was known for giving women attorneys a fair opportunity to make a living, appointed Mary Eva Miller to represent the defendant.

At the trial that ensued, there were no witnesses for the defense, and the evidence was overwhelming that the defendant had committed some type of crime. Mary Eva Miller's client was found guilty on the indictment and sentenced to serve five years in the penitentiary.

Mary Eva Miller subsequently discovered a flaw in the indictment, so she filed a motion to set aside the judgment. The judge, however, refused to grant a writ of habeas corpus for the return of the prisoner until he heard Miller's argument. After the hearing on the motion to set aside the judgment, the judge granted the writ, and the prisoner was returned. As a result, the judgment and verdict were set aside, and a new trial was ordered. Mary Eva Miller's client was then allowed to plead guilty to petty larceny, which resulted in a sentence of only a few months. The State's Attorney's Office informed Miller that that was the first time a writ of habeas corpus had ever been granted in the Criminal Court for the return of a prisoner from Joliet under similar circumstances.

Mary Eva Miller's legal services in that case were rendered without compensation because her client's wealthy eastern family refused to help him in any way. As for the client, after he was released from prison, he got a job both to support himself and to pay Miller's legal fees. Later in her career, Mary Eva Miller also made a name for herself in her criminal law practice when she represented newsboys during the pressmen's strikes and thwarted the State's Attorney's efforts to secure verdicts against her clients.

Mary Eva Miller's civil practice was also thriving, particularly in the area of probate law. After she had been in practice for thirteen years, she attracted nationwide attention for receiving the largest fee ever paid to a female attorney, $42,000. She had won a probate case on behalf of the heirs for millionaire Judge Bross and secured a court order for the immediate distribution of three million dollars.

Given Mary Eva Miller's commitment to the social issues of her time, however, the case that she herself probably considered her biggest success was one in which she received absolutely no pay, but made a significant change in tort law. In *People ex rel. Barnes v. Chytraus*, 228 Ill. 194, 81 N.E.2d 844 (1907), Mary Eva Miller represented Minerva Barnes, a poor woman who had been born into slavery.

Barnes had been injured through the negligence of the Chicago City Railway Company and had a meritorious cause of action against the railway company. Barnes sought leave in the Superior Court to file suit as a poor person. To that end, together with her application, she submitted both her own affidavit stating that she was poor and unable to pay the costs and expenses to prosecute her case and an affidavit in the same tenor from her attorney.

Judge Axel Chytraus denied her application because she had failed to comply with the Superior Court's rule for filing as a poor person. That rule required, among many other things, that the attorney submit a detailed affidavit attesting to the applicant's poverty and declaring that the attorney had ascertained that the applicant is a poor person and, if the attorney had not personally known the applicant for at least one year, an additional affidavit of a citizen of good standing. Moreover, the Superior Court's rule provided that no suit would be dismissed or decree entered or disposed of by settlement until court costs were first paid. That rule, which worked to the benefit of corporations in personal injury suits, was so burdensome and oppressive to both the lawyer and the client that it was virtually impossible to comply with it fully, thereby depriving the poor of their day in court. In response to Judge Chytraus' denial of Barnes' application, Mary Eva Miller filed a mandamus action, challenging the validity of the Superior Court's rule. The Illinois Supreme Court granted the mandamus petition, declaring the Superior Court's rule null and void. Of this decision, Mary Eva Miller was quoted as saying: "It restored the rights of the poor to sue, a right, which the court had shamelessly deprived them." (Mary S. Logan, *The Part Taken by Women in American History* [New York: Arno Press, 1972] p. 748)

Mary Eva Miller's tremendous sense of justice can also be gleaned from other facts of her life. She ran in the campaign for Municipal Court judge on the Socialist ticket, and she wrote for a suffrage publication in Chicago. She also went on automobile tours throughout Chicago and the State of Illinois to speak out for woman suffrage and devoted a great deal of time to the Illinois Suffrage Association, which she organized in Cook County.

Through her work with the suffragists, Mary Eva Miller became interested in the Norwegian Danish Young Women's Christian Home, of which she eventually became the vice president. The Home was founded to provide a safe and clean residence for Norwegian and Danish servant girls in Chicago. The Home also served to investigate applications for servant girls to determine whether the positions offered by the employers were safe, because some employment agencies had been exploiting young women by luring them into dens of white slavery.

Mary Eva Miller is also remembered for her involvement in a number of organizations. She was an accomplished public speaker, having spoken at a number of events, including a congress at the Art Institute in 1893 and the National Council of Women held in Washington, D.C. in 1895. She was a member of the Chicago Men's Association of Commerce, the Women Lawyers' Association, and the Chicago Political Equality League. For a number of years, she was also associated with various other women's clubs.

At 6:30 a.m. on March 17, 1914, at the age of forty-eight, Mary Eva Miller died in the Frances Willard Hospital in Chicago of pneumonia and heart illness. She was interred in Marshall, Michigan. One can only speculate that she believed herself near death. Interestingly, she executed her final will, in which she revoked all former wills, on March 14, 1914, only three days before she died. In fact, she may have been in the hospital at the time of her last will because, from their testimony in the Probate Court on April 28, 1914, the witnesses to her will — Dr. B. H. Orndorff and J. F. Harvey, a student — did not seem to know her very well. Moreover, one gets the sense that Mary Eva Miller must have looked much younger than her years, because both witnesses estimated her age to be about thirty-five.

The will left all her sizeable estate, valued at over $35,000, to her family. Interestingly, she left her office furnishings as well as one-half of the accounts due from her law business to her nephew, Louis Miller, who may have been following in his Aunt Mary Eva's footsteps in the legal profession.

Mary Eva Miller was, by the standards of any point in time, an accomplished lawyer and an outstanding member of her community. Indeed, her life was committed to using her extraordinary skills to make this world a better place. Her untimely death was certainly a loss. The words of one of her fellow members of the Women Lawyers' Association sums up the general sentiment of women lawyers at the news of Mary Eva Miller's death: "We are shocked and exceedingly sad for we feel that Miss Miller was needed, that she was so willing, and was capable of doing good service not only for her sex but for all humankind." (*Women Lawyers' Journal* vol. 30 [April 1914] p. 51)

MAE ISABELLE REED

By Marilyn Kuhr

A private practitioner in small-town Illinois and later in Ohio, Mae Isabelle Reed represents the phenomenon of quiet, steady law practice by an early woman lawyer.

Mae Isabelle Reed was born in 1875 in Princeton, Illinois, a farming community located in Bureau County. Her father was from Connecticut and her mother from Massachusetts. After graduating from high school in 1891, Reed taught public school in Princeton, which had a school system unusual for a pioneer settlement community. Its three-story high school was built in 1867 and taught commercial law, bookkeeping, stenography, Latin, Greek, French, and German. Its first woman board member served in 1892. Students were drawn from a wide area, and there were military organizations for both boys and girls.

In 1895, Reed moved to Ottawa (then the county seat of LaSalle County, Illinois) and took a position with probate court Judge Samuel Hall. Hall, born in DeKalb County in 1851, had graduated from Jennings Seminary in Aurora in 1871, and studied law in Dixon. He was admitted to practice at Ottawa in 1879 and practiced both in LaSalle, where he was city attorney and was first elected to a probate judgeship, and in Ottawa.

After studying law with Judge Hall, Reed was admitted to practice by the second district appellate court in Ottawa on November 4, 1897. In September 1898, she opened an office at 102 Post Office Building. Reed specialized in probate and chancery matters, but was also available for "conveyancing, briefing, abstracting, general steno and court reporting." She is shown on LaSalle County property records as a witness to transactions—for example, to the sale by widow Mary Louise Riggs of several lots in North Ottawa on April 27, 1899.

Reed practiced at the Post Office Building and boarded at 1103 Post, Ottawa, through approximately 1901, when she moved to Columbus, Ohio, to practice with the law firm of Morton, Irvine & Blanchard. Her practice with that firm would continue for at least the next twenty-nine years. 1920 census records for Franklin County, Ohio showed Reed living alone in a home she owned at 348 Wilson Street, Columbus, Ohio. She was then forty-five and unmarried, and worked on a salaried basis as an attorney.

The place and date of Reed's death are unknown.

MARION E. GARMORY

By Julie A. Bauer

Marion Garmory was one of several early women lawyers from Rockford, Illinois. In addition to practicing law, Garmory was active in business. She believed strongly in the value of a business education for women.

Marion Elizabeth Garmory was born on January 7, 1872, in Rochelle, Illinois. She was the third child of John and Sarah (Moffett) Garmory. Garmory's parents were born in Scotland, but had lived in England where Marion's sister, Margaret, and her brother, Hugh, were born. The Garmorys arrived in the United States shortly before Marion's birth.

Marion Garmory

Garmory's parents were "earnest, intelligent and industrious Scotch people, sturdy and substantial, who believe[d] in so bringing up their children that they shall be intelligent, self-reliant and self-supporting" (*Chicago Legal News*, vol. 30, [1898] p. 238). John Garmory worked as a school janitor in Rochelle; his wife kept house. Garmory later described her early years in Rochelle as "uneventful." She graduated from Rochelle High School in 1889 with distinguished honor.

In 1892, the Garmory family moved to Rockford, Illinois. Marion Garmory worked as a stenographer for Robert K. Welsh, a lawyer (and later circuit court judge) in Rockford. Garmory soon began studying law under Welsh. She assisted Welsh in preparing his most important cases. Garmory studied law "not from any belief or hope that I would ever attain fame or fortune as a lawyer, but as a means of education and advancement in my work, and because of the enjoyment and satisfaction I acquired from it." (*ibid.*, p. 238)

Garmory sat for the bar examination on March 1, 1898 at Ottawa, Illinois. Twelve persons applied for admission to the bar at that time. After the applications of three candidates were rejected on the ground that they did not comply with the Supreme Court Rules, the remaining nine applicants (eight men and Garmory) took the examination. Five passed, with Garmory at the head of the class, having obtained the highest average. The *Chicago Legal News* reported that "her standing (did) not rest upon the markings of the examiners alone; the members of the class with one accord acknowledged that this high honor was justly conferred upon her." (*ibid.*, p. 238)

After her admission to the bar on April 20, 1898, Garmory entered the private practice of law in Rockford.

In 1915, following the deaths of her parents, Garmory moved into the home of Bailey B. and Anna (Ruhl) Page, 906 Haskell Avenue, Rockford. Garmory's close friendship with the Pages would last for the rest of their lives.

Trained as a veterinarian, Bailey Page was a prominent businessman in Rockford. He worked in the quarrying business, serving as president of Northern Illinois Supply Company. Garmory served as the trustee of two of Page's companies, Northern Illinois Supply Company and Rockford Sand and Gravel Company. Garmory also served as secretary and manager of Rockford Frame and Fixture Company.

After Bailey Page's death in 1933, Garmory continued to live with Anna Page and manage her financial affairs. Anna Page was an avid conservationist, farmer, and nature lover. In June 1945, the two women purchased the Stark farm, a 160-acre farm near Kingston in DeKalb County, Illinois. They called the farm "Hilltop Farm" and raised hogs and grew corn and oats there.

Following Anna Page's death in 1948, Garmory purchased the house at 906 Haskell Avenue. She also served as the executor of Anna Page's estate. Page, who had previously donated the land from her husband's quarry to the Rockford Park District, left 180 acres of farmland northwest of Rockford to the state for park purposes. After the state decided that the property was too small for a state park, the Rockford park district acquired the land. Today, it is the Anna R. Page Conservation Forest, located at North Springfield Avenue and Safford Road in Rockford, Illinois.

Marion Garmory was one of the founding members of the Rockford Woman's Club, a non-profit organization that promotes and encourages philanthropy, civic and cultural improvements, and education. The club also played an important role in the social lives of Rockford women. Garmory spoke to club members on the value of a business education to women, pointing out the importance to women of investments, and a thorough understanding of the laws governing the administration of estates.

Garmory was also a leader in the woman suffrage movement in Rockford. She was a member of the Second Congregational Church in Rockford, the Winnebago County and Illinois State Bar Associations, and the Illinois Farm Bureau. Garmory never married, but she remained close to the families of her brother and sister. Garmory died on March 13, 1959, at Rockford Memorial Hospital at the age of eighty-seven. She had been hospitalized following a fall in her home seven weeks earlier. She is buried, along with her family members and the Pages, at Greenwood Cemetery, Main and Auburn Streets, Rockford.

ELLEN G. ROBERTS

By Mary Alice Kenny

Ellen Gertrude Roberts, the ninety-eighth woman admitted to the Illinois bar, was a practicing lawyer in Chicago. In addition to her civil litigation practice, Roberts was a scholar and an avid reader. Though she only lived forty-three years, Roberts became a well-respected member of the Illinois legal profession.

Born September 29, 1869, in Kansas City, Kansas, Ellen Roberts was one of seven children, two boys and five girls. Her father was Thomas B. R. Roberts.

Roberts attended the Kansas City Public High School where she became the first student to graduate at the age of fifteen. After graduation from high school in 1884, she became a schoolteacher in Kansas City and then decided to study business.

Roberts eventually came to Chicago and became a bookkeeper for the Virginia Hotel and, later, for the Victoria Hotel. While working as a bookkeeper, she studied law at the Chicago College of Law. So adept was she at the law that she was admitted to the Illinois bar in 1900 before she completed her course work. Roberts, nonetheless, continued her education and graduated from the newly renamed Chicago-Kent College of Law in 1902, when she was awarded the Flood Prize for Scholarship. Throughout her life, Roberts was known as a student of other subjects besides law and collected and maintained a large and valuable library.

Ellen Gertrude Roberts

Roberts practiced law in Chicago from 1902 to 1913, moving offices to various parts of the city several times. Roberts joined the established rank of Chicago lawyers as she became a member of the Illinois State Bar Association and Chicago Bar Association. Additionally, Roberts was a worthy Matron of the Queen Esther Chapter No. 41 Order of the Eastern Star, the sister organization to the Masons. She also was a member of the State Microscopial Society of Illinois.

Roberts gained some notoriety during her legal career for her involvement in the case of "Sentimental Tommy" Foulkes. Foulkes was an Iowa farmer who was directed, by a stranger, to Dr. F. M. Steward for treatment on his eyes. Roberts was the building agent for Dr. Steward, who was located at Fifty-sixth and Indiana Avenue. She allegedly collected money from Foulkes as an agent of Dr. Steward.

Foulkes brought an action in tort against Dr. Steward for the treatment on his eyes. Foulkes claimed that he was fraudulently induced to believe that his eyes were diseased. The Circuit Court of Cook County awarded him $2,274 on December 29, 1899. The case was reversed and remanded on appeal on October 13, 1913 because Foulkes' testimony was self-contradictory and opposed to the testimony of other witnesses.

On February 12, 1913, Roberts died at the age of forty-three from an unsuccessful operation for cancer at St. Bernard's Hospital. The *Chicago Bar Memorial* published an article "In memoriam" for Roberts, a tribute reserved only for a select few of the members. Respected Chicago lawyer Mary M. Bartelme wrote the memorial.

ISABEL 'BELLE' QUINLAN

By Shelli Boyer

Wife of a railroad engineer and the mother of two young children in the late 1800s, ambitious Isabel Quinlan dedicated her life to the law. In 1901, she became the one hundreth woman admitted to the Illinois bar and followed that achievement with a legal career that spanned nearly half a century and included a two-year term as mayor of Benton, Wisconsin.

"Belle" Quinlan was born Isabel Greer in Indianapolis, Indiana on March 12, 1859. According to some sources, she was the fourth cousin of thirty-first American President Herbert Hoover. At the age of seventeen, she married James Quinlan, an engineer on the Burlington railroad, and moved to Chicago. The Quinlans had two children, Marie Katherine and John Martin. The family moved many times over the next twenty years, finally settling in Benton, Wisconsin, a small mining town near Galena, Illinois, in 1907.

Belle Quinlan was admitted to the Wisconsin bar in 1916. After her husband's death a year later, she gave herself intensely to her career and the community of Benton, earning a reputation as a feisty litigator and quite successful attorney. Although her practice consisted almost entirely of suits on behalf of miners against mining companies, in one notable case, Quinlan sought damages for a client whose land had been damaged by silt and sludge from a local mine. Even though, at the time, juries traditionally reduced the amount of damages claimed in such cases, Quinlan's client was awarded $1300 more than she had requested.

Quinlan was known for her broad-minded views and her civic interest. When she was not fighting for justice or hosting theater parties, she actively participated in improving the quality of life in Benton. She served as both Circuit Court Commissioner for Lafayette County, Wisconsin and president of the Benton Village Board, and was at least partially responsible for organizing both the library and the sanitation system in Benton. In 1922, she was elected mayor of Benton; for reasons no one recalls, however, she lost her bid for re-election 172 to 55.

Most notable, however, was Belle Quinlan's founding of the Fortnightly Club. The club met every two weeks to discuss books and contemporary issues, in an attempt to bring some semblance of culture to the small Wisconsin town. In 1920, Belle Quinlan served as the first president of the Club, which still exists in Benton today, almost eighty years later.

In her day, Belle Quinlan was known as a spirited, yet stubborn woman who adamantly refused to reveal her age. Those who remember her laugh and say, "in practice you did not cross Belle." She practiced law into her nineties and, according to newspaper accounts, "was highly respected by attorneys, the courts and her clients."

Belle Quinlan died on New Year's Eve in 1954, at the age of ninety-five, survived by her son Martin, four grandchildren, seven great grandchildren, and three great-great grandchildren.

PRACTICAL CONCERNS

by Gwen Hoerr McNamee

Women's entrance to the formerly male legal profession posed a number of practical concerns. As women lawyers began to create a role for the 'Good Old Girl,' they also had to determine her public persona. One of the most visible issues centered on hats. When women were first admitted to the bar the custom of the day was that women wore hats whenever they were in public, but judges required that attorneys remove their hats when entering a courtroom. Women lawyers in the Equity Club discussed this issue struggling to resolve the inconsistency. In June 1889, attorney Margaret L. Wilcox articulated the issue as "'The bonnet' or 'not the Bonnet' in the courtroom." She then set forth her opinion on the issue:

> I give you fair warning that I shall wage unending warfare for the freedom of women lawyers. If one should chose to lay aside her bonnet in the courtroom, whether on account of a heated atmosphere, or the shabbiness of the bonnet, or because she knows, intuitively, that the jury to be addressed would be prejudiced against her argument by either the extremely fashionable style of her hat, or its lack of style; whether one should plead with bonnet on, feeling confident that its beauty and becoming style lends persuasion to her tongue, or conscious that her hair needs the friendly concealment of a hat, in either case, I maintain that it is the inalienable right of each lady to follow her "own sweet will." Her keen intuition will guide her aright. (Margaret Wilcox, "Dear Equity Club" [June 1, 1889] reprinted in Drachman, *Women Lawyers*, pp. 177-8)

Chicago attorney Catharine Waugh McCulloch addressed the issue in a more straightforward fashion indicating she believed a bonnet detracted from a woman's credibility. She acknowledged that "some seem to think that a bonnet is absolutely necessary on a woman's head to redeem her from the curse deserved for lifting up her voice on the rostrum." McCulloch, never one to be restrained by mere social convention, indicated she removed her hat whenever she appeared in court. (McCulloch, "Fellow Citizens" [May 2, 1888] reprinted in Drachman *Women Lawyers* pp. 134-35)

Women lawyers additionally had to establish a public space for their presence. Ellen Martin and Mary Fredrika Perry were denied admission to Harvard Law School in 1873 because it was unacceptable for men and women to use the library at the same time. The availability of facilities for women working in the city was also a concern. In 1892, several women formed the Business and Professional Woman's Club to address some of these needs. In 1902, Club president Mary Bartelme announced that the organization had acquired three floors in the Atwood Building located on the north east corner of Clark and Madison. These quarters provided restroom facilities, a cafeteria, a reading room, and a gymnasium, all services desired by working women that were otherwise unavailable.

Practical issues plagued women lawyers well into the twentieth century. In 1923, when Bartelme was elected the first woman judge in the state, the *Chicago Herald and Examiner* published a story on these issues, asking prominent members of the bar, "How should a lawyer address a woman judge?" and "How should she dress in court?" (November 8, 1923) A reporter even asked the new judge what she was going to wear on the bench, a question certainly never posed to a male judge. Bartelme, with a history of forging new paths, decided not to don a robe in the day-to-day operations of her courtroom. In 1947, the hat issue resurfaced. The *Chicago Daily News* reported that a judge in Los Angeles ordered a woman lawyer to remove her hat before she could speak in his courtroom.

FIRST 101 WOMEN LAWYERS IN ILLINOIS

1. **Alta M. Hulett** admitted June 6, 1873
2. **Mary Fredrika Perry** admitted September 17, 1875
3. **Ellen A. Martin** admitted January 8, 1876
4. **Abbey S. Colton** admitted January 15, 1877
5. **Alice D. Merrill** admitted June 13, 1878
6. **Marietta B. R. Shay** admitted June 17, 1879
7. **Cora A. Benneson** admitted June 5, 1880
8. **Phebe M. Bartlett** admitted September 18, 1880
9. **Ada H. Miser Kepley** admitted January 13, 1881
10. **Lousia Lusk** admitted June 11, 1881
11. **Josephine S. Dollarhide** admitted January 11, 1882
12. **Bessie Bradwell Helmer** admitted June 15, 1882
13. **Kate Kane Rossi** admitted March 24, 1884
14. **Laura B. Shepard** admitted May 14, 1884
15. **Alice C. Nute** admitted March 20, 1885
16. **Emma Strawn** admitted June 9, 1885
17. **Mary C. Geigus Coulter** admitted September 17, 1885
18. **Catharine V. Waite** admitted June 16, 1886
19. **Catharine Waugh McCulloch** admitted November 9, 1886
20. **Letitia L. Burlingame** admitted May 9, 1887
21. **Mary Merrill Schwenn** admitted June 14, 1887
22. **Anna McCoy** admitted June 13, 1888
23. **Mary A. Ahrens** admitted June 12, 1889
24. **Bertha E. Curtis** admitted June 12, 1889
25. **Minerva A. Doyle** admitted June 12, 1889
26. **Myra Colby Bradwell** admitted March 21, 1890
27. **Lillien Blanche Fearing** admitted June 10, 1890
28. **Flora V. Woodward Tibbitts** admitted June 10, 1890
29. **Emma J. Bauman** admitted October 21, 1890
30. **Cora B. Hirtzel** admitted October 21, 1890
31. **Laura M. Starr** admitted June 9, 1891
32. **Katherine E. Wallace** admitted June 9, 1891
33. **Sarah M. Knapp** admitted October 22, 1891
34. **Alice M. Albright** admitted June 14, 1892
35. **Louisa Dennert** admitted March 16, 1892
36. **Mary Lee Colbert** admitted June 14, 1892
37. **Effie Henderson** admitted June 14, 1892
38. **Lois A. Marcoot** admitted June 14, 1892
39. **Mary M. Negus** admitted June 14, 1892
40. **Marion H. Drake** admitted June 14, 1892
41. **Charlotte C. Holt** admitted March 28, 1893
42. **Minerva K. Elliott** admitted June 15, 1893
43. **Cecelia Hedenberg Whitlock** admitted June 15, 1893
44. **Zetta Strawn** admitted June 15, 1893
45. **Mary Kennedy Brown** admitted Jan 15, 1894
46. **Mary Margaret Bartelme** admitted June 15, 1894
47. **S. Emma Corrington** admitted June 15, 1894
48. **Ida Platt** admitted June 15, 1894
49. **Loise Foskette** admitted June 15, 1894
50. **Jeannette A. Jaques** admitted October 22, 1894
51. **Florence E. Jaques** admitted October 22, 1894

52. **Mabelle Thatcher Little** admitted January 11, 1895
53. **Linda A. Dent** admitted March 29, 1895
54. **Florence E. Embrey** admitted June 6, 1895
55. **Nora Palmer** admitted June 6, 1895
56. **Florence Kelley** admitted June 12, 1895
57. **Mary Eva Miller** admitted June 12, 1895
58. **Margaret Tailor Shunt** admitted November 21, 1895
59. **Nellie B. Kessler** admitted January 16, 1896
60. **Lillie C. Spink** admitted January 16, 1896
61. **Helen Honor Tunnicliff Catterall** admitted March 28, 1896
62. **J. Pyle Bowen aka Mary E. Squire** admitted June 10, 1896
63. **Nellie Carlin** admitted June 10, 1896
64. **Genevieve Melody** admitted June 10, 1896
65. **Anna Marian Mullin** admitted June 10, 1896
66. **Grace Reed** admitted June 10, 1896
67. **Eva May Reynolds** admitted June 10, 1896
68. **Mildred Elwell Tremaine** admitted June 10, 1896
69. **Jessie L. Davis** admitted June 10, 1896
70. **Emma Smith** admitted November 6, 1896
71. **Edith May Cork** admitted May 7, 1897
72. **Virginia Dixon** admitted June 5, 1897
73. **Belle Brandon Reiley** admitted June 5, 1897
74. **Victoria A. Desalliond** admitted June 16, 1897
75. **Elizabeth L. Kenney** admitted June 16, 1897
76. **Alice St. Clair Lenaghan Shoreman** admitted June 16, 1897
77. **Emma Blood** admitted November 4, 1897
78. **Helen M. Kearns** admitted November 4, 1897
79. **Carrie Libby Rapp** admitted November 4, 1897
80. **Mae Isabelle Reed** admitted November 4, 1897
81. **Minnie Maud Hallam** admitted Feb 15, 1898
82. **Marion E. Garmory** admitted April 20, 1898
83. **Antoinette L. Funk** admitted October 15, 1898
84. **Isabel A. Helmich** admitted October 15, 1898
85. **Eliza C. Field** admitted October 20, 1898
86. **Minnie Ross Powers** admitted Feb 22, 1899
87. **Ruth Dick Hall** admitted June 7, 1899
88. **Estelle V. Pease** admitted October 14, 1899
89. **May F. Power** admitted October 14, 1899
90. **Marie L. Rawson Wood** admitted October 14, 1899
91. **Josephine E. Mosher Steven** admitted October 14, 1899
92. **Jane C. Trull** admitted October 14,1899
93. **Margaret C. Wich** admitted October 14, 1899
94. **Clara J. Breese** admitted June 7, 1900
95. **Agnes A. Graham** admitted June 7, 1900
96. **Bertha L. Chatfield** admitted October 12, 1900
97. **Isabelle H. Reid** admitted October 12, 1900
98. **Ellen Gertrude Roberts** admitted October 12, 1900
99. **Margaret A. Ketchum** admitted June 5, 1901
100. **Isabel Quinlan** admitted October 15, 1901
101. **Hattie Belle Frahm** admitted October 15, 1901

PROFESSIONAL ASSOCIATIONS

As women worked to establish themselves in the legal profession and fought against their remaining legal and cultural restrictions, some formed organizations offering emotional support, practical advice, and professional mentoring. Excluded from male professional associations, women formed separate organizations to collectively address the legal and cultural restrictions they faced. The first of these associations was the Equity Club, founded in 1887 by Letitia Burlingame of Joliet, then a law student at the University of Michigan, one of the few, but growing number of professional schools that admitted women. Female attorneys across the country wrote letters on relevant issues to the club for compilation and publication to the members. The Equity Club dissolved in 1890, replaced by more formal local and national organizations that advocated activism as well as support.

In 1892, the United States planned to celebrate the 400th anniversary of Columbus's arrival in the Americas at a World's Columbian Exposition to be held in Chicago the following year. A Board of Lady Managers comprised of politically moderate, wealthy women decided the fair would emphasize women's domestic, philanthropic, and artistic activities as representative of women's role in the world. Professional women who contested this portrayal formed the Queen Isabella Association in a united effort to include a tribute to Columbus's patron, Queen Isabella of Castile, at the upcoming fair. Denied space on the fair grounds by the Board of Lady Managers, the Association established its own club house two blocks away where they highlighted the work of women doctors, lawyers, and educators, and advocated women's suffrage. In August 1893, over thirty women lawyers from across the country attended a conference with speeches given by leading women lawyers and activists including Elizabeth Cady Stanton.

Other organizations were formed that combined the goals of professional support and political activism. The National Association of Women Lawyers (NAWL), founded in 1899 and headquartered in New York, focused on the international community of women lawyers within and beyond the borders of the United States. In 1911, it began publishing the *Women Lawyers' Journal* addressing general legal issues, advocating women's rights, and highlighting the advancement of women in the profession. Still in existence, the NAWL will celebrate its centennial anniversary next year. The Women's Bar Association of Illinois (WBAI), founded in 1914, also provided support for women in the legal community, advocated legal reforms and advanced the rights of women. The leader in the fight to allow women to sit on juries in Illinois, the WBAI finally achieved this goal in 1939. Still vital today, the WBAI has been in existence for eighty-four years.

NAWL with Chief Justice William Howard Taft 1923

National Association of Women Lawyers

Following is the biography of Lettie Burlingame, founder of the Equity Club. Like the other women who organized and led women's professional associations, Burlingame recognized the power of the collective effort of women in championing a cause and the benefit of supporting its members.

LETITIA LAVILLA BURLINGAME (1859-1890)

By Gina Raith

Throughout her thirty-one years, Letitia Burlingame felt passionately about life, work, religion, poetry, and women's issues. A strong advocate of women in the law, Burlingame is best known for starting the first national organization for women attorneys in America.

Letitia Lavilla Burlingame, born August 6, 1859, in Lockport, Illinois, was the second of two daughters born to Harmon R. and Olive C. Burlingame. Burlingame's Christian parents fostered her intellectual pursuits, including poetry, music, German, and French. They raised her to become a voracious reader and a prolific writer. At the tender age of twelve, she wrote an essay that she called "Juvenile Efforts, My Composition on School." For her high school graduation, Burlingame wrote and sang the class song. She also wrote an essay entitled "Genius Not Self Developing" in which she admonished her classmates to surmount obstacles, and to appreciate that he who does well, does his best.

Letitia Burlingame kept diaries throughout her adolescence and beyond. The diaries chronicled the events of her life and the world including such topics as her trip to see a theatrical performance Harriet Beecher Stowe's "Uncle Tom's Cabin," the assassinations of Czar Alexander II of Russia and President James Garfield, and the death of Ralph Waldo Emerson.

Her writings reveal that she was a pious, virtuous soul, constantly striving for self-improvement. New Year's Day inevitably brought on a distinct period of reflection and goal-setting. Each year, she adopted a resolution from the Bible and attempted to earnestly pursue it throughout the year. Her January 1, 1878, diary entry sets out one of her annual pledges: "Whatsoever thy hand findeth to do, do with all thy might."

After graduation, Burlingame taught high school. She considered the wages extremely low and resigned after teaching for only a year. When faced with the decision between entering the Conservatory of Music in Boston and studying law, she chose the latter. She believed that as an attorney, she could

contribute more to humanity. Letitia Burlingame was also drawn to the pillars of the profession: research, logic, and reasoning. In 1883, her legal career commenced with studying law at Fithian & Avery, a respected Joliet law firm. Three years later, she entered the school of her first choice: The Law School of the Michigan University at Ann Arbor (today known as University of Michigan Law School). At that time, she was one of only seven women in the law department at Michigan University.

Letitia Burlingame's family remained an ongoing source of support throughout her education. When she went to Ann Arbor, her mother, Olive Burlingame, followed her, and ran a boarding house for university students. Olive's husband, meanwhile, stayed in Joliet to hold down the homestead during the two years that his wife and daughter were in Ann Arbor.

While in law school, Letitia Burlingame managed to practice music each day, and continued reading literature between legal treatises. She excelled in Club Court, and was elected Chief Justice. She also took part in Moot Court, in which she scored a perfect one hundred — foreshadowing what was to become a successful, albeit brief, career as a trial lawyer.

Burlingame graduated from Ann Arbor in 1886 and was admitted to the Michigan bar that May. Once again, she had the honor of writing the class poem, this one entitled "The Temple of Justice." Initially, she opted to stay in Ann Arbor, and on October 6, 1886, she hosted an all-women's dinner party which secured her place in history. During that dinner party, Letitia Burlingame proposed the idea of forming the Equity Club, a correspondence club through which women studying or practicing law could become acquainted. The seven founders present that evening considered Equity Club to be an apt name and a reflection of what women were bringing to the practice of law — a heightened sense of fairness and civility. Burlingame, a leader among her peers, was chosen to be the first chair, a job she relished.

To become a member, women had to be studying or practicing law, had to pay two dollars in annual dues, and had to submit one letter per year. What started as a local correspondence club soon blossomed into the first national organization for women attorneys, as the founders began to receive dues and letters from women throughout the country. The founders even received some letters from women practicing abroad, thereby officially making the Equity Club the first international organization of women attorneys as well. Burlingame translated letters from women in Germany into

Lettie Burlingame

PROFESSIONAL ASSOCIATIONS

English for the Equity Club Annual. The Equity Club also held meetings which addressed such topics as the duties of women lawyers in society.

For four consecutive years, from 1887 to 1890, the Equity Club published and distributed to each member an "Equity Club Annual" as a means of communication for women lawyers, who were few and far between. The Annual was a compilation of all the Equity Club letters received from members each year. The letters reflect that women practicing law in the late 1800s had concerns not unlike those harbored by women practitioners today. In addition to noting the inherent challenges with the profession, many lamented the difficulty of balancing family and career while maintaining mental and physical health. Others wrote of sexuality. The Equity Club bridged the communication gap that would otherwise have prevented the mutual support and exchange of ideas between geographically dispersed women lawyers.

Not surprisingly, Letitia Burlingame contributed letters in each of the four years of the Equity Club's existence. In her letter of April 23, 1887, she waxed prophetic:

> The local branch of the Equity Club... has been a source of strength to me, for while I have the kindest feelings towards all men and women, it seems that we who have common aims should stand very close together, not merely for material assistance we may give each other, but for the sympathy and encouragement which shall better fit us for whatever difficulties we may encounter. (reprinted in Drachman, *Women Lawyers* p. 46)

On May 9, 1887, Burlingame was admitted to practice in Illinois, with plans to specialize in equity. On the first Monday of May, 1888, she commenced practicing in Joliet, making her the first woman attorney in Will County, Illinois. After only a year, Burlingame opened her own law office. Her work was primarily handling civil matters in the circuit court. She took on a case of first impression regarding the constitutionality of a trust deed. Undaunted by being vastly outnumbered by her male counterparts, Burlingame preferred courtroom work and encouraged other women to spend more time litigating. She is known to have won every case she pursued. She even led one client to victory in a jury trial, despite the fact that five lawyers represented the opponent.

In her Equity Club letter of May 17, 1888, Burlingame wrote: "I think women ought to go into the court room. Where are they needed more? If your heart, O women versed in law, fails you at the threshold of the forum, what of her whose all, and often more than all, is there at stake? Shall not your courageous dignity sustain her in her hour at trial?" And in her last letter to the Equity Club, dated April 22, 1889, she observed: "Friction only fires progression, and the dullest flint when struck emits a spark."

Her words also resonated through several public speaking engagements. While maintaining a successful practice, Burlingame lectured on temperance and suffrage on behalf of the Woman's Christian Temperance Union and the Joliet Equal Suffrage Association. She spoke in churches and penitentiaries, giving her last speech to women in prison just one week before her untimely death.

Letitia Burlingame's active mind, writer's gift, and ongoing professional accomplishments belied a frail physical condition, which plagued her throughout her life. Seemingly aware of the fleeting time she would have in this world, on her seventeenth birthday Letitia Burlingame wrote that she wished to die at an early age. Her wish was unfortunately fulfilled. She lost a battle to a severe bout of Russian influenza on December 12, 1890, dying in her parents' home at age thirty-one.

Letitia Burlingame's valuable stories, letters, poems, and essays live on through a memorial arranged for publication by her mother in 1895. Entitled *Lettie Lavilla Burlingame: Her Life Pages, Stories, Poems, and Essays* (Joliet, Ill.: J. E. Williams & Co., 1895) the book also contains highlights from some of her speeches.

Burlingame's eloquent, altruistic sentiments transcend time and convention. In 1878, at the age of eighteen, she wrote:

> *Did you ever feel a longing of both heart and soul*
> *To reach some far away, some rich and lovely goal?*
> *Has Ambition's fluttering dart with its living fire*
> *Ever pierced your glad heart with a fond and fierce desire,*
> *To know all that the world can know,*
> *To go as far as man can go,*
> *To sing a song beyond compare,*
> *To live a life both grand and fair?*

Letitia Burlingame both knew and lived that life.

LEGAL ADVOCACY AND SOCIAL REFORM

Women trained in the law but without full rights and privileges of citizenship were acutely aware of the problems facing women and children during the period of intense industrialization in the 1880s. Far beyond the mere practice of law for a fee, women lawyers — often working with enlightened male colleagues and lay women reformers — expanded the paradigm of legal work to include social reforms specifically addressing the needs of women and children. One of the first of these efforts was the Protective Agency for Women and Children (PAWC). Established in 1886, the PAWC provided legal assistance and practical support for young girls working in the factory sweatshops and for abused women fleeing their husbands. One of the leaders of the Agency was lawyer Mary A. Ahrens, who consistently addressed the needs of women and children throughout her career. Charlotte Holt, the first "Agent" of the organization, ran the day to day operations for five years and then decided to go to law school so she could more effectively provide assistance to those in need. Admitted to the bar in 1893, Holt drafted the first legislation in Illinois that treated children's criminal cases separately from adult cases.

Women lawyers also joined with reformers in the fight to protect the rights of laborers. Florence Kelley, a member of the social activist community that resided at Jane Addams' Hull House in Chicago, was one of the most proficient labor reformers. She earned her law degree in 1895 so she could more effectively advocate and enforce the labor reforms she established.

Furthering the work of Ahrens, Holt, and Kelley, Chicago women lawyers and reformers established the first Juvenile Court in the country in 1899. Lawyer Mary Bartelme, the first Illinois woman Public Guardian and one of the court's founders, became the first woman judge's assistant in 1913. Bartelme established a "girls' court" where all the participants were female, including the police officers and the prison guards. Additionally, Bartelme founded the Mary Clubs, group homes for girls who did not require institutionalization, but had nowhere else to go. She earned the nickname "Suitcase Mary" for her practice of giving each girl who went to a foster home a suitcase with clothes and essentials.

Nellie Carlin, appointed Public Guardian in 1913, furthered Bartelme's work as she consistently fought for women's rights and established additional programs to assist women with children.

Following are the biographies of the advocates Ahrens, Kelley, Bartelme and Carlin. Missing is the story of Charlotte Holt. Though her work was crucial to the success of the PAWC and the legislation she drafted established the foundation for the nation's first juvenile court, much of Holt's life remains a mystery. As with many of the first generation of women lawyers, the historical record contains few remnants of their lives and work.

The Children's Amendment

to the Constitution of the United States

By FLORENCE KELLEY

THE resolution introduced by Senator McCormick, proposing a child-labor amendment to the Constitution, was drafted and endorsed by a large group of responsible organizations, and it is the only pending child-labor resolution of which this is true. These organizations include the National Consumers' League, the National Child Labor Committee, the National Parent-Teachers Association, the United Council of Women, the League of Women Voters, the American Federation of Labor, the National Board of the Y.W.C.A., and the General Federation of Women's Clubs. The resolution introduced by Mr. McCormick reads:

"The Congress shall have power to limit or prohibit the labor of persons under eighteen years of age, and power is also reserved to the several States to limit or prohibit such labor in any way which does not lessen any limitation of such labor or the extent of any prohibition thereof by Congress. The power vested in the Congress by this article shall be additional to and not a limitation on the powers elsewhere vested in the Congress by the Constitution with respect to such labor."

Mrs. Kelley as General Secretary of the National Consumers' League has worked tirelessly for many years to uphold standards of health and work for women and children in industry

Florence Kelley and The Children's Amendment

University of Illinois at Chicago The University Library Department of Special Collections

MARY A. AHRENS

By Denise R. Jackson

Mary A. Ahrens, admitted to practice law in Illinois on June 12, 1889, graduated in a class of four female and sixty male students. She led an interesting and full life before and after admission to the bar.

Mary Adelaide Ahrens was born in Staffordshire, England on December 29, 1826. At about the age of fifteen, she came to the United States with her family, led by her father, the Reverend William H. Jones. The Jones family settled in Galesburg, Illinois, which, at that time, had a population of about eight hundred people.

Mary Ahrens married for the first time in 1857 while living in Galesburg. Her husband's name was Philip Fellows and together they had three children, two sons and a daughter. For almost two decades, Mary Ahrens remained at home with her children and studied horticulture. While at home she also undertook the study of medicine, eventually earning her diploma.

Between 1863-1864, Ahrens enrolled as a special student at the Galesburg Seminary. The seminary was the part of Galesburg College that admitted women. Mary Ahrens was considered a special student because she was not enrolled in a degree seeking program.

During her last years in Galesburg, Mary Ahrens was married a second time to Louis Ahrens, a younger man. She was fifty years old and he was forty-two years old when they wed.

Mary A. Ahrens

From James Bradwell, *Portraits of Twenty-Seven Illinois Women Lawyers* (1900), University of Illinois at Chicago The University Library Department of Special Collections

Soon after marrying Louis, Mary A. Ahrens enrolled in Union College of Law, which later would become Northwestern University School of Law. She graduated with honors in 1889, at the age of fifty-six. At that time, her class, which included four women, was known for graduating the largest number of women in any class.

Before graduating from law school, Ahrens had not given much thought to practicing law. Instead, she is said to have wanted to use her skills lecturing on the legal status of women. Ultimately, she decided to blend her legal education with her interest in the legal status of woman. Even before graduating from law school, Mary Ahrens was very involved in many relevant and important issues of the period. She was a founding member of the Illinois Woman's Press Association, which was organized by women writers. The organization, founded in 1885, began informally and its members included newspaper and magazine writers, editors, and artists whose mission was the advancement of the literary interests of

women. While the name of the organization suggests statewide membership, the majority of its members were Chicagoans. The organization existed for forty-four years.

Ahrens was also involved in the Protective Agency for Women and Children (PAWC), which was created in 1886. The PAWC, founded by the Chicago Woman's Club (CWC) with the support of eighteen additional women's organizations, was established to provide legal assistance for those who could otherwise not afford it. Handling a variety of cases, the agency assisted women who were wronged by their husbands and represented girls who sought redress from the harsh and unfair conditions of their labor in the garment and other industries. The PAWC also assisted victims required to testify in court and helped former clients find work and shelter. In many ways, the PAWC helped women regain their self-respect and establish their independence. Mary Ahrens sat on the original governing board of the PAWC, representing the Cook County Woman's Suffrage Association, and served in that capacity for two years. In 1889, the PAWC created a new governing structure with officers. Ahrens, then sixty-three years old, was named vice-president. She held that office until 1892.

In 1891, Mary A. Ahrens spoke at the annual meeting of the Illinois State Bar Association. There she gave a toast on the topic "Women in the Learned Profession." Her words resonate so strongly today that the 1891 toast was featured in the *Illinois Bar Journal*, Vol. 79 (1991). Ahrens remarked:

> It may be that you look at woman askance, and think that she has not taken the proper steps to prepare her[self], but she is able to demonstrate today, that she can reason always step by step from the lowest platform up to the heights where you yourself stand; she is in the professions today; she has come there to stay, and she is there through her own exertions; and now that she is there, she is entitled to recognition, which it is due that she should receive, and gentlemen do welcome her wherever she makes herself fit, and prepares herself to go.

As an attorney, Ahrens was known for her efforts to settle cases outside the courtroom and short of litigation. Even before graduating from Union College of Law, Ahrens had a reputable name as an attorney and had cases waiting for her when she was admitted to the bar. Ahrens did not specialize in a particular area of the law but worked on all sorts of cases representing people from all walks of life, particularly women, the indigent, and those with no one else to turn to for legal guidance. In *Case and Comment* vol. 21 (1914) p. 430, Ahrens is quoted as saying that she "considers law a good profession for a woman who enters it in the right spirit and with the natural qualification. There are lions in the way, but the woman who goes bravely forward will find when she reaches them that they are chained."

Mary A. Ahrens was also a suffragist, concerned about women securing the right to vote. She served as chair for the Woman's School Suffrage Association, which sought women's right to vote in Illinois school elections. In June 1891, after a long battle by the Illinois Woman Suffrage Association, women were granted the right to vote for school officers. Women did not yet have the right to vote for school superintendents. Therefore, in 1892, three years after graduating from law school, and after being denied the right to cast a ballot, Ahrens brought a suit against the board of election commissioners of Cook County to obtain the right for women to vote for county superintendent of schools. She lost. The court ruled that the legislature did not have the power or authority to give women the right to vote in an election for county superintendent of schools, adopting the respondent's position that the constitution, and not the legislature, defines the qualifications of voters. This decision did not dampen Mary Ahren's efforts to secure every woman's right to vote. In fact, the very year that Ahrens brought suit against the Cook County Board of Election Commissions, she presented one of her papers before the Illinois Woman's Press Association. The paper, titled "Disabilities of Women before the Law," addressed "the need of ballot power for woman." Ahrens was also a member of the Women's Congress Committee of the World's Congress Auxiliary on Jurisprudence and Law Reform of the World's Columbian Exposition.

It is clear that Mary A. Ahrens had a deep commitment to help those less fortunate than herself. During the depression of 1893, she opened the first relief station for men living on the street where the homeless were fed and provided a bed at night. Subsequently, Ahrens recognized that while there were many programs to assist men in the city, destitute women and girls were neglected by most relief associations. Thus, in February 1894, Ahrens founded the Mary A. Ahrens Mission, one of the city's first shelters to assist women and girls. Ahren's goal was to provide women and girls with the assistance they needed without diminishing their self-respect. The mission was favorably received. As the *Chicago Evening Post* reported:

Protective Agency for Women and Children Second Annual Report 1888

University of Illinois at Chicago The University Library Department of Special Collections

There is but one place in Chicago where unemployed girls are welcomed day and night and cared for until they can get work that will support them. This is the new home just opened at 48 Peck Court by Mrs. Mary A. Ahrens. There those in need of assistance can get it without feeling that they are being supported by charity. Arrangements have been made for accommodating fifty or more girls in clean, cozy cots and twice that number can be fed daily. The work is supported entirely by public contributions and promises to be one of the best relief measures undertaken in the city. ([February 2, 1894] p.8)

In order to make the dream of such a home for women and girls become a reality, Ahrens and many volunteers had to renovate, decorate, and furnish the three-story house which included a basement. A former alderman donated the property and an organization dubbed "Friends of Mary Ahrens" provided food, coal to heat the home, and other necessities.

To prevent the women from feeling like they were receiving a free handout, the women paid what they could for room and board. In fact, it was said that Ahrens liked the women to make a contribution because she was interested in helping women who were not satisfied to live on charity.

Mary A. Ahrens was known as a bright, ambitious, and energetic attorney, an intellectual, and an energetic charitable worker. The dedication, quality of work, and tireless exertions of Mary A. Ahrens have made it easier for many women to follow in her footsteps.

FLORENCE KELLEY

By Anne O. Decker

Florence Kelley fought throughout her life to advocate and protect laborers' rights, especially those of working women and children. She designed and helped enforce several key laws toward this purpose, and did so with a fire and uncompromising attitude that left many in awe. During her four years as chief factory inspector of Illinois and thirty-three years as general secretary of the National Consumers' League (NCL), Kelley demonstrated how to improve retail and manufacturing workplace conditions. She showed individuals and groups across the nation the power of rigorous inspections and organized, ethical purchasing practices.

For an era when a high school education was deemed more than adequate for women, Kelley's academic career was startlingly thorough. Kelley received a bachelor's degree in 1882 from Cornell University (majoring in rhetoric, literature, and oratory), studied at Zurich University in the mid-eighties (after an unsuccessful attempt to enroll at the University of Pennsylvania), and attended Union College of Law, graduating in 1894.

After her admission to the Illinois bar the following year, Kelley applied her legal knowledge to legislative reforms, not private practice. Kelley believed that the government had the responsibility, and the capability, of protecting its citizens through the law. (This opinion was foreshadowed by Kelley's college thesis: "On Some Changes in the Legal Status of the Child since Blackstone.") Kelley's faith in the potential of the American political system, combined with her fierce criticisms of the same, produced a potent spirit.

Quakerism deeply influenced the young Kelley. Her mother, Caroline Bartram (Bonsell) Kelley, had been adopted by Quakers when a little girl. More directly political knowledge came from Kelley's Irish Protestant father, William Darrah Kelley, who played a prominent role in Pennsylvanian public life. William Kelley was a lawyer, a judge, and a Jacksonian Democrat, whose business took him (and often his only surviving daughter) across the country observing industrial projects. Although her adult socialism would differ markedly from her father's politics, Kelley learned important life lessons from these early travels: that children were being overworked in miserable conditions, and that governmental intervention was a necessary evil.

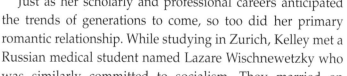

Florence Kelley

University of Illinois at Chicago The University Library Department of Special Collections

Kelley's socialism emerged from the tumult of her political concerns while with Zurich students who talked passionately about socialist developments. Kelley immersed herself in the fever. She began a ten-year correspondence with Friedrich Engels, soon translating into English his text *The Condition of the Working Class in England in 1844* (1887) and an 1848 address by Karl Marx on free trade. Kelley's socialist goals focused on both the personal and the working lives of the exploited because she believed that industrial capitalism penetrated both spheres. Her allegiances within the socialist framework did shift with time; she belonged, for example, to the European-oriented Socialist Labor party, Debs' Socialist Party of America, and the Intercollegiate Socialist Society (serving as president from 1918 - 1920).

Just as her scholarly and professional careers anticipated the trends of generations to come, so too did her primary romantic relationship. While studying in Zurich, Kelley met a Russian medical student named Lazare Wischnewetzky who was similarly committed to socialism. They married on June 1, 1884, and transplanted themselves to New York in 1886, where their three children Nicholas (b. 1885), Margaret (b. 1886), and John Bartram (b. 1888) grew up. Debt set in. Marriage difficulties were exacerbated by repeated political disappointments (such as being kicked out of the Socialist Labor party in 1887). Kelley separated from Wischnewetzky in 1891. She moved to Illinois with the children, received a divorce under the state's relatively lenient marriage laws, and resumed her maiden name.

Illinois not only smoothed the road for divorce-seekers; it also had one of the preeminent social-work movements in the nation, boasting Hull House, Jane Addams, Julia Lathrop, Alice Hamilton, and others who captivated Kelley in late 1891. Kelley's concern about labor conditions expanded freely in this encouraging environment. In 1892, she began investigating the garment industry's sweatshop conditions for the Illinois Bureau of Labor and surveying city slums for the federal commissioner of labor, Carroll D. Wright. Illinois Governor John Peter Altgeld next appointed Kelley as chief factory inspector. Her untiring work in this position until 1897 exposed numerous industrial abuses (including disease-infested conditions), and inspired, on one occasion, warning gunshots.

Through these projects and others, Kelley directly impacted legislative reforms such as: Illinois' 1893 factory act cutting women's work hours, banning child labor, and monitoring tenement sweatshops; *Muller v. Oregon's* affirmation of the ten-hour work day for women, highlighted by the famous "Brandeis brief" (1908); minimum wage legislation across the country; the Keating-Owen Child Labor Act of 1916 (struck down two years later); the Sheppard-Towner Maternity and Infancy Act of 1921; and woman suffrage. These developments were not always permanent, but continued to clear the ground for future legislative improvements and attitude changes about acceptable work conditions for women and children. It is interesting to note that Kelley firmly opposed the Equal Rights Amendment: she considered it potentially dangerous in asserting workplace equality before conditions were actually equal, thus leading to the suppression of actual abuses and the undermining of hard-earned protective legislation for women. Kelley argued that the amendment would benefit white-collar female professionals but threaten the blue-collar working women whose rights she championed.

Kelley's public works were multiple and varied. They straddled the personal and the political; highly opinionated editorials would flow as easily from her pen as congressional reports and sociological surveys. Her pieces fluidly moved from written to spoken. The audiences at her talks could be in the dozens or the hundreds, and were diverse in character, from the American Federation of Labor to church groups, the National Association for the Advancement of Colored People to consumer leagues. The one constant was a direct, impassioned style.

The following list of her spoken and written topics (not exclusive) demonstrates Kelley's primary interests and her unabashed beliefs over five decades: "Need Our Working Women Despair?" (1882), "The Need of Theoretical Preparation for Philanthropic Work" (1887), "White Child Slavery" (1889), "An Address in Memory of Thomas Paine" (1889), Hull House maps and papers (1895, as a principal coordinator), "The Working Child" (1896), "Working Women's Need of the Ballot" (1898), "Use and Abuse of Factory Inspection" (1903), "The Young Bread Winners' Need of Enfranchisement" (1905), "How Can We Best Utilize the Press?" (1905), "What Women Might Do with the Ballot" (1911), "What Should We Sacrifice to Uniformity?" (1911), "Progress of Labor Legislation for Women" (1923), "Challenge of the Working Children" (1930), and "The Child and the Machine" (1931).

Feared and scorned as a socialist by many, and rejected by others for her uncompromising positions on the elimination of child labor and the betterment of women's work, Kelley was also praised for these same stances. Today, following an increased understanding of pervasive industrial abuses, the effective legislative activity of the New Deal, and a heightened awareness of consumer power, the appreciation is even greater.

After 1905, Kelley occasionally would retreat from the political fray to Naskeag Point near Brooklin, Maine. The fiery Kelley is buried there today, although it is difficult to imagine her ever at complete rest.

MARY BARTELME

by Brian I. Hays, Michael N. Levy and Gwen Hoerr McNamee

Mary Margaret Bartelme, an exceedingly bright and compassionate lawyer who established a number of firsts for women, reached the pinnacle of her career in 1923 when she became the first woman judge in Illinois and the second one in the nation. She served on the juvenile court bench for ten years and dedicated her career to assisting dependent and delinquent girls and boys. Bartelme summarized her philosophy about her life work when she remarked, "There are no bad children, there are confused, neglected children, love-starved and resentful children. These are the ones who find their way into court and what they need most, I try to give them, understanding and a fresh start in the right direction."

Mary Margaret Bartelme was born to Jeannette Theresa Hoff Bartelme and Balthazar Bartelme in a farmhouse near Fulton and Halsted Streets in Chicago on July 24, 1866. Both of her parents were French immigrants. Her father was a well-known builder and contractor. She had a sister, Adeline Bartelme (Tilt) and a brother, Alfred. In her youth, the family moved to River Forest, where Bartelme would reside until she retired.

Bartelme graduated with honor from West Division High School in Chicago at the age of sixteen. She then attended the Cook County Normal School and later continued her education under private instruction. At the age of nineteen, Bartelme became a teacher in the Chicago Public Schools. She taught for three years at the Armour Street Public School and for two years at the Garfield Park Public School.

In 1892, Bartelme embarked on a new career. Grieving over her mother's recent death, Bartelme found it too difficult to continue teaching. She first considered studying medicine as she had an aptitude for chemistry. In recalling this transformative period in her life, Bartelme explained that when she went to a woman physician to learn about the profession, the doctor told her to talk to a lawyer before she made her decision. Bartelme then consulted Myra Bradwell, editor of the *Chicago Legal News*. Bradwell took a deep interest in Bartelme and encouraged her to choose a career in the legal profession. "One visit to [Bradwell]", said Bartelme "and I was determined to take up the study of law." *Chicago Tribune* (November 8, 1923). Months later Bartelme enrolled at the Union College of Law where she was the only woman in her class.

Bartelme graduated from law school two years later, in 1894, and her thesis on spendthrift trusts, which reviewed a doctrine announced in the celebrated case of *Nichols v. Eaton*, won a prize and was published in the *Chicago Legal News*. That same year Bartelme was also the recipient of the *American Law Register and Review* of Philadelphia $75 prize for the best annotation of a case decided that year for her annotation on *Singe v. Singe*, 1 Q.B. 466 (1894). She was admitted to the Illinois bar in 1894.

Bartelme began her legal career practicing probate law as a partner at the prosperous firm of Barnes, Barnes & Bartelme. She was immediately successful in practice and developed a reputation as an excellent attorney. Bartelme so impressed her colleagues that, without her knowledge, she was recommended her for the position of Public Guardian. After just three years of private practice, Bartelme began her long career in public service in 1897, when Governor Tanner appointed her to the position of Public Guardian of Cook County, the first woman Public Guardian in the country.

LEGAL ADVOCACY AND SOCIAL REFORM

Bartelme excelled in her new position, bringing an energy and compassion that was lauded by the press as well as those she assisted. Bartelme explained that in the narrowest interpretation, her duties included administering the estates of minors who were left without guardians, however, she expanded her duties to include what she termed "maternal" service, answering demands that other children asked of their mothers. In fulfilling her duties as Public Guardian after only a few months, Bartelme began to envision a new system of care for children that would provide them with suitable homes where they would receive an education and kind treatment. Bartelme personally acted on her ideals when during this time she took into her own home and then adopted two sisters, ages nine and ten, that had been abandoned by their family. Bartelme raised the two girls as a single parent, saw them both get married and have children, and maintained a close relationship with them and their families her entire life.

Bartelme's work as Public Guardian won public praise as well. Within three months of taking the position, Bartelme's supporters were described as "more than delighted with the efficiency, conscientiousness and thoroughness with which her official responsibilities have been discharged." (*Chicago Evening Post* [April 28, 1997]). Bartelme served in that post for sixteen years, under four different governors, earning the title of "the county's most conscientious servant."

Mary Margaret Bartelme

From James Bradwell, *Portraits of Twenty-Seven Illinois Women Lawyers* (1900), University of Illinois at Chicago The University Library Department of Special Collections

During her tenure as Public Guardian, Bartelme also began to influence the justice system. In 1897, Bartelme was one of six women who comprised the Juvenile Court Committee. The committee was organized by educator Lucy Flower and included social reformer Julia Lathrop (who later became the first director of the United States Children's Bureau), as president, and other members Jane Addams, founder of the Hull House settlement in Chicago, Sara L. Hart, wife of businessman Henry Hart of Hart Schaffner and Marx, and philanthropist Louise deKoven Bowen. The committee furthered the work begun by lawyer Charlotte Holt and the Protective Agency for Women and Children and drafted legislation setting forth a new system of handling the cases of children, mandating that they not be confined in jails or police stations. Years later, Bartelme recounted the experiences of the committee in lobbying the Chicago City Council on behalf of the bill. These unsophisticated men were so overwhelmed by these determined and educated women that one councilman remarked, "It sure is up to us gentlemen to do whatever youse want. It ain't often that such distinguished citizens come before us men and you ain't got no reason to be afraid, that you will get whatever you

ask for." (Speech by Mary Bartelme, [May 1932] Mary Bartelme Papers) Through their collective effort including assistance from woman's clubs, lawyers and other men and women professionals, the bill passed, and in 1899 Cook County created the nation's first Juvenile Court.

The committee purposefully had not included any apportionment in the bill for fear that a financial request would cause its defeat. Thus, after the court was established it was up to the committee to fulfill the requirements of the new law and find a place to house the juveniles as an alternative to jail. Bartelme and the committee fitted up an old house on West Adams Street in Chicago as a detention home. With the assistance of the Industrial Association, the City of Chicago, and the Cook County government, the home was used for seven years. Bartelme estimated that approximately 2800 children passed through the home annually.

After serving as Public Guardian for sixteen years, in 1913 Bartelme was the unanimous choice of the Cook County Circuit Court to serve as an assistant to the presiding judge. The position was created at the request of Judge Merritt W. Pickney because he felt that a woman was needed to understand the problems of the girls that appeared in Juvenile Court. As reported in *The Survey*, Judge Pickney believed that girls would more readily "unburden their souls to one of their own sex." (vol. 30 [May 17, 1913]) As part of this plan, cases involving young girls were heard in closed sessions and reports of the cases were kept out of the newspapers, in part, to protect girls accused of sexual misconduct from further disgrace. Up until that point, there had been no anonymity in juvenile cases. Bartelme heard the cases of girls up to the age of sixteen and recommended rulings to the judges of the circuit court even though the Illinois Constitution did not provide for elected or appointed woman judges at that time. She served in this position for ten years, first for Pickney and later for Judge Victor Arnold. Bartelme became known for her sympathetic understanding of the troubled girls, achieving a degree of national and international fame for her method of handling cases.

In addition to making her courtroom "a girls' court," in 1914, within a year of taking the position as assistant judge, Bartelme founded a group home that provided an alternative to institutionalization for delinquent adolescent girls. Bartelme formed a committee of volunteers who managed the home and raised funds, opening two additional homes, one in Evanston and one on Prairie Avenue. These three foster homes collectively became known as the Mary Bartelme

Clubs. Two of the homes were for white girls and one was a home for girls of color. Bartelme's objective was to "furnish girl residents [from twelve to eighteen with] a homelike atmosphere, including pet dogs." The girls had to attend school and were taught basic housekeeping skills, but they were free, within certain limits, to come and go as they pleased. Most came from broken households due to the divorce or separation of their parents or were the victims of unfortunate circumstances. Over the years, more than 2,000 girls lived in the three houses.

In addition to providing a new home for the girls who came through her court, Bartelme – sensitive to all the needs of these young women – began a program of handing out a suitcase containing clothes and toiletries for each girl to take with her to her new home. Bartelme enlisted the help of women's clubs to donate the suitcases and sew the dresses for the girls. She earned the nickname "Suitcase Mary" for her efforts to make sure that the juvenile who often owned only the clothes on her back, could enter a foster home feeling presentable. During Bartelme's lifetime over nine thousand suitcases were distributed.

Despite all her innovations, the introduction of a woman assistant judge did elicit some challenges. Complaints were submitted to the grand jury that Bartelme was acting as a judge without holding that office and that children and parents were being deprived of their constitutional rights. A special committee was appointed in 1915 by the Grand Jury to investigate Bartelme's work. The committee not only vindicated Bartelme, but lauded her work. They found, first, that Bartelme "acts at no time in the capacity of a judge and does not exercise the authority of a judge..." The committee further found emphatically that this was a huge improvement over the previous practice of having a male judge and male officials and public hearings of the cases:

> after years of unsatisfactory and disheartening results on the part of the Juvenile Court Judge in the hearing, care and treatment of delinquent girls cases, this old, barbarous and unnecessary plan was done away with and the present plan and procedure of hearing the cases of delinquent girls before a woman assistant (or referee) to the Judge in the presence of other women officials and the parents of the girls was adopted and put in practice. (Grand Jury Committee "To the Judges of the Criminal Court of Cook County," Mary Bartelme Papers)

The Grand Jury followed the recommendations of the Committee and made such a report to the judges of the criminal court of Cook County and Bartelme continued her work for the next eight years.

In 1923, when there was a judicial opening in the Circuit Court of Cook County, Mary Margaret Bartelme decided to run for the seat on the Republican ballot. Dean John Henry Wigmore of the Northwestern University School of Law, among many distinguished lawyers in the city, endorsed her campaign emphasizing her prior experience when he wrote,

> The unanimous opinion of those who have had business in that court [the Juvenile Court of Cook County] is that she has made an admirable judicial officer. She has pointed out a new path in which the woman lawyer may expect to make her mark in the profession. Her high character, her well-balanced judgment, and her tact, combine to make her record in that position a distinguished one. (*Chicago Legal News* [Dec. 12, 1923] p. 165)

Bartelme's supporters crossed race as well as gender lines. Violette Anderson, the second African-American woman attorney in Illinois, wrote an article in *The Colored Women's Exchange News* (October 1923) pledging her support for Bartelme's candidacy as a positive step for all women. Among the many women lawyers who supported Bartelme were Catharine Waugh McCulloch, a prominent Chicago attorney and the first woman justice of the peace in Illinois; Marion Drake, the unsuccessful candidate for alderman in Chicago's first ward; and Bessie Bradwell Helmer; Myra Bradwell's daughter.

Just three years after the passage of the Nineteenth Amendment granting suffrage to women across the country, Bartelme was elected by a margin of fourteen thousand votes and was assigned to serve as a judge in the Juvenile Court, the first woman judge in Illinois. Understanding the power of a judicial seat, Bartelme responded to her election by stating,

> I knew a woman could win. I've never been so happy in my life. I feel that I will be a greater service to Cook County than I have been in the past. The Juvenile Court, probably the most important judicial branch in the city, will be strengthened. I will do more effective work with the wayward girls, the girls who have made slight detour off the straight and narrow path. Armed with the authority of a judge, I'm sure I can do better work.... [W]e will give the youth of this city genuine assistance. ("Mary Bartelme First Woman Judge in Illinois Courts" *Journal Illinois State Historical Society* vol. 17 [1923] p. 247)

Mary Margaret Bartelme's manner of handling cases did not change after her ascension to the bench. She was cited in *The Woman Citizen* as believing that most delinquency was caused by carelessness, ignorance, or indifference on the part of parents, but at the same time held the child's duty to the parent as binding as the parent's duty to child. Bartelme stressed sympathy and understanding over legal lore and technicalities. No one was admitted to her courtroom unless they were associated with the defendant in some manner. The cases were often sad and tragic. Bartelme kept a supply of fresh, white handkerchiefs on the bench to hand to sobbing girls, their families, or even jurors hearing a case. Sometimes a juror was so affected by a case that he would donate his wages to be used for the proper care of the girl whose fate had been decided. Social workers and civic leaders from around the world came to study her methods in the courtroom. For example, in 1926 Queen Marie of Rumania spent a day of her visit to America in Judge Bartelme's courtroom. Bartelme was reelected in 1927 to serve a second term in the circuit court and became known as the "dean of women judges."

Though Bartelme devoted most of her career to helping juvenile girls, she did devote the last few years on the bench to helping boys as well as girls. As the depression intensified in late 1929, the number of children who came through the juvenile court began to increase. Bartelme used the list of seventy-six leading businessmen, published in the *Chicago Daily News* on December 10, 1929 as the men who would see the city through the financial crisis, to solicit their help in the situation of delinquent boys in the city. Bartelme invited these men to an organizational meeting of the "Friends of the Juvenile Court" held January 15, 1930. Successfully recruiting many men committed to the cause of helping those in need, this committee then took on the work of providing money and housing for dependent boys. As with her girls, Bartelme developed deep regard for the boys who came through her court. She often sent presents to those girls and boys who were in group homes for the holidays. Bartelme kept the thank you notes she received and recorded information regarding the well being of many of these juveniles as they matured. By the time of her voluntary retirement in 1933, she had heard over fifty thousand cases and it was said that perhaps no woman in the world was so widely known in juvenile service work or as deeply revered as Judge Mary Margaret Bartelme.

In addition to her work in the development and transformation of the treatment of juveniles within the justice system, Bartelme was a leader in the women's rights movement. As early as 1902, Bartelme was president of the Chicago Business Woman's Club, organized in 1892 and comprised of lawyers, doctors, journalists, and business women who worked in the

city. Because these women worked in professions that had previously been dominated by men, these women not only had to fight for their right to work in these fields, but also had to create a physical space for themselves. Bartelme led the club in efforts to secure a quarters for business women downtown, equipped with restroom facilities, a cafeteria, a gymnasium and a reading room. The club was able to rent three floors in the Atwood building located at 230 Clark Street. Bartelme contributed $3000 of her own money to help the club stay open, though unfortunately, a few years later, the club was forced to declare bankruptcy and disbanded.

Bartelme was also a suffragist. As early as 1895, the year after Bartelme graduated from law school, she wrote an article "Standpoint of a Woman Lawyer" to the *Chicago Tribune* in response their query "why do women want the vote?" Reprinted in the *Chicago Legal News* (vol. 27 [1895] p. 337), the letter explained:

"A Girls' Court" with Mary Bartelme

Collier's Weekly circa 1913 University of Illinois at Chicago
The University Library Department of Special Collections

At all times [a woman] must conform to laws, in the making of which she has no voice, or suffer the penalty for their violation; yet our government is founded on principles which are supposed to make it a government for the people, by the people, and not by one-half of the people for all. Our laws influence and bear upon the lives of both men and women, morally, physically, intellectually and financially, and in these influences women are as deeply interested as men, and should have the right and the responsibility of controlling and directing them by their ballots.

Bartelme's desire for women's role in government and the law extended beyond the ballot. After Bartelme was elected judge in 1923 she remarked,

I hope my election will act as an incentive in interesting women in their government, both local and national, and in everything that pertains to the welfare of their country and the world... The day is coming I believe, when women will share equally with the men the burdens of our courts... Though I may not be living at the time, I expect a woman to some day be president of the United States. *Chicago Daily Journal* (November 7, 1923).

Bartelme also found time to devote to the advancement of women in the professions and to numerous other causes and organizations that either advanced the rights of women and children or influenced the legal profession. She served as a teacher of medical jurisprudence in the Women's Medical School of Northwestern University for several years. Bartelme was also a long-time member of the Women's Bar Association of Illinois, elected president in 1927. Additionally, she was a member of the Illinois State Bar Association, Chicago Bar Association, American Bar Association, Chicago Woman's Club, Cordon Club, Every Day Club, and an honorary member of both the Chicago College Club and Big Sister organizations. Her fundraising efforts helped to support the Mary Bartelme Clubs, the Big Sisters, the Service Council for Girls, and the Oak School for mentally deficient children. Bartelme served on two Chicago Bar Association committees, the Public Service Committee, and the Delinquent Children Committee. She also served as a member of the board of trustees, the director, and the founder of the aforementioned Mary Bartelme Clubs. In addition to many other awards and honors bestowed upon Bartelme, in 1929 Knox College conferred the honorary degree of LL.D. upon Bartelme in recognition of her learning, ability, and contribution to the social sciences and work for the community.

After she retired in 1933, Mary Margaret Bartelme moved to Carmel by the Sea, California with her brother, sister, and niece. Although born a Protestant, Bartelme converted to the Christian Science faith late in life. She dedicated her time to her flower garden that contained roses, fuchsia, and heliotrope. Visitors to her house were often given bouquets to take home. Mary Margaret Bartelme died on July 25, 1954, at the age of eighty-eight after a brief illness. She remained dedicated to young girls right up until the end of her life. One of her last wishes was that in lieu of flowers in memorial of her death, people should make contributions to the Mary Bartelme Clubs. A portrait of Mary Margaret Bartelme, painted by Christian Abrahamsen, hangs at her alma mater, the Northwestern University School of Law in Chicago.

Mary Margaret Bartelme's contribution to women and the legal profession can best be summarized by referring back to the last paragraph of her award winning thesis. She wrote that, "precedent should be highly regarded but as customs and our mode of living changes, the laws administered must be adapted to such change and keep pace with the progress and civilization of the age." Mary Margaret Bartelme led the way in a time of social change both as the first woman judge in Illinois and as an advocate for helping adolescent girls who had become ensnared in the legal system. In her thirty-nine years of practicing law, Bartelme made lasting contributions as a symbol for the growing feminist movement, an agent for procedural change in the courtroom, and

as a tireless reformer and fundraiser that made qualitative differences in the lives of young girls. The girls that she helped continued to affect society long after Bartelme had ceased working in the legal profession. As Jane Addams wrote in tribute to her friend, "Chicago may well be proud of Judge Bartelme's fine contribution."

NELLIE CARLIN

By Edith Canter

The sixty-third woman admitted to the Illinois bar, and the second president of the Women's Bar Association of Illinois, Nellie Carlin was an independent thinker and believer in equal rights who dedicated much of her professional and personal life to efforts to advance the rights of women and children.

Nellie Carlin was born in Chicago on June 24, 1869. She was educated in the Chicago Public Schools and attended the Chicago Athenaeum Business College, studying stenography and bookkeeping. She worked as a bookkeeper for five years with Grant Baking Powder Company and Graham & Sons Bank.

After graduating from Chicago College of Law in 1896, Carlin started her legal career in the offices of Clarence Darrow. In 1900, she formed a partnership with Cora B. Hirtzel, who had been admitted to the Illinois bar ten years earlier.

In 1913, Carlin was appointed Public Guardian of Cook County, only the second woman to hold that position. As Public Guardian, Carlin was responsible largely for representing the interests of orphaned minors in obtaining their rightful estate. In 1916, Carlin ran for judge of the Municipal Court of Chicago. She lost the election by only two hundred votes.

After five years as Public Guardian, Carlin became the first woman appointed as Assistant State's Attorney of Cook County. She served in her new capacity from 1918 to 1921, prosecuting husbands and fathers for failing to support their wives and children or for contributing to the delinquency of children.

Carlin brought to the Public Guardian's and State's Attorney's offices keen insight into the social roots of the problems addressed in the family and juvenile courts. Writing about the Public Guardian's job in *Case and Comment* vol. 21 (October 1914), she noted:

> We are learning that unjust social conditions are in many cases responsible for infractions of the law... We are also learning that unjust economic conditions make bad social conditions and that child labor is the cause of much delinquency of our boys and girls. (p. 375)

Carlin advocated that courts address social problems with tools from both the legal and non-legal spheres. Commenting on her appointment as Assistant State's Attorney, Carlin wrote:

> The problem of our courts as in our daily lives are human problems and need the intelligent vision and the best thought of both men and women for their proper solution. Especially is this true in specialized courts where matters concerning the family (the foundation of our state) are considered and adjusted. While precedent is still one of the guides in law, it is not the only one and we are taking into consideration social as well as legal justice in dealing with many problems in our court (*Women Lawyers' Journal*, vol. 8 no, 2 [1918] p. 16)

Carlin was horrified by the lack of child support given to the children of unwed parents and spoke out publicly against the treatment of those children:

> What a monstrous thing it is to stigmatize the innocent victim of a wrong with the name bastard; why not repeal this law and amend the dependency statute so that when a man is found by a jury to be the father of a child then the man shall be compelled to support that child during its minority... the world is through with destruction, now let us follow the flag of reconstruction and on this banner let us blaze forth this motto: "We stand for the inalienable rights of the child." (*Women Lawyers' Journal*, vol. 8 no. 4 [1919] p. 32)

During much of her career, Carlin was actively involved in organizations supporting the rights of women. From 1915 to 1916, she was president of the Women's Bar Association of Illinois (WBAI), later serving two additional terms as director. In 1936, she was made an honorary member of the WBAI, only the second person to be given that honor. She was the founder of the Women's Protective Association of Illinois, an organization that counseled women offenders in the municipal courts, and was president of the Public Defender's League for Girls, organized to assist girls in criminal or juvenile court proceedings.

A strong advocate for girls, Carlin urged the development of a special court for delinquent girls where their problems would be addressed by women focused on educating the girls

Nellie Carlin

From James Bradwell, *Portraits of Twenty-Seven Illinois Women Lawyers* (1900), University of Illinois at Chicago The University Library Department of Special Collections

and helping them become respected members of society. Through the Women's Protective Association, Carlin advocated the development of the "Shelter House for Women," a home for delinquent girls in the nature of today's halfway houses. She argued forcefully, both within and outside the courts, for fair treatment of girls in the judicial system, invoking the slogan "not sex superiority, but sex equality."

Carlin's view on woman suffrage changed over the years. When she graduated from law school, she proclaimed herself a believer in equal rights. She did not, however, support woman suffrage because she was a follower of Herbert Spencer, an early twentieth century philosopher who questioned the right of the majority to rule. In later years, though, Carlin changed her mind about woman suffrage. She was a member of the Illinois Equal Suffrage Association and was reported to have marched in the great suffrage parade. She also became a director of the activist, pro-suffrage Chicago Political Equality League. In writing a message to the WBAI on its twentieth anniversary in 1934, Carlin praised those who worked for woman suffrage and noted the great opportunities that suffrage brought to women.

Carlin never married nor had children. She did, however, take on the responsibility of raising her orphaned nephew, William Carlin, who went on to become one of Clarence Darrow's partners. In the late 1920s, Nellie Carlin retired from her Chicago law practice and moved to Miami, Florida. There, during her retirement, she continued her community involvement, working to establish a public library. Carlin died in Miami Beach on September 4, 1948.

Carlin's intelligence, independence and activist spirit made her an effective advocate for women and children throughout her career. As the WBAI noted, honoring Carlin in 1936,

> The labor of [Nellie Carlin] over a period of many years has been of such outstanding character that we should give it due recognition on our records that in the future it shall not be forgotten by those who come after us, who do not have to establish the present position of women in public affairs... (Resolution of the Women's Bar Association of Illinois, November 5, 1936.)

THE RIGHT TO VOTE

One of the most inclusive reform movements for women lawyers was the fight for women suffrage. In 1868, when men and women in Chicago first organized to promote woman suffrage, Myra Bradwell and Catharine Van Valkenburg Waite were there, both early leaders in the movement. As the fight went forward, Waite's close friend, Catharine Waugh McCulloch stepped to the fore. In 1893, McCulloch drafted the Illinois law providing women the right to vote in presidential elections. In 1894, McCulloch joined with attorney Ellen Martin and sixteen other members of the Chicago Woman's Club to found the Chicago Political Equality League to aid in the fight for women's full political rights. A number of women lawyers were leaders in this organization. Over the next two decades, countless women lawyers joined with other women professionals and reformers to

Mother Waters

Women's Suffrage Scrapbook Collection
University of Illinois at Chicago The University
Library Department of Special Collections

fight for McCulloch's bill. Prominent among them was lawyer Antoinette Funk, a key member of the Illinois Equal Suffrage Association.

In 1913, McCulloch finally won her battle when Illinois became the first state east of the Mississippi to grant women the vote in national elections. This victory, seven years ahead of the nineteenth amendment, was particularly important to women lawyers. As members of the profession that influenced how laws were interpreted and applied, women lawyers acutely understood how important it was to have a vote in the election of the legislators who enacted the laws and the judges who ruled on the application and validity of those laws. The political sophistication and keen sense of justice demonstrated by Waite, McCulloch, and Funk were reflected not only in their suffrage activities, but throughout their careers.

CATHARINE VAN VALKENBURG WAITE

By Patricia R. McMillen

Mother of five, a successful educator, publisher and real estate developer before entering law school at the age of 56, Catharine Van Valkenburg Waite never ceased in her efforts to promote the varied interests of women, founding, in her daughters and their offspring, a veritable feminist dynasty before her death at the age of eighty-four.

Born in a small town in Ontario, Canada in 1829, Catharine Van Valkenburg emigrated with her family to southeast Iowa around the age of seventeen. After teaching school briefly in her new home, she began college studies at Knox College in west-central Illinois. In 1852, she transferred to Oberlin College (Ohio), which conferred upon her its Bachelor of Philosophy in 1853, just six years after granting to abolitionist and suffragist Lucy Stone the first college degree ever earned by a woman in the United States.

Waite would later tell her law school classmate, Catharine Waugh, how she became the first woman to deliver a graduation oration at Oberlin College, overcoming a prohibition on women's public extemporizing which had been applied even to her illustrious predecessor, Lucy Stone.

Following their marriage in 1854, Mrs. Waite and her new husband, abolitionist attorney Charles Burlingame Waite, settled in the rapidly-growing metropolis of Chicago. Together (and notwithstanding the birth of their first child, daughter Jessie Fremont, in 1856), the Waites quickly became active in the nascent Illinois woman suffrage movement, travelling throughout the state to lecture and advocate, and becoming supporters of Illinois' first local suffrage organization, formed in Earlville, Illinois in 1855.

In Chicago, Mrs. Waite also resumed her career as an educator. In 1859, after teaching briefly at Union Park Seminary, she founded the Hyde Park Seminary, a girls' boarding school in a country retreat just being settled south of Chicago. The Waites moved to the country town that same year, becoming two of the area's earliest residents. The rapid growth of Hyde Park (incorporated in 1861, and annexed by the city of Chicago in 1889) would afford Mrs. Waite ample territory for her later ventures in real estate.

In 1862, however, her life took perhaps its most interesting turn, when Charles Waite's acquaintance with President Abraham Lincoln yielded him an appointment as one of two associate justices of the supreme court of Utah territory. The family—by then including three small daughters—relocated to the frontier town of Salt Lake City, whose Mormon residents that year celebrated the fifteenth anniversary of their mass migration from western Illinois. While her husband represented the federal government to this not altogether welcoming community, Waite took notes for what would eventually become her most renowned publication: a scathing critique of Mormon leader Brigham Young which she titled *The Mormon Prophet and His Harem* (Cambridge: Riverside Press, 1866)

Published after the family returned to Chicago, and dedicated "to the suffering women of Utah," the book focussed the brunt of its wrath upon the practice of polygamy, which Waite criticized both from Biblical and feminist perspectives. An otherwise lukewarm review in *The New York Times*, (June 4, 1866, p.2 col.1) noted Waite's bias with approval, opining that "the hearty hatred [the author] shows for the 'peculiar institution' [i.e., polygamy] is the chief redeeming feature of her book."

Following an unsuccessful application for admission to Rush Medical College of Chicago in 1866, Waite resumed her roles both at the Hyde Park Seminary (which remained open until 1871) and in the suffrage movement. In 1868, she and Charles joined in a resolution calling for formation of a state-wide suffrage advocacy association in Illinois. That organization—the Illinois Woman Suffrage Association (IWSA)—was founded the following year, at a February gathering in Chicago's Library Hall, and quickly deputized Judge Waite (along with Judge James Bradwell, husband of Myra) to present to the 1870 Illinois Constitutional Convention a draft state suffrage amendment. While passage failed, the negotiators did succeed in eliminating sex as a bar to the holding of state offices.

After serving one term (in 1871) as IWSA president, Catharine Waite then became its legislative superintendent, over the next eight years patiently (and unsuccessfully) presenting to each successive Illinois legislature IWSA's resolution for equal suffrage. In 1869, she and Charles also with Myra and James Bradwell lobbied the Illinois legislature to gain passage for a bill, drafted by Myra Bradwell, giving women the right to control their own earnings.

Interestingly, while the Waites were apparently in philosophical harmony on the suffrage question, 1869 gives evidence they may have had strategic disagreements. While Catharine Waite sided with the National Woman Suffrage Association of Elizabeth Cady Stanton and Susan B. Anthony,

that year, in Cleveland, Judge Waite attended the initial meeting of the rival American Woman Suffrage Association and was elected its Vice President.

In 1870, post-Civil-War Reconstruction yielded the Fifteenth Amendment to the United States Constitution, providing, in Section 1, that

> The right of citizens of the United States to vote shall not be denied or abridged by the United States or by any State on account of race, color, or previous condition of servitude.

Across the country, woman suffragists wondered if they, too, might benefit from the new language. In November of 1871, as part of a coordinated multistate effort to test this theory (Susan B. Anthony, in New York, was another test case plaintiff), Catharine Waite applied to the Hyde Park board of elections to be registered as a voter. When her application was summarily denied, she sued, retaining her husband to argue her case.

The opinion of Chief Judge Jameson of the Superior Court of Cook County, denying Waite's petition, was typical of those in similar cases decided at the time. While agreeing that women were citizens of the United States, the judge noted that citizenship did not automatically confer the right to vote: as examples, "children, criminals, lunatics and persons residing in the unorganized territories of the Union, have never been voters." (*The People ex rel Catharine V. Waite v. Horace V. Stebbins et al., Chicago Legal News* vol. 4 [Super. Ct. of Cook County, Illinois, January 12, 1872] p. 97) While refusing to expand the franchise judicially to women, the judge (a former law partner of Charles Waite) instead encouraged the would-be voters to use "the same means which children, women and disenfranchised classes generally have always employed in such cases—and there can be no other—namely, agitation, petition, remonstrance, and if this avail not, then revolution." *ibid*.

Over the next several years, the Waites cooperated on a number of extra-legal ventures, including the birth of their last child, Joseph Van Valkenburg Waite, in 1875. (Joseph's birth brought the number of Waite children to five, joining sisters Jessie, Lucy, and Margaret, and brother Charles Lincoln [b. 1865]. A sixth child [date of birth unknown] did not survive childhood.) Charles' legal career was waning, in its place a varied set of activities as a linguist, philosopher and scholar. In 1881, Catharine's C. V. Waite & Co., Publishing published Charles' magnum opus, *The History of the Christian Religion to the Year 200* (Chicago: C.V. Waite & Co., Publishing, 1881) which would later be translated into French, German, and even Norwegian for use in universities. Catharine's own *Adventures in the Far West and Life Among the Mormons* (Chicago: C.V. Waite & Co., Publishing, 1882) followed the next year. A recasting of her earlier book on Brigham Young, *Adventures in the Far West*, a thinly-veiled autobiographical account of the Utah odyssey of a "Mr. and Mrs. Burlingame", included much additional material, some of which suggested that Waite may, while living in Utah, have risked her family's security in order to foster an anti-polygamy Mormon splinter group, referred to in the later book as the "Josephites."

But at last, law school beckoned. Throughout her adult life, Waite had studied law independently; she once claimed to have "enjoyed reading Blackstone and Kent when most women would have read novels" (letter to The Equity Club, May 4, 1888, collected in the Papers of Caroline I. Reilly [the "Reilly Papers"], Schlesinger Library, Radcliffe College) When Joseph turned ten years old, it was time for Waite to indulge this curiosity full-time. Despite Charles' extended absences on research trips, during which Waite fulfilled the role of single parent along with her other ventures, Waite entered the Union College of Law in 1885, becoming its fifth female graduate in 1886 at the age of fifty-seven. Later that year, she became the eighteenth woman licensed to practice law in the State of Illinois.

Waite's Union College class was the first to include two women law students. Her classmate, Catharine Waugh—for whom Waite served as a sort of surrogate campus mother, warding off unwelcome male attentions but encouraging Waugh's friendship with (and eventual marriage to) their dashing young classmate, Frank McCulloch—later wrote the following reminiscence:

> Though [Waite] had studied law for years and had tried cases in courts of justices of the peace, she had never taken a law degree and so she secured her law degree when she was past fifty years of age. There was none of her young classmates who had a keener mind, a clearer knowledge of law than she. (from an unpublished, undated reminiscence of Catharine Waugh McCulloch, Women's Studies Manuscript Collection of the Schlesinger Library, Radcliffe College)

Recounting an incident in which Waite flirtatiously returned the attentions of her younger male classmates on a spring morning, McCulloch added:

> [Catharine Waite's] sense of humor and her liking for young people made her a good comrade to all her law classmates, [not at all] as stern and cold as some people imagine the early women suffragists to be (*ibid*)

Catharine Van Valkenburg Waite
Sophia Smith Collection, Smith College

Notwithstanding her age, Waite made full use of her law degree in the years following her licensure. Sharing office space at times with her husband or daughter, physician Lucy Clapp Waite (b. 1860), she opened a private law practice, limiting her cases to the pro bono representation of poor women. In November 1886, her publishing company also inaugurated its quarterly law journal, the *Chicago Law Times*. The journal, while short-lived (publication ceased in 1889), favored articles on what today might be called feminist jurisprudence, including developments in marital law, women's political rights, and the progress of women worldwide in gaining access to the bar—a particular interest of Waite, who in 1888 helped found, and served as first president of, the International Women's Bar Association. In a pattern of family cooperation typical of her entire life, Waite called upon her then unmarried daughter Margaret (b. 1862) to be the journal's co-publisher and, occasionally, a contributing author; husband Charles, for his part, authored "Suffrage: A Right of Citizenship" for the journal's inaugural issue, and contributed, as well, accounts of his travels in Europe to each issue.

But Waite's creative energies may perhaps have found their greatest outlet in the real estate business. Around 1890, one biographer lauded her talents thus:

> She has...made her mark in business affairs, operating a real estate business with notable success. She builds houses, rents them, and personally attends to their management. She is her own architect, draughting her plans and putting them into the hands of builders without the aid of any contractors or middlemen. She has built more than fifty houses, and has recently completed the finest business block ever erected in Hyde Park (from a published biographical sketch, source unknown, dated around 1890)

Waite's last major political role was as treasurer of the Queen Isabella Association, founded in 1889 to represent the interests of professional women at the World's Columbian Exposition, to be held in the Hyde Park neighborhood in 1893. Named for Columbus' patron, Queen Isabella of Castile, the Association built its own pavilion just outside the Exposition entrance and commissioned sculptress Harriet Hosmer to create a statue of the Queen. Both projects were financed by public subscription (at $5.00 per share) and by sales of a history written by Association president Eliza Allen Starr (published, of course, by C. V. Waite & Co.). During the Exposition, the Association's pavilion became the site of well-attended international congresses of women attorneys and women physicians, with the medical congress coordinated, fittingly enough, by Dr. Lucy Waite.

Charles and Catharine Waite traveled together to Europe and the Middle East and co-authored one last book, *Homophonic Conversations* (Chicago: C.V. Waite & Co., Publishers, 1903), a travelers' phrasebook, prior to Charles' death in 1909. Four years later—just five months after the passage of the Illinois presidential suffrage bill in June of 1913—Catharine van Valkenburg Waite died of heart failure at the Park Ridge home of her daughter Margaret. She was eighty-four years old.

As mentioned above, Waite's feminist ideals did not die with her, but lived on in her children and grandchildren. Her eldest daughter, Jessie Waite Wright, became an active suffragist in Washington, D.C., addressing the House Judiciary Committee at the age of twenty-three as an Illinois delegate to a woman's suffrage convention in 1880. Daughter Lucy—the first woman graduate of the University of Chicago to attend medical school—became a protégé of Dr. Mary Harris Thompson, first female surgeon in Chicago. A highly-respected gynecologist, Lucy followed Dr. Thompson as Head Surgeon and Medical Superintendent of the Mary Thompson Hospital for Women and Children in Chicago and remained active in women's professional and political organizations all of her life. And closing the circle, psychiatrist Katharine Wright, daughter of Jessie, returned to Chicago to found, in 1947, an outpatient women's mental health clinic (now part of the Illinois Masonic Medical Center) with hours and services geared particularly to working women.

Her grandmother would have been proud.

CATHARINE WAUGH MCCULLOCH

By Maria A. Harrigan

Catharine Waugh McCulloch, a visionary with unwavering determination, led the fight for women's suffrage and the advancement of women in the legal profession. Admitted to the Illinois bar in 1886, she practiced law in both Rockford and Chicago. A mentor and a leader, McCulloch was a founder of the Women's Bar Association of Illinois and was active in many other professional and political organizations. As the first woman justice of the peace and then a master in chancery court , McCulloch spent her life breaking barriers and lending her hand to those following behind her.

Catharine Waugh McCulloch was born Catharine Waugh on June 4, 1862, in Ransomville, New York. She was the first-born of two children and the only daughter of Susan and Abraham Waugh. When Catharine was five years old, the family moved to New Millford, Illinois.

Catharine was known as "her father's little lawyer" from childhood. After graduating from Rockford Female Seminary in 1882, she spent eighteen months as a temperance speaker in northwest Illinois. In 1886, she graduated from the Union College of Law, which later became Northwestern University School of Law.

Waugh attended law school with Catharine V. Waite. Waite was fifty-six when she attended law school and became Waugh's mentor. Waite assisted Catharine Waugh in coping with the male-dominated law school classroom and introduced Waugh to her future husband, Frank McCulloch.

Catharine Waugh was admitted to the Illinois bar on November 9, 1886, one of only eighteen women admitted between 1875 and 1887. Attempting to establish a legal practice in Chicago, she faced a great deal of prejudice from male attorneys. Consequently, she returned to Rockford to begin her law practice, which included mortgage foreclosures, divorces, wills and estates, collection, and probate.

While practicing law, Waugh returned to Rockford Female Seminary and received bachelor's and master's degrees in 1888. In her masters' thesis, entitled "Women's Wages," Waugh wrote about the perceived excuses and real reasons for the inequality between the wages of men and women. Relying on John Stuart Mill's theory of the selfishness of men, she argued that men were accustomed to being served by women and did not want to give that up. She also proposed several ways to remedy the inequality, including an increased emphasis on women's education, woman suffrage, and the expansion of property rights for women. Her interest in and work with the suffrage movement would remain one of the primary passions of her life.

Catharine Waugh married Frank McCulloch on May 30, 1890, at her parents' home in a ceremony performed by Reverend Anna Howard Shaw, a leader in the temperance movement. At first, Waugh refused to use her husband's name. It was not until much later in life that she began using McCulloch. The couple spent their honeymoon in South Dakota, where Waugh conducted a series of lectures for local suffrage groups. After marriage, Frank and Catharine Waugh McCulloch settled in Evanston, Illinois, and Waugh McCulloch joined her husband's law firm in Chicago. In 1898, she was admitted to practice law before the United States Supreme Court.

McCulloch's involvement in the women's suffrage movement, both nationally and locally, expanded after marriage. In 1890, following in the footsteps of her law school mentor, Catharine Waite, she became superintendent of the Illinois Equal Suffrage Association. While superintendent, she drafted a bill providing for women's suffrage in presidential and certain local elections that were not limited to male voters by the Illinois Constitution. Beginning in 1893, the bill was introduced in the Illinois State Legislature on numerous occasions before finally becoming law in 1913. As a result of McCulloch's efforts, Illinois became the first state east of the Mississippi River to grant women suffrage in a presidential election.

McCulloch also spoke on behalf of the suffrage cause in Illinois and surrounding states. In 1908, she addressed the Michigan Constitutional Convention regarding the injustices of the 1850 Michigan Constitution, primarily its failure to grant women suffrage or the right to hold office. She noted the many root causes for this failure, including, the lack of educated, prominent women residing in Michigan and the lack of women's groups such as a suffrage association at the time. Her speech was published in a pamphlet entitled "The Wrongs of Michigan Women."

In her speeches, McCulloch theorized that if women had the right to vote, many of their problems would be alleviated. She was sure that property rights, jury service, guardianship rights, and even children's rights would be implemented at the passage of woman suffrage.

In addition to her work in the suffrage movement, McCulloch ran for Justice of the Peace, winning two successive terms in 1907 and 1909. In 1913, she accepted the position of Law Dean at Illinois College of Law. Her responsibilities included giving lectures to students; those lectures were open to both men and women. She was also the first woman appointed a master in chancery, serving in the Superior Court from 1917 to 1925.

McCulloch was also involved in the introduction and passage of other legislation. For example, she drafted and lobbied for legislation raising the age of consent in Illinois from fourteen to sixteen. She also worked for the passage of a bill assuring joint guardianship by parents of their children. In 1920, she was joined by Esther Dunshee, a fellow suffragist, in introducing a bill that would allow women to serve on juries. After years of effort and struggle by the Women's Bar Association of Illinois, the bill was finally passed in 1939.

McCulloch was involved in many professional organizations. She was the first president of the Illinois Democratic Women's Club. She helped found the Women's Bar Association of Illinois, the Women's City Club, and the Evanston Women's Club. She was a member of the American, Illinois, and Chicago Bar Associations. She was on the executive committees of the Chicago Commons, the Illinois League of Women Voters, the Chicago Church Federation, and the Board of Trustees of Rockford College. She was an active member of the Women's Christian Temperance Union, the Mothers' Club, the Anti-Cigarette League, the First Congregational Church of Evanston, the National Women's Democratic Law Enforcement League, the Civil Liberties Union, the Women's League for Peace and Freedom, and the

Catharine Waugh McCulloch

From James Bradwell, *Portraits of Twenty-Seven Illinois Women Lawyers* (1900), University of Illinois at Chicago The University Library Department of Special Collections

Daughters of the American Revolution. She was also one of thirty-two members of the Equity Club, one of the first national and international organizations of women lawyers in American history.

McCulloch wrote letters to the Equity Club on issues of concern to the members including the struggle of balancing marriage and an active law practice. Many club members remained single because they felt marriage was too large a responsibility in conjuction with a successful career. Other members were married to lawyers with whom they practiced and struggled over whether or not they should appear in court. Some decided to leave courtroom appearances to their husbands, while they remained in the office. While McCulloch personally preferred to conduct business in this manner, she had no objection to women representing clients in court. She did, however, suggest that, just as a male lawyer would, a woman should remove her hat in court.

One of the biggest issues for members was whether to be "lady lawyers" or simply lawyers. In nineteenth century society, business was seen as the male sphere, while charity was seen as the female domain. Some Equity Club members insisted that in order to succeed, they had to adopt the male lawyers' model of success and reject charity work. Other members, McCulloch among them, felt that charity work and social reform should be appropriated into their professional lives and that they should use their legal expertise to help others. In fact, McCulloch devoted much of her legal practice to charity work for poor women clients.

McCulloch had broad political interests aside from her legal practice and other work. In 1936, she and her husband traveled across several continents, visiting New Zealand, Australia, South Africa, South Rhodesia, the Tanzanian Territory, and Kenya. They published a pamphlet explaining various programs established by the governments of the countries they visited. The pamphlet suggested that some of those programs be implemented in the United States. Many of the programs were communist and socialist in nature, involving the regulation and nationalization of businesses, government ownership of utilities, and extensive social aid, including workers' relief. McCulloch also became enamored with the Soviet Union's legal system, which she viewed as very friendly towards women.

McCulloch had a very busy and full family life. She and her husband raised four children, Hugh Waugh (b. 1891), Hawthorn Waugh (b. 1899), Catharine Waugh (b. 1901) and

Frank Waugh (b. 1905). All of them graduated from college. Law coursed through the Waugh McCulloch children's blood. Their three sons became lawyers and worked in the family firm, while their daughter studied music, and eventually married a lawyer.

On May 30, 1940, Frank and Catharine McCulloch celebrated their fiftieth wedding anniversary. That same year, the McCullochs were named "Senior Counselors" by the Illinois State Bar Association.

In 1945, at the age of eighty-two, Catharine Waugh McCulloch died of cancer in Evanston Hospital. Her husband died two years later. They are both interred at Graceland Cemetery in Chicago.

Catharine Waugh McCulloch was an outstanding lawyer and a most dedicated advocate for women's causes. Against almost insurmountable odds, she and her contemporaries entered into and worked within a male-dominated profession, became active in politics and professional organizations, pressed for the passage of and achieved woman suffrage, furthered the cause of women's rights, and fostered discussions of women's issues, many of which are still germane today.

ANTOINETTE LELAND FUNK

By Patricia R. McMillen

Born in 1869 and orphaned at a young age, Antoinette Leland Funk nonetheless survived to become one of Illinois' most prominent women lawyers, a leading suffragist, and a political campaigner who by 1925 would reportedly have "spoken on suffrage, war activities and political issues in every state of the union." (Marquis, Albert Nelson, ed., *Who's Who in America*, 1924-1925 (Chicago: A. N. Marquis & Co., 1924), p. 1242)

Funk began life in Dwight, Illinois, the daughter of Cyrus Leland and Virginia Antoinette (Bouverain) Leland, in May 1869. Raised by relatives after losing both her parents, young Antoinette received an early education in the public schools, then married John Watrous, an actor, in 1887, at the age of 18. Their one child, Anna Virginia, was born in 1893.

Mr. Watrous' untimely death left the young mother widowed, but not for long: on June 5, 1895, wearing a hand-pearled silk wedding dress, Mrs. Watrous was married to Isaac Lincoln Funk, age 32 and a member of an illustrious Bloomington, Illinois family.

Although her second daughter, Rey Leland Funk, was born the following year, Funk apparently saw no reason to postpone her further education, instead entering the two year law course at Illinois Wesleyan University, from which she was graduated in June 1898. Shortly thereafter, her second marriage appears to have foundered, and Funk moved to Pontiac,

Illinois. There, following her admission to the Illinois Bar in October, 1898, she practiced law with C. C. Strawn & Son and appears to have lived, at least for a time, as a boarder in the home of John Keach at 735 Main St., Pontiac, where other guests included six-year-old "Annie V. Funk" and four-year-old "Ray L. Funk". (The 1900 census for the township of Pontiac, Livingston County, Illinois, shows a 31-year-old, twice-married mother of two named "Marie A. Funk" at the Keach address. That this is, however, the census-taker's erroneous name for Antoinette L. Funk seems undeniable, particularly given the indication of the woman's occupation as "Lawyer".)

In 1902, Funk moved around eighty miles northeast of Pontiac, to Chicago, where she opened her first private law office at 120 West Adams Street. According to a memorial published after Funk's death in the *Chicago Law Bulletin*, by her fellow lawyer Grace A. Harte, Funk soon became

> for a number of years, ...probably the most noticeable and dynamic lawyer of her sex to be seen in the courts of Cook county...[sic] She distinguished herself in trial work, and earned the respect of her professional brethren for her intelligence, quick wit, poise, careful preparation and knowledge of the law and decisions in the cases in which she engaged. ("Women's Bar Personal Views and Notes," *Chicago Law Bulletin*, April 13, 1942)

Years later, an article in the Bloomington *Daily Pantagraph* ("Antoinette Funk Quits Federal Post," Bloomington *Daily Pantagraph*, [November 3, 1939] p. 24, col. 5.) would note admiringly her successful defense, while practicing in Chicago, of one Nathan Breen, charged with murder when he shot his sweetheart, Irene Donner, who jilted him after spending all his money. The shooting was admitted, but the defense was temporary insanity due to Breen's treatment by his girl friend. Breen was given a light prison sentence.

In Chicago, Funk also joined the campaign arm of the Democratic National Committee, thus beginning a lifelong involvement in national politics. In 1912, she was active in the unsuccessful Progressive party campaign to re-elect former President Theodore Roosevelt; in 1916, she "stumped the state" for Democrat Woodrow Wilson.

Meanwhile, however, Funk also became a tireless worker in the battle to secure voting rights for women, first in state and then in national elections. In the fight to secure the vote for Illinois women, Funk's name was inextricably linked with that of Illinois Equal Suffrage Association (IESA) president Grace Wilbur Trout, the "noiseless suffragette" who, with Mrs. Sherman Booth and Mrs. Medill McCormick, led the final, successful campaign resulting in passage of the Presidential suffrage bill in the Illinois legislature in 1913.

Following the unsuccessful Roosevelt campaign of 1912, Funk was called to Springfield in May 1913 to assist Trout in lobbying for passage of the pending initiative, drafted by fellow attorney Catharine Waugh McCulloch, to permit Illinois women to vote in United States Presidential elections and in all elections not otherwise prohibited by the Illinois state constitution. The Springfield lobbyists methodically worked the state's legislators, and managed to push the bill through the state Senate by May of 1913. They then organized a massive telephone campaign aimed at persuading Speaker William McKinley to call the bill for a vote in the Illinois House. As Trout later reported, over one weekend spent by Speaker McKinley in Chicago, the phones at home and in his Chicago office rang every fifteen minutes, day and night, with pro-suffrage calls placed "by leading men as well as women." (Grace Wilbur Trout, "Sidelights on Illinois Suffrage History" in *Journal of the Illinois State Historical Society*, vol. 13 [1920] p. 145, at 162) Needless to say, the Speaker quickly capitulated, and by the end of June 1913, the bill had been signed into law. Fifteen thousand women were said to have marched in the victory parade on Michigan Avenue in Chicago, led, according to Grace Harte's *Chicago Law Bulletin* memorial cited above, by "Antoinette Funk's carriage, bearing large banners."

Antoinette Leland Funk

Sarah Rehtmeyer Collection

In November 1913, Funk addressed the 45th National American Woman Suffrage Association (NAWSA) convention in Washington, D.C. on the subject of the Illinois victory. The convention delegates promptly elected her to the NAWSA Congressional Committee, whose purpose was to work for an amendment to the U. S. Constitution affording women the right to vote in national elections.

Working, again, with McCormick and Booth—this time in Washington, D.C.—Funk found herself in the midst of controversy when, in early 1914, she drafted an amendment which she hoped would be accepted by Congressional factions primarily opposed to woman suffrage on the basis of states' rights. Funk's amendment which became known as the "Shafroth-Palmer Amendment" after its introduction in the U. S. Senate by Sen. John F. Shafroth of Colorado and in the House of Representatives by Rep. A. Mitchell Palmer of Pennsylvania, attempted to meet the objections of states'-rightists (primarily Southern Democrats) by providing for state-by-state ratification of the federal suffrage amendment by a majority of its registered voters.

Although preliminarily passed upon by NAWSA's Official Board prior to its introduction in Congress in early 1914, Funk's amendment outraged delegates at NAWSA's general convention, held in Nashville later that year. Withdrawing its support for Funk's strategy, NAWSA returned to its earlier (and ultimately successful) position which made universal suffrage binding upon all states once the federal amendment had been ratified by the legislatures of 36 states (three-quarters of the 48 states then included in the union).

Disunity on strategic details did not, however, deter Funk's efforts to ensure support throughout the United States for some form of universal suffrage. Her report to the 1914 NAWSA convention boasted of her travels during the preceding summer, when, she said, she covered eight thousand miles in two months to speak to voters and potential voters throughout the Midwestern and Western U. S. She deplored the efforts of the western brewery interests, in particular, to oppose women's votes, but proudly described the support evident during a one-day visit to the South Dakota state fair:

Every prize-winning animal, every racing sulky, automobile and motorcycle carried our pennants... The squaws from the reservation did their native dances waving suffrage banners, and the snake charmer on the midway carried a Votes for Women pennant while an enormous serpent coiled around her body. (Quoted in Ida Husted Harper, ed., *The History of Woman Suffrage, volume V* (New York: National American Woman Suffrage Association, 1922), pp. 420-421.)

No doubt, it was in recognition of Funk's enthusiasm that the 1914 NAWSA convention re-appointed her as vice-chair of the Congressional Committee, a position she continued to fill until her resignation in 1916.

During Funk's tenure with NAWSA in Washington, her close working relationship with Grace Wilbur Trout apparently gave way to renewed alliance with Trout's rival, Chicago suffragist Catharine Waugh McCulloch. In a letter written to McCulloch in 1915, Funk expressed her view that Trout had allied herself with "all sorts of queer associations that...we could not endorse; that the time is here when a smaller organization than Trout's, made up of a better class of women, could in a few years put a snuffer on the undesirables and amalgamate all the rest." (Letter to Catharine Waugh McCulloch, March 17, 1915) In the same letter, Mrs. Funk inquired as to the willingness of Chicago suffragist Elvira Seass Stewart to join the national cause in Washington, and described sources of funding for Stewart's salary, including "some small articles of silver and gold..."—apparently, jewelry donated by suffrage supporters—"that will perhaps bring us...$25". (*ibid.*) In a later letter, Funk turned again to McCulloch to explore a question of suffrage policy—a question that, perhaps, betrayed a certain otherwise-hidden motivation for Funk's enthusiastic embrace of the suffrage movement:

> It seems to me that our Association, and indeed, all suffragists, whether they belong to us or not, ought to stand as strongly for prohibition as for suffrage... I am not able to understand why in the past these two movements have not gone along together. Don't you think that they should do so in the future? If not, why not? I know you have a much more extensive viewpoint on the matter of suffrage history. Please tell me. (letter to McCulloch dated April 2, 1915)

With other women—suffragists and antisuffragists alike—Funk loaned her talents to the nation during World War I. As one of eleven women (including Trout) appointed in 1917 to the Women's Committee of the Council of National Defense, she assisted in the effort to "coordinat[e] the women's preparedness movement." She also served as vice chair, executive officer, and "Director—Propaganda and Speakers' Department" of the National Woman's Liberty Loan Committee, raising funds to assist in the nation's war effort.

Following the war, Funk remained active in national politics, serving in the Education Department of the Democratic Party during the unsuccessful Presidential campaign of James Cox in 1919-1920 against Warren Harding, and maintaining at least part-time residence in Washington, D.C. (From time to time she may also have resided in Santa Fe, New Mexico with her eldest daughter, Anna Virginia Huey, and family.) Her government service also continued, with a six-year stint as assistant commissioner of public lands under President Franklin D. Roosevelt's Secretary of the Interior, fellow Progressive (and former Chicago journalist) Harold L. Ickes, beginning in 1933.

In 1939, Funk resigned her position due to ill health, and on March 27, 1942, she died in San Diego, California. She was seventy-three years old.

POLITICAL OFFICE

Viewing politics as a means of reform, as soon as women became lawyers, they started to run for political office. In 1870, through the efforts of Myra and James Bradwell and Catharine and Charles Waite, the legislators at the Illinois Constitutional Convention had removed the prohibition against women holding state offices. In 1881, still decades before women won the right to vote, Ada Kepley ran for State Attorney General on the Prohibition ticket. In 1888, Catharine Waugh McCulloch was nominated by the Prohibition Party in Rockford as its candidate for Winnebago County State's Attorney. The goals of these women as candidates went beyond personal gain; they sought the protection and advancement of women in society.

Installation of Judge Mary Bartelme

Judge Victor Arnold, Catharine Waugh McCulloch, Judge Mary Bartelme,
Sara Hart, Bessie Bradwell Helmer, and Charles Cutting

Chicago Legal News volume 6 (1923) page 165

The first successful campaign for an Illinois woman lawyer occurred in Utah. In 1902, Mary Geigus Coulter was elected to the Utah House of Representatives. She remained active in politics throughout her career. The first successful campaign in Illinois occurred in 1907 when Catharine Waugh McCulloch was elected Justice of the Peace.

Once women won the vote in Illinois, they increased their efforts to attain political office. In 1913, the nation turned its attention to Marion Drake, a young woman lawyer challenging the notorious "Bathhouse" John Coughlin for the alderman's seat in Chicago's corrupt first ward. Drake ran a determined campaign of political and moral reform. Though she had the support of a strong women's movement, she could not overcome Coughlin's powerful political force. It was in response to Drake's candidacy that Coughlin uttered his notorious proclamation, "Chicago ain't ready for reform."

Despite Drake's defeat, her candidacy brought women further into the political scene. Building on this history of political candidacy, other women lawyers were successful in their campaigns for elective office. In 1922, Isabel Quinlan was elected Mayor of Benton, Wisconsin. But it was in 1923, when Mary Bartelme ran for judge in Cook County, that Illinois women lawyers firmly established their presence in elective office.

After twenty years of legal practice that focused on the rights of women and children, Bartelme viewed the bench as a powerful means to further her reform work. Savvy to the cultural restrictions that remained, Bartelme campaigned under a dual philosophy that she was the most experienced and competent candidate, and that as a woman she was naturally more qualified to preside over children in the Juvenile court. With support that crossed gender and race lines, Bartelme won the seat by 14,000 votes.

MARY GEIGUS COULTER

by Suzanne M. Bonds

Mary Anna Clara Geigus Coulter, the seventeenth woman lawyer admitted to the Illinois bar, graduated with honors in 1885 from the law department of the Michigan University (later the University of Michigan Law School). Although she never practiced law in a law office, she was greatly interested in, and participated in, movements for social reform. In 1902, she was elected to the Utah State House of Representatives, where she was chosen chair of the Judiciary Committee. Mary Geigus Coulter used her legislative position to advance reforms in the laws affecting children. She was also active in civic and education associations, which included her election as President of the Utah Federal Women's Clubs.

Mary Anna Clara Geigus was born to John Nicholas and Caroline C. (Wasmund) Geigus on September 7, 1859, in Savanna, Illinois. In 1880, she graduated with an A. B. from Northwestern College, Naperville, Illinois. From 1882 to 1883, Geigus attended Michigan University, taking classes in the Literary Department. She then began studying law, successfully completing her education with honors. In fact, she was

the only female to graduate in the 1885 law class. After graduating from the University of Michigan in 1885, she was admitted to both the Illinois and Michigan bars.

In September 1885, Geigus wrote to Ellen Martin, the third woman lawyer admitted to the Illinois bar, seeking employment. Although it is unclear what response Mary Geigus received from Ellen Martin, Mary Geigus Coulter did not open a law office in Chicago. Instead on October 7, 1985, Geigus married Chester Emory Coulter, M.D. and moved to Ogden, Utah, where she spent most of the remainder of her eighty-six year life in community service.

Mary Geigus Coulter

From *Women Legislators of Utah 1896-1993*, compiled by Delila M. Abbott and Beverly J. White (1993) with permission

Coulter began her career as a teacher in the public school system in Utah. She founded and became president of the Alglaia Club and, in 1900, was elected president of the Utah Federated Women's Clubs. She enjoyed being involved in the community and was even elected vice president of the National Association of Women Lawyers headquartered then in New York City during a period of time when she was living only temporarily in New York.

Coulter was also interested in social issues and the arts. Her memberships along these lines were varied. They included the National Arts Club of New York City, Order of Women Legislators, European Literati and Booklovers, and the Societe Academique d'Histoire International of France.

In 1902, Mary Geigus Coulter was elected to the Utah House of Representatives. During her three-year tenure she was appointed chairman of the Judiciary Committee. While serving in state government, she sponsored and formulated legislation addressing social reforms, education, and child labor. One issue of particular interest was the betterment of social conditions for abandoned and neglected children.

Coulter was elected twice as the delegate to the Republican State Convention, and once for the Progressive Party in 1912. She was also a presidential elector for the Progressive Party in 1912 and a speaker in two national campaigns in Utah, and she was courageous enough to spend two years in the Orient in the early 1900's studying conditions there.

Geigus and her husband had one son, Halvor Geigus. In 1916, Halvor was a Captain in the Coast Defenses. By 1944, he had attained the rank of Major. It has been written that one of

Mary Geigus Coulter's major satisfactions of her later life was to see her son recognized as a writer of distinction in the fields of both drama and fiction.

On July 25, 1946, some thirty-one years after her husband had succumbed to Bridget's disease, Mary Geigus Coulter died after a prolonged illness. At the time of her death a local Ogden, Utah newspaper appropriately stated: "She will be remembered by all who knew her as a woman of rare attainments. . ."

MARION DRAKE

By Scott Schmidt

Suffragist, Progressive, and social activist, Marion Drake's greatest triumph, ironically, came in political defeat, as her unsuccessful campaign for the seat of a corrupt Chicago alderman focussed the nation's attention on the realities of Chicago vice.

Marion Drake was born in Beloit, Wisconsin, in 1864, the eldest daughter of Massachusetts natives Manly Drake (b. 1843) and his wife, Marie E. (b. 1840). In 1870, along with Marion's younger brother, Lyman, and Manly's widowed mother Mary Ann, the family moved to Chicago, where Manly originally found work at the Board of Trade and, later, in the real estate business.

Young Miss Drake worked as a stenographer before enrolling in the Chicago College of Law. She graduated from law school in 1892 and was admitted to the Illinois bar in June of that year.

After graduating, apparently at or near the top of her class, Miss Drake followed her law school dean, former Illinois trial and appellate court judge Thomas A. Moran, into practice with the firm of Moran, Kraus & Mayer. In addition to Moran, the name partners of the firm included founder (and former Chicago corporation counsel) Adolf Kraus and the brilliant young attorney Levy Mayer, whose long career would stress representation of business and financial clients, many in precedent-setting battles. In one such case, argued during Drake's tenure with the firm, Mayer succeeded in having Illinois' "eight-hour law" (prohibiting manufacturers from employing women for more than eight hours per day, or forty-eight hours per week) struck down as an unconstitutional infringement on citizens' freedom of contract. *Ritchie v. The People of the State of Illinois*, 155 Ill. 98 (1895). The firm founded by Kraus and Mayer in 1881 survives today as Mayer, Brown & Platt, one of Chicago's larger and more prestigious law firms.

Marion Drake

From James Bradwell, *Portraits of Twenty-Seven Illinois Women Lawyers* (1900), University of Illinois at Chicago The University Library Department of Special Collections

In 1895, Drake was selected to give the commencement address for her law school alma mater. Her speech, entitled "The Lawyer as Philanthropist", stressed the importance of lawyers' participation in civic affairs and deplored their growing concern with profitability—themes still relevant to lawyers today.

Perhaps as a result of this strong belief in the progressive social role of lawyers, and her support of protective labor legislation for women and children Drake resigned from the Moran firm in 1898 and established her own practice, opening her first office at 189 West Madison Street. In the following years, she founded a court reporting business, and became active in politics and in such civic organizations as the Immigrant Protective League. She served as first ward chair of the Women's City Club of Chicago, a progressive organization dedicated to civic and moral reform, and was a member of the Chicago Law Institute, a voluntary organization of lawyers which maintained a library, desks and meeting rooms for lawyers' use in the Chicago City Hall.

But Miss Drake's civic agenda would culminate in the Chicago aldermanic election of 1914. In May of 1913, the Illinois legislature granted limited voting rights to women, permitting them to register and vote in all elections not otherwise prohibited by the state constitution. As soon as the bill was signed into law, activist women throughout Illinois began preparations to mobilize women to vote at their earliest opportunities, including, in Chicago, the general municipal elections scheduled for April 1914.

In northern Illinois, Drake became the first President of the Cook County Suffrage Alliance, an organization formed in early 1914 to encourage women's campaigns for office. With the assistance of the Alliance and other such organizations, and despite ongoing attacks on the new law's constitutionality (Drake's former employer, Levy Mayer, represented anti-suffrage liquor interests in one such attack), over 200,000 women were registered throughout the state, and petitions filed on behalf of female candidates in eight Chicago aldermanic races. According to the account of Lloyd Wendt and Herman Kogan in *Lords of the Levee* (Indianapolis: The Bobbs-Merrill Co., [1943] cited herein as *Lords of the Levee*), candidates included Harriet Vittum, head resident of the Northwestern University Settlement and Woman's Club president, in the 17th ward, and "one-time seamstress" Bernice Napieralski in the 12th.

But the toughest race of all—the contest to unseat the First Ward's eleven-term alderman, the notorious "Bathhouse John" Coughlin—would be mounted by Marion Drake herself. In 1914, the First Ward stretched from Lake Street on the north to 29th Street on the south, from the lakefront to the Chicago River, and encompassed not only Chicago's main mercantile and business districts, but a red-light district known as "the Levee." Brothels, gambling houses and saloons lined the Levee's streets, and political clout determined which of them would survive the city's periodic clean-up campaigns. In this context, "the Bath"—a former promoter, himself, of some of the District's more questionable entertainments—had managed to hold onto his seat for twenty-two years, enjoying the gracious support of fellow businessmen, including Michael "Hinky-Dink" Kenna, as well as of their loyal patrons and employees.

Drake's first challenge was to secure the nomination of the pro-suffrage, reform-minded Progressive party. Out of the woodwork stepped contender Karl N. Wehle, brandishing a stack of nominating petitions. A thorough canvass of the purported signers of Wehle's petitions showed that only three of the signers were legitimate; and the Progressive nomination went to Drake.

Leasing a store-front office, with a big window in which a live Drake "sat complacently eating corn and lettuce leaves" (*Lords of the Levee*, p. 307), the new candidate set to work. Not, herself, an ardent prohibitionist—her support for the sale of beer probably lost her the votes of more doctrinaire "drys"—Miss Drake was supported by a wide variety of feminists, from socialites to settlement workers. As one writer would later comment:

> Hundreds of women flooded into the district. The campaign had the quality of both a revival and a fairy tale, for in one blow they hoped to slay the monster vice and to demonstrate the political strength of domestic ideals. (Adade Mitchell Wheeler, *The Roads They Made: Women in Illinois History* (Chicago: Charles H. Kerr Publishing Co., 1977).

Newspapers across the nation reported the race, and Miss Drake won the support of both the *Chicago Daily Tribune* and the liberal Municipal Voters' League for her campaign to clean up the First Ward. Coughlin's response—now famous—was pithy: Chicago, he said, "ain't ready for reform."

That her strategy, however, had some effect on even the hardened Coughlin was evident when, a week before the election, he complained to federal postal authorities that

ON THE EVE OF THE BATTLE.

[Copyright: 1914: By John T. McCutcheon.]

VOTE FOR COUGHLIN VENALITY, VICE AND VICTORY

'SAVE ME! SAVE ME!'

SELF-RESPECTING VOTERS OF THE FIRST WARD

BATH HOUSE JOHN

FIRST WARD

MARIAN DRAKE

Maid Marian to the rescue.

Marion Drake and "Bathhouse John" Coughlin

Chicago Daily Tribune (April 6, 1914)

campaign posters depicting him "as a horrible beast, shown sucking money from defenseless women", were obscene. As one later historian would paint the scene:

> "I never did that to no woman!" wailed Bathhouse. "I'm a good family man." But the federal officials turned down the plea. "It's not obscene, but you might try suing for libel," was their advice. (*Lords of the Levee*, at 309-310)

In the end, organized vice prevailed, Coughlin winning handily in a five-way race amid accusations of tampering and vote-buying; but the political education of Illinois women received an important lesson.

Following her electoral defeat, Drake remained active in local politics. As president (and, it would seem, one of very few members) of the non-partisan "Can't-Stand-for-Thompson Club", she opposed the 1915 election of Coughlin-Kenna supporter William Hale "Big Bill" Thompson for mayor of Chicago, holding a rally in the First Ward. Her open letter to "The Women of Chicago Who Think and Lead" called Thompson "of all the candidates for mayor,...the one utterly beyond the pale." Unfortunately, once again, clout prevailed, and Thompson went on to rule Chicago for three scandal-ridden terms.

Never married, Drake lived the rest of her life in Chicago, retiring from active law practice in 1938 at the age of seventy-four.

Note: Patricia R. McMillen also contributed to this article.

OTHER PROFESSIONS

Though the majority of women practiced law once they obtained their licenses, some who were admitted to the bar pursued careers in other professions. The diverse endeavors of these women included the fields of education, business, farm management, and even medicine.

There were some who combined their practice of law with other pursuits. A number of these women were successful writers, editors, and publishers. Some used their writing to advocate legal and social reforms, writing books and articles and publishing legal periodicals. Others used writing to fulfill their creative talents. From poetry to feminist law journals, women lawyers expressed their ambition in a variety of ventures.

The following biographies begin with women who used their legal training to enhance their careers in other professions. Genevieve Melody and Grace Reed were both scholars and educators. Both used their legal training to further their careers as teachers and then principals in the Chicago Public Schools, and in their political and social reform activities. Anna Mullin obtained her legal training to assist in her commission business. Zetta Strawn, who practiced for a short time as a business lawyer, ultimately applied her legal training to her responsibilities as a farm manager in Ottawa, Illinois.

There was at least one of the early women lawyers, Jane Crombie Trull, who abandoned her legal training completely to pursue an alternate profession. Trull opted to obtain her medical degree and practiced medicine in Elgin, Illinois for over twenty years.

Many other women lawyers supplemented their law practice or devoted their entire careers to the printed word. Marietta B. R. Shay, who was admitted to the Illinois bar in 1879 and practiced law in Streator, Illinois, was the first woman in the United States to write a law textbook for use in law schools. L. Blanche Fearing was an accomplished poet in addition to a practicing attorney. Bessie Bradwell Helmer, though she practiced law on a limited basis in her husband's office, dedicated her career to editing and publishing the *Chicago Legal News*. Helen Tunnicliff Catterall, who was a scholar and a practicing attorney, spent the last ten years of her life compiling and editing the legal case history of slavery in the United States for the Carnegie Institute.

These women all reveal yet another layer of influence of the first generation of Illinois women lawyers.

GENEVIEVE MELODY

By Maureen Hanlon

Genevieve Melody was a remarkable woman who was educated in the law, but chose to devote her career to education. Melody was born on September 8, 1872, in Chicago and had two brothers, Paul Melody, and Monsignor John Webster Melody, and a sister, Nellie Melody Burke. She attended elementary school at Douglas School and graduated from South Division High School. After taking some classes at Milwaukee and Downers College and Lake Forest University, she began her career as a teacher at Hyde Park High School in 1892, where she taught mathematics and literature. Later she taught at Division High School. In 1895, she was named head of the history department at Chicago Normal College. In 1896, she received her law degree from Kent College of Law and was admitted to the Illinois bar on June 10th of that year. After her graduation from Kent, Melody was featured in the *Chicago Legal News* and indicated she expected to enter the practice of law in Chicago.

Little is known about Melody's career from 1896 until 1898, when she enrolled in classes at the University of Chicago. As an undergraduate, Melody was enrolled in the College for Teachers which was the only college at the University of Chicago at the time. Most of Melody's courses were in math and history. She received a total of nine credits for her two years of study at the Kent College of Law. Thirty-eight credits were needed to graduate. The University of Chicago awarded Melody a Bachelor of Philosophy in December 1902, and she received Honorable Mention for her senior college work. The University of Chicago Alumni directory for 1903 lists Melody as a high school teacher residing at the Continental Hotel in Chicago.

After graduation, Melody continued taking courses at the University of Chicago and received a Masters of Philosophy in June 1908. The thesis for her masters degree was entitled "Jefferson as a Political Leader." A. C. McLaughlin, a preemi-

Genevieve Melody

From James Bradwell, *Portraits of Twenty-Seven Illinois Women Lawyers* (1900), University of Illinois at Chicago The University Library Department of Special Collections

nent educator, was the professor responsible for consulting with Melody on her thesis. In 1913, the Alumni Directory at the University of Chicago lists Melody as the Principal of Park Manor School residing at 606 Vincennes Avenue. Melody exhibited an enduring dedication to her continuing education. Throughout World War I, she took at least one or two classes a year. Melody continued to take classes until 1928, mostly in the subject areas of history, psychology, philosophy, and advanced education.

In 1925, Melody was appointed the fourth Principal of Calumet High School giving her the distinct honor of becoming the first woman principal of a co-educational high school in the City of Chicago. In the fall of 1926, Calumet High School opened a new high school building at 8131 South May. In November 1926, pupils from Calumet High School marched between the old and new school buildings carrying their books, drawing boards, sports equipment and as much of their belongings as they could carry. One can only imagine Melody joining in this parade. On March 31, 1927, Melody gave a talk, entitled "Vital Reasons for Attending High School," on the Chicago Federation of Labor radio station WCFL.

While on a trip to Sweden, Genevieve Melody died suddenly on July 22, 1933, apparently from a heart ailment. She was sixty-one years old. On Sunday afternoon, November 5, 1933, the students of Calumet Senior High School held a memorial service in honor of Melody and reflected on her career at Park Manor, Calumet High School and her relation to school and society. The theme of the memorial was "for those remembered there is no death." The memorial service probably would have pleased this remarkable woman who graduated from law school in 1896 and chose to pursue a successful career as an educator where she influenced the lives of many children .

GRACE REED

By Lorraine Schmall

Educator and suffragist, Grace Reed used her law degree as background for a career spanning nearly fifty years in the Chicago Public Schools.

Grace Weston Reed was born in 1863 in Chicago to Charles L. Reed and Paulina Reed. Her father was a bookkeeper. Her mother, Paulina, born in Bavaria, was the first German elementary school teacher in Chicago and spent her entire life teaching in the Chicago public schools.

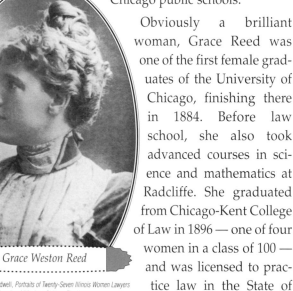

Grace Weston Reed

From James Bradwell, *Portraits of Twenty-Seven Illinois Women Lawyers* (1900), University of Illinois at Chicago The University Library Department of Special Collections

Obviously a brilliant woman, Grace Reed was one of the first female graduates of the University of Chicago, finishing there in 1884. Before law school, she also took advanced courses in science and mathematics at Radcliffe. She graduated from Chicago-Kent College of Law in 1896 — one of four women in a class of 100 — and was licensed to practice law in the State of Illinois in the same year.

A *Chicago Legal News* article describing the Kent class of 1896 described Reed as a vigorous student with a clear head for business.

It appears, however, that school administration, rather than law, was Reed's life's passion. Although a newspaper report about the 1895 Chicago-Kent graduates commented that Reed found teaching public school "uncongenial," she held the position of principal of Calumet Avenue School, both before and after her graduation from Chicago-Kent Law School in 1896. The fact that Reed was appointed a principal as early as 1895 suggests recognition either of her superior ability or her law degree. Her biographical entry in the catalogue for the Chicago Historical Society notes only that she taught in the Chicago public schools, or worked as a principal, from 1885-1931. She was a member of the Chicago Principals' Club, a highly intellectual forum, which during the time of Reed's membership, sponsored symposia with speakers such as John Dewey, Dwight Perkins, and Jane Ada. A 1927 biography of famous Illinois women identified Grace Reed as one of Chicago's best-known educators. Additionally Reed was officially recognized by Governor Frank Lowden for her achievements as a public school principal; and Reed was, while alive, sufficiently preeminent as an educator to be

mentioned in a book by Charles Wacker (now out of print) titled *The Tale of One City*.

In addition to the Chicago Principals' Club, Reed belonged to the Ella Flag Young Club, an organization devoted to the progressivism and professionalism of public school teachers and founded by Ella Flagg Young, one of the first women superintendents of public instruction in the United States. Reed also belonged to the Henry Dearborn Chapter of the Daughters of the American Revolution.

In addition to her career in education, Reed was an active suffragist and was described in the *Chicago Tribune* as a woman who carried "equal suffrage ideas to the Nth degree." She publicly demanded equality for women in such positions as fire fighters, police officers and "every branch of the American Government." At some point, she was urged to run for Alderman of the First Ward in Chicago, although it is unclear whether she ever did.

This lawyer-educator risked her position for her ideals. Although most prominent women in the early twentieth century were leaders in the temperance movement, Reed maintained a staunchly contrary position. In 1911, the *Chicago Tribune* reported that over 1000 people had demanded her removal as principal of the Francis E. Willard School because she made the mistake of remarking in 1909, that "a saloon keeper who is a man of good character is as much entitled to respect as anyone." Her resignation was never demanded by the Board of Education because, according to President Schneider of the School Board, she "towers mountains higher above her critics."

Although little is recorded of Grace Reed's legal work, it is possible that, late in life, she at least had thoughts of reviving her legal career. Her name was listed in Sullivan's law directory beginning in 1917 through 1929, and she belonged to the Women's Bar Association of Illinois for at least some period of her adult life.

Grace Reed never married. She died in 1933.

ANNA MULLIN

By Kathy H. Lee

A successful teacher and business woman, Anna Marian Mullin studied law not to practice the profession, but to enhance both her intellectual and business skills.

Anna Marian Compton Mullin was born in Chicago on November 9, 1855. Her father was John A. Compton, a Canadian from St. Johns; her mother was born in England. Anna Compton soon became the epitome of persistence, self-motivation, leadership, and ambition. She earned a college degree in English literature. Not content, she also became a Latin scholar.

Anna Compton Mullin

On December 22, 1870, at age twenty-five, Anna Compton married William C. Mullin. They lived on Chicago's south lakefront, at 3860 South Ellis Avenue. Anna taught in Chicago public schools for several years. Unsatisfied, she then sought a career in the commission merchant business. Locating her office at 243 South Water Street, Mullin worked hard, taking off only one day in a six year period, and did well.

In 1893, Anna Mullin enrolled at Chicago College of Law, the law department of Lake Forest University. Mullin did not intend to practice law, but believed that her knowledge of law would assist her in business. She received her bachelor of laws from the law school on June 3, 1896.

Exactly one week following her graduation from law school, Anna Mullin was admitted to the Illinois bar. She soon accepted the position of treasurer at a new college settlement, the "Forward Movement", on the West Side of Chicago. The Forward Movement sponsored a summer camp in Saugatuck, Michigan for working class youth of Chicago, placed poorer children in farm homes in summer months, and planned wholesome evening recreational activities for city youth over the winter months. Mullin devoted much time and energy to this venture, utilizing her experience in teaching, business, and law.

Mullin died on February 2, 1927, from a heart condition. At the time, she was living at 1465 East 50th Street. She was buried next to her husband at Oakwood Cemetery, 71st Street and Cottage Grove.

Patricia McMillen also contributed to this article.

ZETTA STRAWN

by Kristen Brown and Faith E. Buegel

Lizetta ("Zetta") Strawn was born to a prominent family in Ottawa, Illinois, in 1857. Though the family's initial pursuit in the area was farming, by the late nineteenth century, the Strawns were launching a legal dynasty that included Silas Strawn of the firm Winston, Strawn & Shaw. Zetta Strawn graduated in 1893, at age thirty-six, from the Union College of Law, now known as Northwestern University School of Law. Shortly after graduation, Strawn received admission to the

Illinois bar and worked for a short time in the law offices of Ellen A. Martin in Chicago. She was also admitted to the bar in Kansas, though she never practiced there.

Zetta Strawn was considered a good business lawyer, however, instead of pursuing a career in the law Strawn focused her energy on managing a large farm. After her father's death, she was responsible for her family's 190 acres in Ottawa township and, between 1905 and 1909, managed an even larger parcel of farm land in Iowa.

Zetta Strawn's father, Robert Chalfant Strawn, came to Ottawa with his parents, Joel and Lydia, in 1825. Zetta Strawn's grandfather, Joel, was the first member of the Strawn family to move to Illinois from Ohio, but many relatives followed. LaSalle County history is replete with information about Joel and his siblings. Many of the Strawn descendants still live in the LaSalle County area.

Robert Strawn married Elizabeth Rhoades in 1847. Respected and prosperous, Robert and Elizabeth had four children: Lydia (1850-1921); Nellie (1862-1932); Theo (1870-1925); and Zetta (1857-1931). The elder Strawns farmed for many years before moving into the town of Ottawa. Both of Zetta Strawn's parents died of old age and were memorialized in the local newspaper as loyal, honored, and intellectual.

Strawn's brother Theo also graduated from Northwestern University School of Law, three years later than his sister. He was admitted to the bar in 1896, and practiced in Ottawa for several years. Following his legal career, Theo became one of the largest individual orange growers in Florida. Zetta Strawn's sisters, like Zetta, never married. The three ladies, who lived together in the family home in Ottawa until their deaths and were known about town as the Strawn Sisters. Local children could hitch a ride with the sisters in their old, open Hupmobile, which the sisters also used to drive their cows out to pasture.

Zetta Strawn passed away in Ottawa in September 1931, at the age of seventy-four having been one of the first women in Illinois licensed to practice law, and as an accomplished business woman in her own right.

JANE CROMBIE TRULL

By Mae Hung

Although licensed to practice law before the turn of the twentieth century, Jane Crombie Trull found her life's work in a medical practice that spanned more than twenty-five years. Jane Crombie Trull was born on September 28, 1864, in Decatur, Macon County, Illinois, the first daughter, and second child, of Albert D. Trull and Julie L. Harrell. Originally from New Hampshire, Mr. Trull worked as a railroad station agent. He and Mrs. Trull had been married in Macon County on April 11, 1861. Ultimately, their marriage would produce eight children, five boys (two of whom died in infancy) and three girls (one of whom died in early childhood).

When Trull was one year old, the family moved to Wayne, a town in northwest DuPage County, Illinois. Trull lived there with her family until the age of sixteen, when she moved to Chicago. Without attending college, she entered the Chicago College of Law in September 1896, working as a cashier during the day. She was graduated from the law school in 1899, a member of the College's tenth graduating class, and was admitted to practice in Illinois in mid-October of that year.

Apparently, however, the law did not interest Trull, and she enrolled the next year at Bennett College of Eclectic Medicine and Surgery, then located at Ada and Fulton Streets on Chicago's near west side. "Eclectic medicine" was, at the turn of the twentieth century, the third largest branch of medical practice in the United States, following regular medicine and homeopathy. In addition to early acceptance of women as medical practitioners (Bennett College, chartered in 1869, had from the beginning graduated women students along with men), the specialty, native to America, stressed herbal remedies, and "campaigned against the excessive drugging and bleeding of the regular profession." Though practitioners of eclectic medicine were viewed with some skepticism by the regular profession, by 1890 they had won appointments on the attending staff of Cook County Hospital and served there as interns. (Bennett College was, nevertheless, converted to a regular medical school in 1907, and in 1915, became the Loyola University School of Medicine.)

Trull was graduated from Bennett College in 1905. After becoming licensed to practice as a physician and surgeon, she moved to Elgin, Illinois in 1907 to establish a medical practice. She would spend the rest of her life in Elgin, actively practicing medicine for all but the last two years and living in the rooms above her medical office.

Although Dr. Trull never married, she was active in numerous fraternal associations, including the First Universalist Church, the Elgin chapter of the Eastern Star (an organization affiliated with the Masons), the Royal Neighbors of America, the Elgin Physicians' Club, the Memorial Women's Relief Corps, the White Shrine, and the Women's Club of Elgin.

In 1928, Dr. Trull retired from active medical practice due to failing health. She moved into the home of her friend, Mrs. M. E. Fisher, on St. John Street in Elgin. According to her obituary, however, Dr. Trull was ill suited to retirement:

> Always active, and unusually versatile, a physician who had always enjoyed a large practice and who particularly enjoyed contacts with people; Dr. Trull found retirement irksome... [so] when she gave up her practice,... Dr. Trull began the study of chiropody [i.e., podiatry] and in a year

was qualified to practice as a chiropodist. She was engaged in this practice to a more or less extent, at the time of her death. (*Elgin Daily News*, [September 6, 1930] p. 1)

Dr. Jane Crombie Trull died of apparent heart failure in September 1930, just short of her sixty-sixth birthday. She was survived by her two brothers, Clarence (who lived, with his wife and two children, in the Trull childhood home in Wayne) and Ziba Trull.

Note: Gwen Hoerr McNamee and Patricia McMillen contributed to this article.

MARIETTA BROWN REED SHAY

By Judith Gaskell

Marietta Brown Reed Shay was the first woman to graduate from the Illinois Wesleyan University College of Law and the sixth woman to be admitted to practice in Illinois. Her 1881 book, *Student's Guide to Common Law Pleadings*, was one of the first American law books written by a woman.

Marietta Brown Reed was born on March 12, 1849, in Fall River, Massachusetts, to Isaac and Nancy Reed. Between 1850 and 1860, the Reed family moved to a farm in South Ottawa, Illinois. According to the 1860 census, Marietta Reed had two older sisters, Minerva and Flora, and two younger sisters, Irene and Ida.

On June 6, 1869, Marietta Reed married John Henry Shay, a Civil War veteran and Congregational minister. The Shays had five children. Wellington was born in July of 1870; Arthur H. in February of 1872; Ethel G. in June of 1876; and Ralph R. in December of 1880. The birthdate of a second daughter, Ruth, is unknown.

From 1877 to 1879, the Shays studied law at Illinois Wesleyan University College of Law, which was popularly called "The Bloomington Law School." Upon completion of the two-year course of study, Illinois Wesleyan law students, such as the Shays, were automatically admitted to the Illinois bar. Students attended lectures, did moot court exercises, studied major texts such as Blackstone's *Commentaries*, and were required to pass a comprehensive exam at the end of their senior year. Mrs. Shay was the winner of the $50 first prize for best final examination. Both Shay and her husband graduated on June 19, 1879, and were admitted to practice on that same day.

Shay's book, *Student's Guide to Common Law Pleadings, Consisting of Questions on Stephen, Gould and Chitty*, was published in Chicago, in 1881, by Callaghan and Company. This 250-page book was printed and distributed by the *Chicago Legal News* and sold for $2.00. On the title page the author was listed as M.B.R. Shay, LL.B. Contemporary book reviewers showed no awareness that the author was a woman. The review in the October 22, 1881, vol. 13, issue of the *Chicago Legal News* stated that

> [t]he author has shown great care and good judgment in the preparation of the questions, and we have no hesitation in recommending the work to any one studying either Stephen, Gould, or Chitty.

The book was used as a textbook at Illinois Wesleyan and probably was based upon the work Mrs. Shay had done while studying law.

In 1881, the Shay family moved to Streator, Illinois, where John Henry Shay became the first pastor of the new First Congregational Church. Mr. Shay left the ministry in 1885 to practice law with the firm of Burns, Ong & Shay. Mrs. Shay also practiced law for several years around that time and was listed as a lawyer in the 1900 census. Their son, Arthur H. Shay, was later a well-known solo practitioner in Streator.

Marietta Brown Reed Shay died on May 27, 1939, at the age of ninety and is buried in Riverview Cemetery in Streator. While Shay's legal text is no longer in common use, she led the way for women to participate in law as educators, as well as students.

LILLIEN BLANCHE FEARING

By Denise R. Jackson

Lillien Blanche Fearing was an accomplished lawyer as well as a poet. Her writings about life in Chicago at the turn of the century reflected her spirit and courage as she overcame the restrictions caused by her blindness to find success in two professions.

Born in Davenport, Iowa on November 27, 1863, Lillien Blanche Fearing, also known as L. Blanche Fearing, was blinded when she was five years old. According to the local Davenport, Iowa newspaper, *The Davenport Democrat and Leader*, Blanche was an active child. She and her older brother often played together in the family yard. One day, Blanche and her brother were playing with a rope. Her brother began swinging the rope swiftly over his head until it made a whirling noise. At the same time, Blanche began walking towards her brother. As they continued to play, Blanche got too close to the rope and it struck her in one of her eyes. Within a week, Blanche had lost sight in that eye. Several weeks later, she lost sight in the other eye.

According to the Davenport newspaper article, after losing her sight, Blanche was pampered by family and friends. She especially enjoyed being entertained and read to. She developed a remarkable memory which allowed her to repeat most things verbatim. When Blanche's capacity for memorization was recognized, her family took great efforts to insure that she received an education. This included several months at the state institution, Vinton School for the Blind. There she mastered the writing method used by the blind. In addition, when she visited her family, she would read her original manuscripts to family and friends. It is said that Blanche could read as quickly as she could talk. Clearly these skills helped her, as she graduated from Iowa College in 1884.

Fearing is said to have published her first poem at the age of eight. In addition to her written talents, she was also known for her talent in bead work, her skilled work with needle and thread, her china painting and, ironically, her ability to blend colors so beautifully.

In addition to her older brother, Blanche's family included her father, Henry Fearing of Marietta, Ohio; her mother, the former Mary A. Ferris of Meadville, Pennsylvania; a younger brother and a sister, whose name was Marien Edna. Her parents were married in Davenport on May 16, 1852. Her father, born February 2, 1823, was one of the oldest settlers of the village of Davenport, Iowa. When Blanche's family moved to Chicago, making their home at 430 Chicago Avenue, her father remained in Davenport. He later joined the family in Chicago in 1890, some two years after their arrival.

L. Blanche Fearing

From James Bradwell, *Portraits of Twenty-Seven Illinois Women Lawyers* (1900), University of Illinois at Chicago The University Library Department of Special Collections

Once in Chicago, Blanche entered Union College of Law, where her sister and mother attended classes with Blanche and read all of her assignments and cases to her. Blanche graduated with honors in 1890, at the age of twenty-seven, after taking the same required courses and exams as all graduating students. At her graduation banquet, Blanche sat in the seat of honor next to United States Supreme Court Chief Justice Melville W. Fuller. She was one of four students who had graduated with identical records and the school could not decide who would receive the single scholarship prize. Ultimately, the school decided to divide the prize among all four students. Fearing was the first woman to receive the scholarship prize, and upon her admission to the Illinois bar on June 10, 1890, became the first blind woman admitted to practice law anywhere in the world.

While it is noted that L. Blanche Fearing was a genius in the study of law, more is known of her as a poet and author. In addition to the publication of her first poem at age eight,

Lillien Blanche Fearing wrote *The Sleeping World and Other Poems* (Chicago: AC McClurg & Co.) in 1887. The book, inscribed to her mother, marked the beginning of a series of writings. Her next literary effort was completed after graduating from law school. In 1892, Fearing wrote *In the City By the Lake* (Chicago: Seale & Gorton) composed of two books: *The Shadow* and *The Slave Girl*. Like her earlier works, *In the City By the Lake* was also dedicated to a family member, this time Fearing's sister, Marien. The following year, Fearing wrote *Awake and Asleep* under the pseudonym of Raymond Russell. It is her only known work written under a pseudonym.

Two years later, in 1895, Fearing wrote *Roberta*, a long poem whose main character was named Roberta Green. Fearing's last work, of which little is known, was titled *The Isle of Shoals*, and was described, in a *Chicago Tribune* article, as an idyl, or short poem describing a simple, pleasant, peaceful scene or domestic life.

The issue addressed in each of these works was how the underprivileged coped with the evils of the city. Addressing issues of poverty and slavery, Fearing delivered a message of courage and triumph. Her poems and other writings attracted the attention of Oliver Wendell Holmes and John G. Whittier. Fearing is also named as a noteworthy poet in the *History of Chicago*.

In addition to her literary pursuits, Lillien Blanche Fearing maintained a law office in the Journal Building in Chicago. However, according to the *Chicago Tribune*, poor health plagued Lillien Blanche Fearing. Accompanied by her mother, she went to Eureka Springs, Arkansas, at the time known for its curative baths. Unfortunately, her health continued to deteriorate, and Lillien Blanche Fearing died in Eureka Springs on August 1, 1900 at the age of thirty-seven.

In her poem, "In the City by the Lake," the final lines epitomize who Fearing was, her accomplishments, her spirit and her enduring legacy.

Oh, then teach
All capable of bearing the bright arms
Of reason, fearless, independent thought!
If you would lead men surely angelward,
Teach them to think, not what to think, but how.

BESSIE BRADWELL HELMER

By Jennifer A. Widmer and Maureen P. Cunningham

Bessie Bradwell Helmer was the daughter of two renowned lawyers, Myra and James Bradwell. The Bradwells were known for securing legal rights for women and for supporting women's professional advancement. Growing up in such a household, it is not surprising that Helmer devoted her life to the advancement of women through higher education. Helmer obtained both a master of arts and a law degree.

Although she was the twelfth woman to be admitted to the Illinois bar, Helmer opted not to practice law in a courtroom. Instead, she applied her knowledge to legal editorial pursuits, and she followed her parents into a life of public service dedicated to legal and social reform.

Bessie Bradwell was born in Chicago on October 20, 1858. At that time, her mother had been a public school teacher and her father was a young lawyer. In 1861, James Bradwell became a probate judge of the County Court of Cook County, a position he held until 1869. During the Civil War, Myra Bradwell worked tirelessly at raising money for the Union Army's soldiers and their families. Judge Bradwell, an abolitionist, helped slaves escaping from the South. He was the first judge to hold that a marriage made during slavery would be valid after emancipation, and that the children born to a married slave couple were legitimate and would inherit from their emancipated parents. In addition, Judge Bradwell was one of the founders of the Union League Club of Chicago, an organization dedicated to promoting and protecting the federal government.

After the war, Myra Bradwell became known as the first woman to apply for, and be denied, admission to the Illinois bar. In 1868, Myra Bradwell founded the *Chicago Legal News*, the first weekly legal newspaper published west of the Allegheny Mountains. In 1872, Judge Bradwell was elected to the lower house of the Illinois legislature. During his two terms in office, he became the Speaker of the House, and he authored numerous laws securing rights for women. Myra and Judge Bradwell were leading citizens of Chicago and advanced social and legal reforms through their work and their active participation in numerous social clubs and organizations. They served their society and professions with a passion, which they passed on to their daughter.

The 1896 *Album of Genealogy and Biography* painted an apt picture of the young Bessie Bradwell by describing her preference for sitting beside her father as he heard his cases, while other children of the same age played with their toys. At the age of thirteen, she was among those Chicagoans who survived the Chicago Fire of 1871. In 1926, the Chicago Historical Society organized a reception for the survivors of the disaster. Although unable to attend, Helmer sent a letter describing her experiences in detail. "Never shall I forget the sight as I looked back on the burning city. On the bridge, a man, hurrying along, said, 'This is the end of Chicago,' but with all assurance [I] replied, 'No, no, she will rise again.'"

The fire threatened the Bradwell home after they had retired for the evening. Having arisen from bed and put on her best clothes in order to save them from the flames, Helmer hurried with her father to his law office with the hope of saving his rare law book collection. Realizing that the fire would soon be upon them, the pair was forced to abandon their efforts. Before heading to the lake for refuge, however, young Bessie picked up her mother's subscription and account book. Separated from her father, Helmer carried the heavy book for hours through the ruins of the city.

Although their home and businesses were completely destroyed, the family survived. In addition, due to young Bessie Bradwell's efforts, the *Chicago Legal News* survived. Her mother temporarily relocated to Milwaukee, commenced publishing, and delivered the paper to the usual subscribers without missing an issue.

Helmer graduated, as valedictorian, from Chicago High School in 1876. She then entered Northwestern University where she earned her bachelor of arts in 1880. In a letter she sent in 1925 to her friend Marion Talbot, Dean of Women at the University of Chicago, Helmer recalled that when she was in college, the twelve women in her class were "a serious minded crowd" who felt as if they were on trial. In 1893, Bessie Helmer was selected a member of Northwestern's chapter of Phi Beta Kappa. As she wrote to Marion Talbot in 1896, she was very pleased when she was elected, not so much because of the honor, but because Northwestern insisted on awarding the honor upon its graduates irrespective of gender.

Helmer enrolled at the Union College of Law, now Northwestern University School of Law, in 1880. She was the only woman in a class of fifty-three students. Even more remarkable, and a testament to her intellect, Helmer was unanimously selected to be valedictorian by her classmates upon her graduation in 1882. In her commencement address, Helmer analogized the charge given to lawyers with that of the mission of the priesthood, stating,

> The lawyer must combine with wealth of intellect and mental culture, a keen perception of justice, of right, of fidelity. The basis of law is morality - practical morality, as applied to the relations of man with man. And the true lawyer, worthy of the name and office, is a legal priest, administering at the altar of justice and righteousness, in the highest sense known to man in his relations to his fellows. (*Chicago Legal News* vol. 15 [1882] p. 337)

On June 15, 1882, Bessie Bradwell Helmer was admitted to the Illinois bar. Shortly thereafter, she traveled to Europe. Upon her return, Helmer earned a master of arts degree in 1883. Helmer chose not to practice law in the traditional sense. Instead, she followed in her mother's footsteps by pursuing

Bessie Bradwell Helmer
Chicago Tribune Photo

editorial endeavors, frequently taking over the management of the *Chicago Legal News* while her parents traveled abroad or tended to other business.

Bessie Bradwell married Frank Ambrose Helmer, also a lawyer, on December 23, 1885. The wedding was a lavish affair. The guest list included judges and prominent businessmen of the time, such as Mr. and Mrs. H. C. Tiffany, the Honorable and Mrs. H.B. Hurd, and, Judge Bradwell's former law partner, Governor John L. Beveridge.

Several sources mention that Bessie Helmer assisted her husband in his law practice. Presumably this was Helmer's occasional occupation since, in addition to her work on the *Chicago Legal News*, she also served as editor of Hurd's Revised Statutes of Illinois from 1905 to 1923, and she edited nine volumes of the Illinois Appellate Court Reports. Upon her mother's death in 1894, Helmer became the president of the Chicago Legal News Company, and an assistant editor of the paper. She worked with her father, who took over as editor-in-chief, until he retired in 1903 because of ill health.

Upon her father's death in 1907, Bessie Helmer became editor, a position she held until the last issue was printed on July 16, 1925. Under her leadership, the *Chicago Legal News* continued to proclaim the accomplishments of women lawyers throughout the nation. The publication debated and encouraged woman suffrage, jury service for women, quality public school education, the elimination of political corruption, ethical standards for the legal and journalism professions, and other social and legal reform. Throughout World War I, Helmer printed articles written by members of the Chicago and Illinois bars which gave firsthand accounts of the war, and of the service of their fellow bar members. Following the war, many of the articles Helmer printed focused on issues of international law.

The Helmers had one daughter, Myra Bradwell, named after her distinguished grandmother. Although she did not continue the tradition of legal studies that her grandmother and mother had undertaken, she embarked on literary pursuits and attended Vassar College. Myra Bradwell Helmer excelled at golf and became one of the most skillful women players in America, winning the Western Golf Championship in 1913.

Bessie Helmer was a member of the Illinois State Bar Association (honorary), the American Bar Association, and the Illinois Press Association. In addition to her professional pursuits, Helmer was involved in many social and philanthropic groups. She served as secretary of the Soldier's Home

OTHER PROFESSIONS

in Chicago where she worked with her mother to raise funds for nursing wounded soldiers and for providing assistance to the many widows and orphans left after the Civil War. Helmer also held the position of vice-chairperson of the World's Congress Auxiliary on Government Reform, and was a member of the Daughters of the American Revolution, the Republican Club, and the Chicago Woman's Club. But the most notable of her associations was with the Western Association of Collegiate Alumnae (WACA).

Helmer was instrumental in the growth and development of WACA, which was organized in Chicago in 1883. The membership comprised college-educated females who shared the belief that to advance in society, a woman needed to be educated.

With that purpose in mind, in 1887, WACA established a fellowship to assist women of outstanding ability in pursuing further education. WACA granted the first fellowship to Ida Street in 1888. The fellowship coffers, however, frequently ran dry and the fellowship fund was referred to as the "sinking fund."

Understanding the importance of the fellowship to young women seeking to advance their place in society through education, Helmer took an active interest in the fellowship committee. In June 1890, she proposed to raise funds for the fellowship by holding an author's reading. The reading took place on March 7, 1891 and raised $459.64 for the fund. In 1891, Helmer became chairperson of the Committee on Fellowships, a position she held until 1907. In 1893, at her request, the membership agreed to make yearly pledges to the fellowship fund, thus ensuring its survival.

Helmer was responsible for WACA's eventual joinder with the nationally organized Association of Collegiate Alumni (ACA), known today as the American Association of University Women (AAUW). While Helmer was state director for Illinois in 1889, and with the support of the membership, WACA was disbanded and re-organized as the eighth branch of the ACA. During her tenure as the chair of the Fellowship Committee, Helmer also established European fellowships for young women.

Helmer served as president of the ACA in 1890-1891, and she served as the president of the Chicago branch in 1894-1895. The Chicago branch of the ACA became well known for its efforts in petitioning colleges and universities to open their doors to women, in seeking to establish a reform school for girls in Illinois, in campaigning to end child labor, and in making the public aware of the need for compulsory education and competent teachers. Jane Addams, known for her work at Hull House, was a visitor and occasional speaker at ACA meetings. As a result, the Chicago branch supported an internship program to assist Addams in her work among Chicago's poor.

Due to Bessie's failing health caused by a heart condition, she and Frank Helmer moved to Battle Creek, Michigan to live with their daughter who had settled there after marrying Dr. J. Stuart Pritchard in 1915. Frank Helmer died of cancer on September 29, 1925. After a period of treatment at the Battle Creek Sanitarium, Bessie Helmer died on January 10, 1927. Three days later, she was buried at Rosehill Cemetery in Chicago.

Like her parents, Bessie Bradwell Helmer was a woman known for her intelligence, strong character, and dedication to advancing the rights and professional development of women. Because of her efforts, generations of women have been given the opportunity to pursue their education and their dreams.

HELEN HONOR TUNNICLIFF CATTERALL

By Gwen Hoerr McNamee

A woman of many talents, Helen Honor Tunnicliff Catterall engaged in a career that included teaching, photography, writing, and the practice of law. Throughout her life, Catterall used her talents to aid those in need and in the fight to establish rights for African-Americans.

Helen Honor Tunnicliff Catterall was born March 3, 1870, to Damon George Tunnicliff and Sarah Alice Bacon. Her father, a lawyer and judge, encouraged Catterall, the oldest of his three daughters, to study law. Catterall's sister, Ruth, studied medicine and later became a distinguished physician in Chicago conducting research in infectious diseases for the John McCormick Institute. Catterall's paternal grandmother, Marinda Tilden Tunnicliff, was a distant cousin of New York Governor Samuel J. Tilden, who gained public prominence for overthrowing the "Tweed Ring," a group of corrupt New York City politicians, in the early 1870s.

Catterall was raised in Macomb, Illinois. An excellent student, she was also a talented violinist and dedicated much of her spare time to philanthropic work. With her sister Sarah, Catterall conducted sewing classes on Saturday afternoons at the St. Agnes School in Macomb. Oral tradition in Macomb also depicts Catterall and the Tunnicliff family as strong supporters of racial equality. The Tunnicliff residence is believed to have been part of the Underground Railroad during the antebellum period.

Catterall left Illinois to go to college at Vassar. Adept in photography, Catterall photographed the exterior and interior of St. Paul's Episcopal Church in North Andover, Massachusetts while a student at Vassar. She brought the photographs back home to Macomb, where they served as inspiration for her congregation, then preparing to build a church. St. George's Episcopal Church was completed in the fall of 1895. Modeled after St. Paul's, St. George's was designed by Boston architects Arthur Rotch and George Thomas Tilden (possibly a distant relative of Catterall's). Both architects had worked with the renowned architect Henry Hobson Richardson who died in 1886.

After graduating in 1889, Catterall returned to her family home and began legal studies in her father's law office. In 1893, she moved to Chicago, where she pursued postgraduate work in political economy at the University of Chicago, holding a fellowship from 1893 to 1895. Catterall then resumed her legal studies at the University of Chicago.

During this time Catterall drew up the municipal code for her home town. To accomplish her task, Catterall collected all the laws governing the city of Macomb, including acts of the Illinois General Assembly that specifically related to Macomb, the general ordinances of the city, and all the special ordinances passed by the city council. In 1897, the Macomb City Council published her work as "The Municipal Code of Macomb, Illinois." In March 1896, Catterall passed her bar examination and was admitted to the Illinois bar.

It was during her study at the University of Chicago that Catterall met Ralph Charles Henry Catterall, an instructor and doctoral candidate in history. The two were married on June 24, 1896, at St. George's Episcopal Church in Macomb.

After their marriage, Catterall and her husband stayed in Chicago until 1902, when Ralph took a position as an assistant professor of history at Cornell University in Ithaca, New York. During the next several years, Catterall devoted herself to linguistic studies to assist her husband in his work and to raising their son, Ralph T. Catterall.

In 1903, the University of Chicago Press published Professor Catterall's book, *A National Bank*, on the history of the second bank of the United States. The *New York Times* published a favorable review of the book. In 1905, Ralph became head of Cornell's history department. Years later, in Catterall's obituary, the *New York Times* stated that she was also a professor at Cornell University during the family's years in New York; however, her department is unknown.

In 1914, Ralph Catterall died of a cerebral hemorrhage at the age of forty-eight. After her husband's death, Catterall resumed her legal studies, entering and graduating from the Law School of Boston University. She was admitted to the Massachusetts bar in 1915 and practiced for a time in Massachusetts. Catterall's legal work influenced her son, Ralph, who went on to study law himself and became a judge in Richmond, Virginia.

In 1923, the Carnegie Institute of Washington hired Catterall to compile and edit judicial cases for a book on the history of slavery in the United States. Catterall moved to Richmond, Virginia. She became a member of the Woman's Club of Richmond and of the American Historical Association.

Though her health had begun to fail, Catterall worked on the Carnegie project for the next ten years. The goal was to present an unbiased view of the institution of American slavery through the written judicial opinions that interpreted and created laws regarding slavery. Through the cases she compiled, Catterall also sought to illustrate "the life of the negro" under slavery. Though she died shortly before the fourth and final volume of her work was finished, it was completed and published after her death, consummating the important study entitled *Judicial Cases Concerning American Slavery and the Negro* (Washington D. C.: Carnegie Institution of Washington, 1936; republished New York: Octagon Books, Inc., 1968).

On November 10, 1933, Helen Tunnicliff Catterall died in Richmond, Virginia. In the preface to the final volume of her *Judicial Cases*, a colleague wrote a tribute to Catterall that captured her achievements in so many endeavors:

> The faithfulness and accuracy with which she worked, the acuteness of her perceptions in legal matters, and the varied learning which she bore so lightly and modestly, deserve most grateful commemoration...

125 YEARS AND BEYOND

The first generation of Illinois women lawyers operated from a dual position: as women they remained outside of the male culture of the legal profession; as lawyers they maintained inside access to powerful tools of change. As most men and women adhered to the male professional culture, women found within it opportunities as well as limitations. Early women lawyers used their dual identity to advance women's crusade for full citizenship and all its rights and privileges.

Since Alta Hulett's admission to the bar 125 years ago, women lawyers in Illinois have continued to grow in numbers and influence. Advancing the rights of women, breaking new barriers and successfully practicing law, women are setting new standards in the legal profession both in Illinois and throughout the country. In 1977, Esther Rothstein was elected the first woman president of the Chicago Bar Association. In 1992, Mary Ann McMorrow became the first woman elected to the Illinois Supreme Court. But as Chicago lawyer Delores Hannah recently remarked, it is still too long between the first and the second. It took thirteen years before Laurel Bellows became the second woman elected president of the Chicago Bar Association. We are still waiting for the second woman to be elected to the Illinois Supreme Court.

Nationally, the figures are not much different. Justice Sandra Day O'Connor was appointed to the Supreme Court of the United States in 1981. Over a decade later, in 1993, Justice Ruth Bader Ginsberg became the second woman justice on our highest court.

This book resonates with pride for past accomplishments, and with both hope and concern for the future. Women have taken tremendous strides toward achieving full rights and privileges of United States citizenship and establishing a culture in the legal profession that includes both men and women. Yet there is still a long way to go and time alone is not the answer. As the foremothers of the Illinois legal profession have taught us, there must be a continuous, conscientious effort to eliminate all forms of discrimination and to forge new paths of opportunity and success for women. It is in this spirit that we celebrate the 125th Anniversary of women lawyers.

Esther Rothstein
President of the Chicago Bar Association
1977-1978

Laurel Bellows
President of the Chicago Bar Association 1991-1992,
Founder and Chair of the Alliance for Women 1992

Patricia Bobb
President of the Chicago Bar Association 1997-1998

SOURCES

INTRODUCTION

Elizabeth Cady Stanton, Susan B. Anthony and Matilda J. Gage, editors, *History of Woman Suffrage* volumes 1, 2, and 3 (Rochester, NY: Charles Mann (1881); Steven Buechler, *The Transformation of the Woman Suffrage Movement* (New Brunswick, NJ: Rutgers University Press, 1986); Julia Lathrop Speech, (1923) Mary Bartelme Papers, University of Illinois at Chicago Special Collections box 4, folder 66, quoting Oliver Wendell Holmes.

THE FIGHT TO GAIN ENTRANCE

Information on Arabella Mansfield is from Louis A. Haselmayer, "Belle A. Mansfield" *Women Lawyers' Journal* vol. 55 (Spring 1969) p.46. Information on Myra Bradwell's case includes *In re Bradwell* 55 Ill. 535 (1870); Myra Bradwell, "A Woman Cannot Practice Law or Hold Any Office in Illinois," *Chicago Legal News* vol. 2 (Feb 5, 1869) p. 145; Bradwell v. Illinois, 83 U. S. (16 Wall.) 442 (1872). Sources for Alta Hulett and her work include Public Laws of Illinois 578 (1872); Elizabeth Boyton, "Woman's Kingdom," *Chicago Inter-Ocean* (March 31, 1877), p. 6; Charles D. Mosher, *Centennial Historical Albums of Biographies of the Chicago Bar* vol. 6 (1876) p. 49 Chicago Historical Society Archives and Manuscripts; and Catharine Waugh McCulloch, "Alta Hulett," Grace Harte Papers, Women's Studies Manuscripts Collection, Schlesinger Library, Radcliffe College.

MYRA COLBY BRADWELL

Biographies of Bradwell can be found in *Notable American Women, 1607-1950: A Biographical Dictionary* (Cambridge, MA: Belnap Press, 1971), vol.1; Jane Friedman, *America's First Woman Lawyer; the Biography of Myra Bradwell* (Buffalo: Prometheus Books, 1993); Charlotte Adelman, *The Women's Bar Association of Illinois — The First 75 Years* (Paducah, KY: Turner Publishing Company, 1992); Herman Kogan, "Myra Bradwell: Crusader at Law," *Chicago History* (1974); and Frederic B. Crossley, *Courts and Lawyers of Illinois* (Chicago: The American Historical Society, 1916). Crossley also includes a biographical sketch of James Bradwell. Obituaries of Bradwell include "Death of Myra Bradwell," *American Law Review* vol. 28 (1894) p. 278, and "Myra Bradwell," *Chicago Legal News* vol. 26 (1894), p. 200-202. Discussions of Bradwell's work include: Nancy T. Gilliam, "A Professional Pioneer: Myra Bradwell's Fight to Practice Law," *Law and History Review*, vol. 5 (Spring 1987), pp. 105-133; Frances Olsen, "From False Paternalism to False Equality: Judicial Assaults on Feminist Community, Illinois 1869 — 1895," *Michigan Law Review* vol. 84 (1986), pp. 1518-41; Nadine Taub and Elizabeth Schneider, "Women's Subordination and the Role of Law," in David Kairys, ed., *The Politics of Law: a Progressive Critique* (New York: Pantheon Books, 1982, 1990); and Ellen Carol DuBois, "Taking the Law into Our Own Hands: Bradwell, Minor and Suffrage Militance in the 1870s" in Nancy A. Hewitt and Suzanne Lebsock, eds., *Visible Women: New Essays on American Activism* (Urbana: University of Illinois Press, 1993), 19-40. Works discussing Bradwell's involvement in the suffrage movement include Steven M. Buechler, *The Transformation of the Woman Suffrage Movement: The Case of Illinois, 1850-1920* (New Brunswick: Rutgers University Press, 1986); and Aileen Kraditor, *The Ideas of the Woman Suffrage Movement, 1890-1920* (New York: Doubleday, 1965). Articles on Bradwell's fight for admission to the bar include Ellen Martin, "Admission of women to the Bar," *Chicago Law Times* vol. 1 (1887); Karen Berger Morello, *The Invisible Bar* (New York: Random House, 1986); D. Kelley Weissberg, "Barred from the Bar: Women and Legal Education in the United States 1870 -1890," *Journal of Legal Education* vol. 28 (1977) pp. 485-507; Charlotte Adelman, "A History of Women Lawyers in Illinois," *Illinois Bar Journal*, (May 1986), pp. 424-428; and Meg Gorecki, "Legal Pioneers; Four of Illinois' First Women Lawyers," *Illinois Bar Journal* (October 1990), p. 512. Information about the 1893 World's Columbian Exposition and the Queen Isabella Association is from Jeanne Madeline Weimann, *The Fair Women* (Chicago: Academy, 1981) and the Queen Isabella Association Papers at the Chicago Historical Society Library. There are also numerous articles written by Myra and James Bradwell throughout the *Chicago Legal News*, including "A Woman Cannot Practice Law or Hold Any Office in Illinois," vol. 2 (February 5, 1869), p. 145.

ALTA MAY HULETT

Biographical sketches of Alta Hulett were written by Charles Mosher in vol. 6 of the *Centennial Historical Albums of Biographies of the Chicago Bar* and by Laura Hubbard (unpublished, 1881). Both are located in the Chicago Historical Society Archives and Manuscripts Department. Other biographical sketches include: Catharine Waugh McCulloch, "Alta M. Hulett," Grace Harte Papers, Mary Earhart Dillon Collection, Schlesinger Library Radcliffe College; "Rockford's First Woman Lawyer," Rockfordania file, Rockford Public Library; Hazel Hyde, "First Women Lawyers of Rockford" *Nuggets of History* (January-February, 1966); and Robert Lindvall, "Alta M. Hulett," *Nuggets of History* (Spring 1978). Obituaries appeared in the *Chicago Tribune* (March 28, 1877), and the *Chicago Inter-Ocean* (March 31, 1877). Information on Hulett is included in the following articles: Ellen Martin, "Admission of Women to the Bar" *Chicago Law Times* vol. 1 (1887); McCulloch, "Lawyers of Rockford College," Grace Harte Papers; Meg Gorecki, "Legal Pioneers: Four of Illinois' First Women Lawyers," *Illinois Bar Journal* (October 1990); Charlotte Adelman, "A History of Women Lawyers in Illinois," *Illinois Bar Journal* (May 1986); and Herman Kogan, "Myra Bradwell: Crusader at Law," *Chicago History* (Fall 1974).

Newspaper accounts of Hulett's lecture "Justice vs. the Supreme Court" were published in the *Rockford Gazette* (November 30, 1871), the *Rockford Journal* (December 2, 1871) and the *Rockford Register* (December 2, 1871). Myra Bradwell described the events of Hulett's bill becoming law in "Liberty of Pursuit Triumphant in Illinois," *Chicago Legal News* (March 23, 1872). The events are also recorded in the *Journal of the House of Representatives* (March 21, 1872). Hulett's admission to the bar was reported in the *Chicago Tribune* (June 7, 1873). *The History of Woman Suffrage* edited by Elizabeth Cady Stanton et. al., also recounts Hulett's work and the changes in the Illinois law on their chapter on Illinois in volume III. A description of the Chicago Philosophical Society appears in a paper by Rima Lunin Schultz, "Kate Newell Doggett's Challenge to the Patriarchy and the Women's Rights Movement in Chicago 1868-1884," given at the Illinois History Symposium in 1995. The papers of the Philosophical Society are at the Chicago Historical Society. Correspondence regarding the society is in the Sam Willard Papers, also at the Chicago Historical Society. The description of San Diego women lawyers, honoring of Hulett appears in the *75 Year History of National Association of Women Lawyers 1899 — 1974*, Mary H. Zimmerman, ed. (Lansing: National Association of Women Lawyers, 1975) pp. 468-9. An alternate version of this article appears in *Historical Encyclopedia of Chicago Women* Rima Lunin Schultz and Adele Haste, eds, (Bloomington: Indiana University Press, forthcoming).

ADA MISER KEPLEY

Ada H. Kepley; Charlotte Adelman, *A Farm Philosopher*, "A History of Women Lawyers in Illinois", *Illinois Bar Journal* (1986); *Chicago Legal News* vol. 2 (1870) p. 320; *Chicago Legal News* vol. 2 (1870) p. 353; *Chicago Legal News* vol. 3 (1870) p. 13; *Chicago Legal News* vol. 3 (1870) p. 60; Brief Histories of Some County Bars and Other Legal Organizations in Illinois and a Brief History of The Illinois State Bar Association — 1877 to 1977, The Illinois State Bar Association (1977); ALR v5 1870-71; *Chicago Law Times* vol. 2 (1888) pp. 301-07; *Chicago Law Times* vol. 1 (1887) pp. 79-92 ; Lelia J. Robinson, LL.B., "Women Lawyers in the United States", *The Green Bag* vol. 2 (1890) p.10; Meg Gorecki, "Legal Pioneers: Four of Illinois' First Women Lawyers", *Illinois Bar Journal* (1980); The First Women Law Students, The Invisible Bar; Frances E. Willard and Mary A. Livermore, *A Woman of the Century Fourteen Hundred Seventy Biographical Sketches Accompanied by Portraits of Leading American Women In All Walks of Life* Buffalo: Charles Wells Moulton, (1893); Virginia G. Drachman, *Women Lawyers and the Origins of Professional Identify in America The Letters of the Equity Club, 1887 to 1890* Ann Arbor: University of Michigan Press, (1993); *Chicago Legal News* vol. 2 (1870) pp. 20-21; *Chicago Legal News* vol. 2 (1869) pp. 44-45; *Chicago Legal News* vol. 32 (1900) p. 340.

THE LAW SCHOOLS THAT DID ADMIT WOMEN

Samuel Haber, *The Quest for Authority and Honor* (Chicago: University of Chicago Press, 1991) pp. 101-05, 193-222; Burton J. Bledstein, *The Culture of Professionalism: The Middle Class and the Development of Higher Education in America* (New York: WW. Norton, 1978) p.96; Jerald Averbach, *Unequal Justice: Lawyers and Social Changes in Modern America* (London: Oxford University Press, 1976); Frank Ellsworth, *Law on the Midway: The Founding of the University of Chicago Law School* (Chicago: The Law School of the University of Chicago, 1977); *Chicago Legal News*, vol. 2 (July 2, 1870) p. 320 and Leila Robinson, "Women Lawyers in the United States," *The Green Bag* vol. 2 (1890) pages 10-31; Catalogue of Lake Forest University (1889 and 1890-91); Herman Kogan, *The First Century: The Chicago Bar Association, 1874-1974* (Chicago: Rand McNally & Company, 1974), 46-47; conversation with Dr. Bob Mawry, Archivist, Illinois Wesleyan University; and Lyn Schollett, "Chicago's Early Women Lawyers: 1870-1920," unpublished manuscript, Northwestern University School of Law.

THE PRACTICE OF LAW

Ellen Martin, "Admission of Women to the Bar" *Chicago Law Times* vol. 1 (1887) p. 76; "Ellen Martin," *Chicago Legal News*, vol. 48 (1916) p. 333; and "Miss Ida Platt," *Chicago Legal News* vol. 352 (1894) p. 26.

MARY FREDRIKA PERRY

Chicago Legal News vol. 15 (1883) p. 339; "M. Fredrika Perry," *Chicago Legal News* vol. 15 (1883) p. 347; Obituary in the *Chicago Tribune*, (June 9, 1883); James B. Bradwell, "Women Lawyers of Illinois," *Chicago Legal News* vol. 32 (1900) p. 339; Virginia G. Drachman, *Women Lawyers and the Origins of Professional Identity in America* (University of Michigan Press: Ann Arbor 1993); Ellen Martin, "Admission of Women to the Bar," *Chicago Law Times* vol. 1 (1887) p. 79; *Chicago Legal News* vol. 12 (1880) p. 434, quoting the *Chicago Inter-Ocean*.

ELLEN MARTIN

Ellen Martin's writings include "Admission of Women to the Bar," *Chicago Law Times*, vol. 1, (1886) p. 76, a letter to the Equity Club May 25, 1888, published along with additional information about Ellen Martin in Virginia Drachman, *Women Lawyers and the Origins of Professional Identity in America; The Letters of the Equity Club, 1887 to 1890* (1993) and "The Women Voters at Lombard," *Chicago Legal News*, vol. 23, (1891) p. 270. This event is also recorded in "The Ladies of Lombard," *The Daily Inter-Ocean* (April 11, 1891) and "Women and Municipal Suffrage," *Chicago Legal News*, vol. 23, (1891) p. 278. Ellen Martin's remarks at a service in honor of Miss Perry are recorded in "M. Fredrika Perry." *Chicago Legal News*, vol. 15, (1883) p. 347. Martin is discussed in John P. Downs and Fenwick Y. Hedley, *History of Chautauqua County and its People* (1875), Ada M. Bittenbender "Woman in Law" in the *Chicago Law Times*, vol. 2, (1887) p. 301, Lelia J. Robinson, "Women Lawyers in the United States" *Green Bag* vol. 2, (1890) p. 10, James B. Bradwell, "Women Lawyers of Illinois" *Chicago Legal News*, vol. 32 (1900) p. 339, John William Leonard, *Woman's Who's Who of America (1914-15)*. An obituary was written for Miss Martin in the *Chicago Legal News*, vol. 48 (1916) p. 333. Martin is also discussed in Bessie Louise Pierce: *A History of Chicago Volume III*, (New York: A.A. Knopf, 1937); Lillian Budd, *Footsteps on the Tall Grass Prairie: A History of Lombard, Illinois*, (Lombard, IL: Lombard Historical Society, 1977; Adade Mitchell Wheeler, *The Roads They Made...Women in Illinois History*, (Chicago: Charles H. Kerr Publishing Co., 1970), and Karen Berger Morello, *The Invisible Bar: The Woman Lawyer in America 1638 to the Present*, (New York: Random House, 1986). The founding of the National League of Women Lawyers is noted in *The American Lawyer*, vol. 1, (1893) p. 25. A discussion of the Queen Isabella Society can be found in Jeanne Madeline Weimann, *The Fair Women*, (Chicago: Academy, 1981). Archives on the Queen Isabella Association and some of their journals chronicling Ellen Martin's involvement as well as yearbooks of the Chicago Political Equality League are at the Chicago Historical Society. Archives on Ellen Martin are kept at the Lombard Historical Society. Ellen Martin's papers are in the Bentley Historical Library, University of Michigan. An alternate version of this article appears in *Historical Encyclopedia of Chicago Women* Rima Lunin Schultz and Adele Haste, eds, (Bloomington: Indiana University Press, forthcoming).

CORA AGNES BENNESON

Personal Papers and Journals of Cora A. Benneson, viewed June 1996 in Quincy, Illinois. Helen Warning, "Pioneer Women of Quincy: Cora Benneson Predicted Modern Woman Would Develop Own Faculties," *The Quincy Herald-Whig*, (February 20, 1997) at 6D, "Death of a Pioneer" *The Quincy Weekly Whig*, (May 18, 1893). *Illinois State Historical Society Journal*, vol. 12, pp. 307-309. *Portrait and Biographical Record of Adams County, Illinois* (Chicago, 1892). Mary Esther Trueblood, *Representative Women of New England* (1904). Virginia Drachman, *Women Lawyers and the Origins of Professional Identity in America: The Letters of the Equity Club 1887 to 1890* (1993), letter to the Equity Club December 12, 1887.

KATE KANE ROSSI

Biographical sketches of Rossi were written by James Bradwell in the *Chicago Legal News* vol. 32 (June 2, 1900) p. 340 and by Catharine Waugh McCulloch in the Grace Harte Papers, Mary Earhart Dillon Collection, Schlesinger Library, Radcliffe College. Articles on Rossi in the *Chicago Tribune* include "Causes Stir in Mayor's Office" (February 28, 1908), "Woman is Released on Bond" (February 29, 1908), "Woman Attacks a Policeman" (May 7, 1910), and her obituary "Mrs. Kate Rossi, Woman Lawyer Since 1894, Dies" (November 23, 1928). Articles on Rossi that appear in the *Chicago Record Herald* include, "Woman Lawyer Not Guilty" (May 8, 1908), "Kate Kane Rossi Attacks Cop" (May 7, 1910), and "Woman Seeks Job as Chief of Police" (April 15, 1911). A notice of Rossi's death appeared in the *Chicago Daily News* (November 22, 1928). Articles on Rossi that appeared in the *New York Times* include "Milwaukee's Woman Lawyer" (April 22, 1883), "Miss Kane's Revenge" (April 23, 1883), "Kate Kane at Liberty" (April 24, 1883), "Kate Kane Brings a Libel Suit" (April 25, 1883), "Miss Kane Again in Jail" (May 1, 1883), "From the Woman Lawyer's Dungeon" (May 14, 1883), and "Kate Kane Released" (May 21, 1883). Information on Lavina Goodell and her relationship with Rossi is included in Catherine B. Cleary, "Lavina Goodell, First Woman Lawyer in Wisconsin," *Wisconsin Magazine of History* vol. 74, (Summer 1991) pp. 243-271. Information on Rossi also appears in "The Legal World Moves," *Chicago Legal News* vol. 30 (1897) p. 80, Alice L. O'Donnell, "A Long Way, Baby: Women and Other Strangers Before the Bar," *Yearbook 1977* (Washington, D. C.: Supreme Court Historical Society, 1977), and Charlotte Adelman, *WBAI 75: The First 75 Years* (Paducah, KY: Turner Publishing Company, 1992).

MARY MERRILL SCHWENN

Virginia G. Drachman, *Women Lawyers and Professional Identity* (University of Michigan Press: Ann Arbor, 1993) pp. 6 and 46; O.C. Burlingame, *Lettie Lavilla Burlingame: Her Life Pages, Stories, Poems and Essays* (Joliet, IL: 1895) at 318; Cullin Cain, "The Strange Case of Mary Schwenn — Law Graduate, Kansas Lawyer, Kirkwood Recluse," *St. Louis County Leader*, (Oct. 29, 1937); Probate Record for Mary (Merrill) Schwenn; Newspaper Obituary Notices for Mary (Merrill) Schwenn, William Sherman Merrill and Thompson A. Merrill; "Mrs. Lease to Resume the Practice of Law" *Chicago Legal News* vol. 27 (1895) p. 337; and Richard Stiller, *Queen of Populists: The Story of Mary Elizabeth Lease* (New York: Thomas Y. Crowell Company, 1970).

CORA B. HIRTZEL

Much of the description of Cora Hirtzel's legal practice is derived from "A Woman as Corporation Counsel Thornton's Assistant," *Chicago Legal News*, vol. 29 (June 5, 1897) p. 341. The formation of her practice with Nellie Carlin was announced in *Chicago Legal News* vol. 32 (January 20, 1900) p. 185. Information on telephone service is from the article "Telephones" in volume 19 of the 1996 *World Book Encyclopedia*. Other sources used include census records.

EFFIE HENDERSON

Chicago Legal News, vol. 32 (June 2, 1900) p. 341; *Illinois Wesleyan Alumni Roll, University Bulletin - Series XVII* (November 5, 1919); Henderson family genealogy book (1897); *History of McLean County, Illinois*, (1879) p. 992; *Historical Encyclopedia of Illinois and History of McLean County, Volume II*, pp. 847-848, (1908) 1089; *Bloomington-Normal City Directories* (1893-1902); *Daily Pantagraph*, (June 15, 1892) p. 8; *Daily Pantagraph*, (February 14, 1938) p. 3; *Daily Pantagraph*, (February 15, 1938) p. 21. Miss Henderson's reported cases are: *Nelson v. Davidson*, 160 Ill. 254 (1896); *Nelson v. Riddell*, 160 Ill. 306 (1896); and *Nelson v. Davidson*, 160 Ill. 389 (1896).

IDA PLATT

Information on Ida Platt is included in the following articles: "Miss Ida Platt," *Chicago Legal News* vol. 26 (1894) p. 352; "The Legal World Moves," *Chicago Legal News* vol. 30 (1897) p. 80; Monroe A. Majors, *Noted Negro Women Their Triumphs and Activities* (Salem: Ayer Company, Publishers, Inc., 1896, 1893); "Colored Members of the Chicago Bar," *American Law Review* vol. 30 (1896) pp. 922-23; "We Envy Each Other," *Raleigh Gazette*, (August 14, 1897); *Chicago City Directory 1894 - 1912, Chicago Law Directory 1911-1928*; "Miss Violette Anderson" *Chicago Legal News* vol. 52 (1920) p. 405; Edith Sampson, "Are Our Women Holding Their Own?" in *1927 Intercollegian Wonder Book*, Frederic H. Robb ed.(Chicago: The Washington Intercollegiate Club of Chicago, Inc., 1927); *American Law Review*, vol. 30 (1896); "Ida Platt" *N.Y. Amsterdam News*, (January 26, 1957), p.9; *Michigan Law Review*, vol. 84, No. 4&5, (1986); and Charlotte Adelman, *WBAI - Women's Bar Association of Illinois - the First 75 Years*. Information on Chicago College of Law is from "The College Forum," *Chicago College of Law*, vol. I (1894). Sources for the position and treatment of African-Americans in Chicago in the late nineteenth and early twentieth centuries is from Ernest Rather, *Chicago Negro Almanac and Reference Book*; Estelle Hill-Scott, *Occupational Changes Among Negroes in Chicago*, (1939); Kletzing, and Crogman, *Progress of a Race: The Remarkable Advancement of the Afro-American* (1897); Geraldine Segal, *Blacks in the Law - Philadelphia and the Nation*, (University of Pennsylvania Press 1983); William Henri Hale, "The Career Development of the Negro Lawyer in Chicago," (A dissertation University of Chicago, September 1949). Information on women in the American legal profession is from: Women's Studies Manuscript Collection, (Schlesinger Library, Radcliffe College) Illinois Equal Suffrage Association, "Women Lawyers in Chicago" (1908); *National Bar Journal*, "Women as Practitioners of Law in the United States," vol. I, no.1 (1941); and Karen Morello, *The Invisible Bar: the Woman Lawyer in America: 1638 to the Present* (New York: Random House, 1986). Information on Chicago Public Schools is from Mary Herrick, *The Chicago Schools: A Social and Political History*, (Chicago: Sage Publications, 1971).

LOISE FOSKETTE

General biographical information was found in articles at *Chicago Legal News* vol. 26 (June 30, 1894) p. 352, *Chicago Legal News* vol. 27 (May 11, 1895) p. 321, *Chicago Legal News* vol. 27 (August 3, 1895) p. 418, and *Chicago Legal News* vol. 32 (June 2, 1900) p. 341. Foskette's obituary appeared at *Chicago Tribune* (March 7, 1897) page 6 col. 2. Information concerning the trial of Patrick Eugene Joseph Prendergast for the 1893 murder of five-term Chicago Mayor Carter Harrison I was derived from Paul, Gilbert, Charles Lee Bryson, *Chicago and its Makers* (Chicago: Felix Mendelsohn, Publisher, 1929), pp. 214-215; and Paul M. Green and Melvin G. Holli, *The Mayors* (Carbondale: Southern Illinois University Press, 1987).

MARY EVA MILLER

Mary Eva Miller was recognized in various legal journals: *Chicago Legal News*, vol. 28, (June 1896) pp. 338-39; *Chicago Legal News*, vol. 32, (June 1900) p. 344; *Women Lawyer's Journal*, vol. 30, (Jan. 1914) p. 30 and *Women Lawyer's Journal*, vol. 30, (April 1914) p. 51. In her book entitled, *The Part Taken by Women in American History*, published in 1912 by Perry-Nalle, Mary Simmerson Logan devotes several pages (747-748) to Mary Eva Miller. Mary Eva Miller's obituary appeared in the March 18, 1914 editions of the *New York Times*, the *Chicago Tribune* and the *Chicago Daily News*. Mary Eva Miller's will and probate documents can be found in the Archives of the Clerk of the Circuit Court of Cook County under general number 17732 and docket number 142.

MAE ISABELLE REED

The following sources were utilized in research for this article: George Owen Smith, *A History of Princeton* (self-published in Princeton, IL, 1966); U. J. Hoffman, *History of LaSalle County, Illinois* (1966); and Republican Times of Ottawa, *Ottawa in Nineteen Hundred* (Republican Times of Ottawa, 1900) and *Ottawa Old and New, A Complete History of Ottawa, Illinois, 1823-1914* (Republican Times of Ottawa, 1912-1914). Reed's career is described in James B. Bradwell, "Women Lawyers of Illinois", *Chicago Legal News* vol. 32 (1900) p. 347 and in the *LaSalle County Centennial Directory of Former Ottawans, 1831-1931* (Republican Times of Ottawa, 1931), p. 37.

MARION E. GARMORY

Garmory is discussed in "Examination of Applicants for Admission to the Bar: A Woman Leads the Class," *Chicago Legal News*, vol. 30, (1898) p. 231; "Miss Marion E. Garmory Passed for the Bar at the Head of Her Class," *Chicago Legal News*, vol. 30, (1898) p. 238, and in James B. Bradwell, "Women Lawyers of Illinois," *Chicago Legal News*, vol. 32, (1900) p. 339. Her obituary appeared in the *Rockford Morning Star*, (March 14, 1959). Garmory is also mentioned in "Site for State Park Left By Mrs. Anna Page," *Rockford Morning Star*, (September 12, 1948). She is listed in the 1951 edition of *Sullivan's Law Directory*.

ELLEN G. ROBERTS

Chicago Legal News, vol. 45, (1913) p. 221; *Chicago Tribune*, vol. 72, (1913) p. 2; *Chicago Legal Directory*, 1905-1913; *Chicago Bar Association Memorials* 1909-1913, page 122; *Foulkes v. Steward*, 182 Ill. App. 193 (1st Dist. 1913); and *Proceedings of the Illinois State Bar Association Thirty-Seventh Annual Meeting Springfield, April 8 and 9, 1913*, (Chicago: Chicago Legal News Co., 1913) p. 220

ISABEL 'BELLE' QUINLAN

Milwaukee Journal (January 2, 1955); Unidentified newspaper articles form the 1920s and 1950s; Fortnightly Club Scrap Book; *Women Lawyers' Journal* (May 1922) and Peg Roberts at the Benton Museum.

PRACTICAL CONCERNS

Virginia G. Drachman, *Women Lawyers and the Origins of Professional Identity in America; The Letters of the Equity Club, 1887 to 1890* (Ann Arbor: The University of Michigan Press, 1993) pp. 134-135 and 177-78; Ellen Martin, "Admission of women to the Bar," *Chicago Law Times* vol. 1 (1887) p. 79; "Club Has New Plans," unidentified news clipping, Mary M. Bartelme Papers University of Illinois at Chicago Special Collections, oversize file 113; "Lawyers Discuss New Woman Judge" *Chicago Herald and Examiner* (November 8, 1923) Mary M. Bartelme Papers; "Hats Mix with Law" *Chicago Daily News* (April 10, 1947).

PROFESSIONAL ASSOCIATIONS

Information on the Equity Club is from Virginia Drachman, *Women Lawyers and the Origins of Professional Identity in America* (Ann Arbor: The University of Michigan Press, 1993). Information on the Queen Isabella Association is from Jeanne Madeline Weimann, *The Fair Women* (Chicago: Academy, 1981), 28-30 and the Queen Isabella Association Archives, Chicago Historical Society Library. Mary H. Zimmerman, ed. *75 Year History of National Association of Women Lawyers 1899-1974* (Lansing: National Association of Women Lawyers, 1975) discusses the history of the NAWL while Charlotte Adelman, *WBAI 75 The First 75 Years* (Paducah, KY: Turner Publishing Company, 1992) sets forth the history of the WBAI.

LETITIA LAVILLA BURLINGAME

Lettie Lavilla Burlingame: Her Life Pages: Stories, Poems, and Essays, Olive C. Burlingame ed. (Joilet, IL: J. E. Williams & Company, 1895); Lelia J. Robinson, "Women Lawyers in the United States," *The Green Bag*, vol. 2 (Boston, 1890) p. 10; and Virginia Drachman, G., *Women Lawyers and the Origins of Professional Identity in America: The Letters of the Equity Club, 1887-1890* (Ann Arbor: University of Michigan Press, 1993).

LEGAL ADVOCACY AND SOCIAL REFORM

Information on the Protective Agency for Women and Children is from Elizabeth Pleck, "Feminist Responses to 'Crimes against Women,' 1868-1896," *Signs* vol. 8 (1983) pp. 451-470; *Protective Agency for Women and Children First Annual Report 1886-7* (Chicago: Dean Brothers Blank Book and Printing Co., 1887) Chicago Historical Society Library; Henriette Greenbaum Frank and Amalie Hofer Jerome, *Annals of the Chicago Woman's Club* (Chicago: Chicago Woman's Club, 1916), 133-35. Both the PAWC and the Annals of the CWC also provide information on Charlotte Holt. Information on *Florence Kelley is from Kathryn Kish Sklar, Florence Kelley and the Nation's Work: The Rise of Women's Political Culture, 1830-1900* (New Haven: Yale University Press, 1995) pp. 280-285. Sources for the founding of the Juvenile Court and on the work of Mary Bartelme include Elizabeth J. Clapp, "Welfare and the Role of Women: The Juvenile Court Movement," *Journal of American Studies* vol. 28 (1994) pp. 359-383; "A Court for Girls with a Woman Judge," *Collier's The National Weekly* circa 1913, Mary M. Bartelme Papers, University of Illinois at Chicago Special Collections box 5 folder 103; Mary Bartelme, "Radio Talk," 3 November 1923, Mary M Bartelme Papers, box 2 folder 36 and "'Pretty Clothes' in a New Suitcase, Cheer Girl in Juvenile Court," news clipping source unknown, 14 October 1923, Mary M. Bartelme Papers, box 4 folder 77.

MARY A. AHRENS

Sketches of Ahrens appear in: *A Woman of the Century, Leading American Women in all Walks of Life*, Frances E. Willard and Mary Livermore eds. (Buffalo: Charles Wells Moulton, 1893); Lelia Robinson "Women Lawyers in the United States," *The Green Bag*. vol. 2 (1890) p. 10; James Bradwell, "Women Lawyers of Illinois," *Chicago Legal News* vol. 32 (1900) p. 339; and "Mary Ahrens, Lawyer and Philanthropist," *Case and Comment* vol. 21 (1914) p. 430 . Recitation of speech given by Ahrens in 1891, Thomas Clancy, "Women in a Learned Profession," *Illinois Bar Journal* vol. 79 (September 1991). Bessie Louise Pierce *A History of Chicago, The Rise of a Modern City (1871-1893)* vol. 3 (New York: A.A. Knopf, 1937) p. 373. Henriette Greenbaum Frank and Amalie Hofer Jerome *Annals of the Chicago Woman's Club for the First Forty Years of Its Organization 1876-1916* (Chicago: Chicago Woman's Club, 1916); Albert Nelson Marquis, *The Book of Chicagoans* (Chicago: A.N. Marquis & Co., 1917); *The People ex rel. v. English et al.* 139 Ill. 622 (1892); 'Home for Poor Girls,' *Chicago Evening Post* (February 2, 1894) page 8; Elizabeth Pleck, 'Feminist Responses to Crimes Against Women,' 1868-1896,' *Signs* vol. 3 no. 3 (Spring 1983) pp. 451-470.

FLORENCE KELLEY

Karen Altman, "Women Public Speakers in the United States: Florence Kelley," pp. 294-308; Josephine Goldmark, *Impatient Crusader* (Urbana: University of Illinois Press, 1953); Florence Kelley *Some Ethical Gains Through Legislation* (New York: Macmillan, 1905); *Kelley, Modern Industry in Relation to the Family, Health, Education, Morality* (New York: Longmans, Green, 1914); Kathryn Kish Sklar, *Florence Kelley and the Nation's Work: the Rise of Women's Political Culture, 1830-1900* (New Haven: Yale University Press, 1995); Sklar, "Hull

House in the 1890s: A Community of Women Reformers." *Signs* vol. 10 (1985) pp. 658-677; Louise C. Wade, Florence Kelley *Notable American Women*, (Cambridge: Belnap Press, 1971) pp. 316-319.

MARY BARTELME

"Personals", *The Survey*, Vol. XXX, No. 7, May 17, 1913; Betsy Greenbaum, "The Court of 'Another Chance' Where Judge Mary Bartelme Presides", *The Woman Citizen*, vol. 12, (August 1927), pp. 1214; Anne Shannon Monroe. "When Women Sit in Judgment", *Good Housekeeping*, (April 1920), pp. 46ff.; "Women Who are Making Good in Public Office", *Current Opinion*, vol. LV, No. 2, (August 1913), p. 95; "Mary Bartelme First Woman Judge in Illinois Courts", *Journal of the Illinois State Historical Society*, vol. 17, p. 246 (editorial); Professor B. Elizabeth Lane, untitled submission to *Women Lawyer Journal*, vol. 2, No. 4, (February 1913), pp. 1, 67; Karen Morello, *The Invisible Bar* (New York: Random House, 1986), p. 226; *Chicago Legal News*, (December 12, 1923), p. 165; Sawyers, June. "'Suitcase Mary' Leads a Crusade for Needy Girls"; "Judge Mary Bartelme, 88, Dies in West", *Chicago Daily Tribune*, Vol. CXIII, No. 177, (July 26, 1954), p.1 (obituary); "Mary M. Bartelme, Aided Needy Girls", *New York Times*, Vol. CIII, No. 35,247, (July 26, 1954), p. 17 (obituary); "Memorials", *Chicago Bar Record*, Vol. 36, p. 232 (obituary); the Mary Earhart Dillon papers Schlesinger Library, Radcliffe College scrapbook on Mary Margaret Bartelme of the Women's Studies Manuscripts Collection at the Chicago Historical Society; the archives at Northwestern University Library in Evanston, IL. Articles on Bartelme also include *Chicago Tribune* (November 8, 1923), *Chicago Evening Post* (April, 28, 1897), and the *Chicago Daily Journal* (November 7, 1923). Bartelme's papers are archived at the University of Illinois University Library, Department of Special Collections. Bartelme's May 1932 speech is found at box 3, folder 42 of the University of Illinois archives.

NELLIE CARLIN

Biographical information on Carlin is from *The Bench and Bar of Illinois* Le Roy Hennessey, ed., (Chicago: Bench & Bar Publications, 1920) p. 77; *Chicago Bar Record* vol. 30 no. 5 (March 1949); and James Bradwell, "Women Lawyers of Illinois' Chicago Legal New" vol. 32 (June 2, 1900) p. 344. Obituaries on Carlin appeared in *Chicago Sun Times* (September 6, 1948) and *Chicago Tribune* (September 6, 1948). An obituary on William Carlin was published in the *Chicago Tribune* (October 7, 1963). Article expressing Carlin's activities include from the *Women Lawyers' Journal*: vol. 4 no. 2 (November 1914) p. 87; vol. 5 no. 4 (1915) p. 32; vol. 5 no. 7 (1915) p. 55; vol. 6 no. 8 (May 1917) p. 59; vol. 8 no. 2 (1918) p. 16; vol. 8 no. 4 (1919) p. 32; vol. 9 no. 3 (April 1920) p. 23 and vol. 10 no. 2 (January 1921) p. 11. Articles on Carlin's legal achievements also appeared in the *Chicago Legal News* vol. 28 (1896) p. 339 and vol. 32 (January 2, 1900) p. 185. Information on the Women's Bar Association of Illinois is contained in their archives at the Chicago Historical Society.

THE RIGHT TO VOTE

An excellent account of the Illinois Suffrage movement is Steven Buechler, *The Transformation of the Woman Suffrage Movement* (New Brunswick, NJ: Rutgers University Press, 1986). Information on McCulloch's bill is also included in Frances E. Willard and Mary A. Livermore, *A Woman of the Century* (Buffalo: Charles Wells Moulton, 1893), p. 485. Information on the Chicago Political Equality League is from the *Chicago Political Equality League Annual 1895-1911* (Chicago: Chicago Woman's Club, 1911), Chicago Historical Society Library.

CATHARINE VAN VALKENBURG WAITE

A bound set of the *Chicago Law Times* is held by the Cook County Law Library in Chicago. Copies of Catharine Waite's books, *The Mormon Prophet and His Harem* (Cambridge: Riverside Press, 1866) and *Adventures in the Far West, and Life Among the Mormons* (Chicago: C.V. Waite & Co., 1882), are in the Newberry Library, Chicago, as are copies of some of Charles Waite's books published by C.V. Waite & Co., Publishers. Artifacts (pamphlets, etc.) of the Hyde Park Seminary and of the Queen Isabella Society, as well as a scrapbook of notes by Dr. Lucy Waite on her mother, are held at the Chicago Historical Society.

General biographical information was derived from Dr. Waite's scrapbook, mentioned above; from questionnaires completed by Mrs. Waite and by Dr. Waite and held in the alumni archives at Oberlin College; from entries in Wilson, James Grant, et al., editors, *Appleton's Cyclopedia of American Biography* (New York: D. Appleton & Co., 1888), vol. 6, p. 317; from a published biographical sketch dated around 1890 (source unknown) found in the Papers of Caroline I. Reilly (the "Reilly Papers"), located in the Women's Studies Manuscript Collections of the Schlesinger Library, Radcliffe College, (the "Schlesinger Collection"); from Robinson, Lelia J., "Women Lawyers", *The Green Bag* vol. 2 (1890) p. 10; from the entry in Frances E. Willard, and Mary A. Livermore, *A Woman of the Century* (Buffalo, NY: Charles Wells Moulton, 1893), at 737; from an obituary, published at *Chicago Legal News* vol. 46 (November 13, 1913) p. 117; from entries in *Who Was Who In America*, vol. IV (Chicago: Marquis—Who's Who, Inc., 1968) and in *Notable American Women 1607-1950* (Cambridge: Belknap Press of Harvard University Press, 1971), pp. 523-525; from the records of Graceland Cemetery, Chicago and of the Rock Creek Cemetery Association, Washington, D. C.; and from census records and Chicago and Hyde Park (Ill.) city directories.

Accounts of Mrs. Waite's college and law school years derive from the unpublished reminiscence (n.d.) of Catherine Gouger (Waugh) McCulloch found in the Papers of Grace Harte in the Schlesinger Collection. Mrs. Waite's letter to The Equity Club dated May 4, 1888 is collected in the Reilly Papers.

Hyde Park historical information was derived from Jean F. Block, *Hyde Park Homes* (Chicago: The University of Chicago Press, 1978).

Accounts of the Waites' involvement in suffrage activities were found in Elizabeth Cady Stanton and others, eds., *A History of Woman Suffrage* (Rochester, NY: Susan B. Anthony, 1881), vols. II and III; Adade Mitchell Wheeler, *The Roads They Made: Women in Illinois History* (Chicago: Charles H. Kerr Publishing Co., 1970); and Steven M. Buechler, *The Transformation of the Woman Suffrage Movement: The Case of Illinois, 1850-1920* (New Brunswick, NJ: Rutgers University Press, 1986). The decision in Mrs. Waite's case against the Hyde Park voter registration board, *The People ex rel Catharine V. Waite v. Horace V. Stebbins et al.*, was reported *Chicago Legal News* vol. 4 (Super. Ct. of Cook County, Illinois, January 12, 1872) p. 97.

Biographical information on Charles Burlingame Waite is from entries in Appleton's Cyclopedia (see above) and *Who Was Who In America*, vol. I (Chicago: The A. N. Marquis Co., 1942), and from an obituary in the *Chicago Record Herald*, (March 26, 1909) p. 2 col. 1. Information on the career of Dr. Lucy Waite came from F. M. Sperry, *A Group of Distinguished Physicians and Surgeons of Chicago* (Chicago: J. H. Beers & Co., 1904). Jessie Waite's 1880 address to the House Committee on the Judiciary is reprinted in Stanton, *History of Woman Suffrage, vol. III*, pp. 161-162. Information on the Katharine Wright Center was from the Fall 1992 edition of *Caring*, a quarterly publication of Illinois Masonic Hospital, Chicago.

Other sources consulted for this essay include: Microsoft Encarta, article on "Progressive Party", and Adade Mitchell Wheeler, "Conflict in the Illinois Woman Suffrage Movement of 1913", JISHS vol 76 no. 2 (1983), at 95.

The author thanks Roland Baumann and Edward G. Schwaegerle of the Oberlin College Archives, Carley Robinson of the Knox College Archives, Donald Howard, and Mr. and Mrs. George H. Wright for their gracious assistance in the preparation of this article.

CATHARINE WAUGH MCCULLOCH

Charlotte Adelman, "A History of Women Lawyers in Illinois" *Illinois Bar Journal* (May 1986), pp. 424-428; Ada Bittenbinder, "Women In Law" *Chicago Law Times* vol. 2 (1888) p. 301; James B. Bradwell, "Women Lawyers of Illinois" *Chicago Legal News* vol. 32 (June 2, 1900) p. 339; Virginia G. Drachman *Women Lawyers and the Origins of Professional Identify in America*, (Ann Arbor: University of Michigan Press, 1993), pp. 1-38; 133-137; 173-177; 251-254; Meg Gorecki, "Legal Pioneers" Four of Illinois' First Women Lawyers" *Illinois Bar Journal*, (October 1990) pp. 510-515; Edward T. James, ed. *Notable American Women 1607-1950 A Biographical Dictionary* (Cambridge Belnap Press, 1971) pp. 459-460. Writings by McCulloch include: "Women's Wages" Master's Thesis, Rockford Seminary (November 1888); "Stop the Ruin of Girls" (January 25, 1905); "Women May be Justices of the Peace" (Evanston, 1907); "Some Wrongs of Michigan Women" (January 8, 1908); "Women Suffrage Amendment to the Constitution of the State of Illinois" House Resolution 7, March 11, 1915; "Political Rights of Illinois Women" (1919). Other sources include: McCulloch, Catharine Waugh and Frank. Wedding Announcement *Chicago Legal News* vol. 22 (June, 1890) p. 626; "Social Welfare Legislation and Governmental Participation in Business" (1936); Leila J. Robinson, "Women Lawyers in the United States" *The Green Bag* vol. 2 (1890) p. 10; Job Announcement. *Women Lawyers' Journal* vol. 3 (October 1913) p. 2; Obituary *Sun Times* (April 21, 1945).

ANTOINETTE LELAND FUNK

General biographical information on Antoinette Funk was derived from Albert Nelson Marquis, ed., *The Book of Chicagoans* (Chicago: A. N. Marquis & Co., 1917); Albert Nelson Marquis, ed., *Who's Who in America, 1924-1925* (Chicago: A. N. Marquis & Co., 1924) p. 242; "Antoinette Funk Quits Federal Post," *Bloomington Daily Pantagraph*, (November 3, 1939), p. 24, col. 5; "In Memoriam", in the column, "Women's Bar Personal Views and Notes", written by Grace A. Harte, *Chicago Law Bulletin*, (April 13, 1942); Chicago city directories; census records; and an obituary found in the *New York Times*, (March 29, 1942), p. 45, col. 2. Antoinette Funk's participation in the Illinois suffrage movement is described in Grace Wilbur Trout, "Sidelights on Illinois Suffrage History," in *Journal of the Illinois State Historical Society* ("JISHS"), vol. 13 p. 145 (1920); and in Adade Mitchell Wheeler, "Conflict in the Illinois Woman Suffrage Movement of 1913", JISHS vol. 76 no. 2 (1983), at 95. Funk is also mentioned in "The Noiseless Suffragette," an account of the Illinois victory by Progressive Illinois legislator George Fitch that appeared in the August 9, 1913 edition of Collier's, at 5. Her work in the national woman suffrage movement is covered in Ida Husted Harper, ed., *The History of Woman Suffrage, volume V* (New York: National American Woman Suffrage Association, 1922), pp. 420-421. The letters to Catharine Waugh McCulloch dated March 17 and April 2, 1915 may be found in the Catherine Gouger (Waugh) McCulloch Papers, collected in the Women's Studies Manuscript Collections from the Schlesinger Library, Radcliffe College.

Description of the "Bull Moose" Progressive Party was derived from the article "Progressive Party" in Microsoft Encarta encyclopedia (1996).

The author's gratitude is expressed to Bill Case, of the Funk Prairie Home Museum, Funk's Grove, Illinois, and to Laurel Quaid, Library Assistant, McLean County Historical Society, and Dr. Robert Mowrey, archivist at Illinois Wesleyan University, Bloomington, Illinois, for research assistance with this article.

POLITICAL OFFICE

Information on the Bradwell's and the Waites legislative activities are included in Steven Buechler, *The Transformation of the Woman Suffrage Movement* (New Brunswick, NJ: Rutgers University Press, 1986). Information on McCulloch's political endeavors is included in the Rockfordania File at the Rockford Public Library and is recounted in a news article by McCulloch in the Rockford Star (March 20, 1938). Information on Mary Bartelme's campaign can be found in assorted news clippings, Mary Bartelme Papers at the University of Illinois at Chicago Special Collections department box 4, folder 61.

MARY GEIGUS COULTER

Thanks to the University of Michigan Bentley Historical Library for information, including various Utah newspaper clippings (identity unknown) concerning Mary Geigus, as well as copies of correspondence from Mary Geigus Coulter, Chester Coulter, M.D., and their son, Major Halvor Coulter.

MARION DRAKE

A colorful description of Miss Drake's 1914 campaign against Bathhouse John Coughlin is found in Lloyd Wendt, and Herman Kogan, *Lords of the Levee* (Indianapolis: The Bobbs-Merrill Co, 1943). The campaign is also covered in Adade Mitchell Wheeler, *The Roads They Made: Women in Illinois History* (Chicago: Charles H. Kerr Publishing Co., 1977).

Marion Drake's 1895 commencement address to Chicago College of Law is published at 27 *Chicago Legal News*, p. 351. A copy of her mailing to "The Women of Chicago Who Think and Lead" may be found in the Catherine Gouger (Waugh) McCulloch Papers, collected in the Women's Studies Manuscript Collections from the Schlesinger Library, Radcliffe College, (microfilm of series by University Publications of America).

Levy Mayer's career is recounted in Edgar Lee Masters, *Levy Mayer and the New Industrial Era* (New Haven: 1927).

Other sources consulted include Ida Husted Harper, ed., *The History of Woman Suffrage, volume V* (New York: National American Woman Suffrage Association, 1922); James Bradwell's article, "Women Lawyers of Illinois", *Chicago Legal News* vol. 32 (June 2, 1900) p.339; Harold L. Ickes, *Autobiography of a Curmudgeon* (New York: Reynal & Hitchcock, 1943); numerous articles of the *Chicago Daily Tribune* and directories of the city of Chicago, each on microfilm at the Harold Washington Library Center; and census records.

GENEVIEVE MELODY

Information on Reed appeared in James B. Bradwell, "Women Lawyers of Illinois", *Chicago Legal News* vol. 32 (June 2, 1900) p. 339. Her obituary was reported "Miss Melody, Calumet High Principal, Dies," *Chicago Tribune* (November 6, 1933). Information on Reed is also included in the University of Chicago Library Department of Special Collections and in the *Telumac* yearbook at Calumet High School.

GRACE REED

Grace Reed was included in a biographical compendium by Agness Geneva Gilman and Gertrude Marcelle Gilman, *Who's Who in Illinois: Women Makers of History* (Chicago: The Eclectic Publishers, 1927). Reed made headlines in the *Chicago Tribune*, "Wants Miss Reed to Ignore W.C.T.U.," (December 8, 1908) and "Saloon Defended by School Head" (December 5, 1908); "W.C.T.U. Members Fight Principal," (April 14, 1911); and "Woman Carries Equal Rights Idea to the N— Power," (October 12, 1919). The *Chicago Legal*

News mentions her briefly at *Chicago Legal News* vol. 28 p. 330 (with photo at 331) and *Chicago Legal News* vol. 32 (1900) p. 339. The context in which she worked is exemplified by Adade Mitchell Wheeler and Marlene Stein Wortman's *The Roads They Made: Women in Illinois History* (Chicago: Charles H. Kerr Publishing Co., 1977); in two books about the early development of professionalism in Chicago Public Schools; Edward Pritsch's *Chicago Principals Club: 1899-1935* and Mary Herrick's *The Chicago Schools: A Social and Political History* (Chicago: Sage Publications, 1971); and in *The Bench and Bar of Illinois* John M. Palmer, ed. (Chicago: Bench & Bar Publications, 1899).

ANNA MULLIN

General biographical information was derived from James B. Bradwell, "Women Lawyers of Illinois", *Chicago Legal News* vol. 32 (June 2, 1900) p. 339. Information on the Forward Movement is from *The Commons*, (October 31, 1899) pp. 10-11.

ZETTA STRAWN

Biographical sketch of Robert C. Strawn, *History of LaSalle County*, Michael Cypran O'Byrne ed., (Lewis Publishing Co., 1924). Biographical sketches of the Strawn family, Ottawa: Old and New (The Fair Dealer). Information also appears in Strawn Family Obituaries, "The Fair Dealer," Ottawa, Illinois and "The Daily Republican Times," Ottawa, Illinois; "Fun and Games," Ottawa Township newsletter, (Aug. 24, 1904); LaSalle County Historical Society records. Biographical sketch of Silas Hardy Strawn, Illinois: *The Heart of the Nation*, Hon. Edward F. Dunne (Lewis Publishing Co., 1933). Biographical sketch of Theodore Strawn, History of LaSalle County, U.J. Hoffman (S.J. Clarke Publishing Co., 1906). Information on Zetta Strawn from James B. Bradwell, "Women Lawyers of Illinois," *Chicago Legal News* vol. 32 (June 2, 1900) p. 339; interview with A. L. Perkins, a cousin; and Interview with Robert Jordan, President, LaSalle County Historical Society.

JANE CROMBIE TRULL

Records of the probate of Jane Trull's estate were obtained from the Kane County Probate Court.

Obituaries for Dr. Trull appeared in the *Elgin Daily News*, (September 6, 1930), and the *Chicago Tribune*, (September 7, 1930), p. 16, col. 4. Other general biographical information was derived from James Bradwell, "Women Lawyers of Illinois", *Chicago Legal News* vol. 32 (June 2, 1900) pp., 345-346; a report of Illinois state bar exam results at *Chicago Legal News* vol. 32 (October 21, 1899) p. 72; and census records. Information on the Bennett Medical College was found in *History of Medicine and Surgery in Chicago* (Chicago: The Biographical Publishing Corp., 1922), at 211-212. The description of "eclectic medicine" was derived from Paul Starr, *The Social Transformation of American Medicine* (New York: Basic Books, Inc., Publishers, 1982). Thanks to Diane Shannon at Rush Presbyterian St. Luke's Medical Center Archives for research and assistance with this article.

MARIETTA BROWN REED SHAY

Mrs. Shay is discussed in Ellen Martin, "Admission of Women to the Bar," in the *Chicago Law Times*, vol. 1, (1886) p. 84; Ada M. Bittenbender, "Woman in Law," in the *Chicago Law Times*, vol. 2, (1887) pp. 303-4; and in Lelia J. Robinson, "Women Lawyers in the United States," *Green Bag*, vol. 2, (1900) p. 16. The Shay family is profiled in History of LaSalle County. . . Illinois and Biographies of Representative Citizens . . . vol. 2, (1886) p. 74; and in M.C. O'Byrne, *History of LaSalle County, Illinois*, vol. 2, (1924) p. 209. Mrs. Shay's book, *Student's Guide to Common Law Practices, Consisting of Questions on Stephen, Gould, and Chitty*, published by Callaghan and Company, 1881, is in the collection at the University of Illinois Law Library. The microfilm U.S. census records of 1850, 1860, 1870, and 1900 yielded additional family names, occupations, and places and dates of birth.

LILLIEN BLANCHE FEARING

A Woman of the Century, Leading American Women in All Walks of Life, edited by Frances E. Willard and Mary A. Livermore (Buffalo: Charles Wells Moulton, 1893). Robinson, Lelia J., "Women Lawyers in the United States" *The Green Bag* vol. 2 (1890) p. 10; James Bradwell, "Women Lawyers of Illinois," *Chicago Legal News* vol. 32 (1900) p. 339. Lillien Blanche Fearing, *The Sleeping World and Other Poems* (1887); *In the City By the Lake* (1892). Clarence A. Andrews, *Chicago in Story: A Literary History*, (Iowa City: Midwest Heritage Publishing Company, 1982). Fearing's law school graduation announcement, *Chicago Legal News* (June, 1890). *The History of Chicago*, edited by John Moses and Joseph Kirkland (Chicago: Munsell & Co., 1895). Webster's New World Dictionary of the American Language, idyl, p. 697 (1972). *The Davenport Democrat and Leader*, (March 17, 1892), p. 4; (August 14, 1900), p. 4; (August 15, 1900), p. 7. *The Chicago Tribune*, (August 15, 1900), p. 3.

Special thanks to Mary R. Herr, special collections at the Davenport Public Library, Davenport, Iowa.

BESSIE BRADWELL HELMER

Bessie Helmer wrote of her experiences during the Chicago Fire in a letter, dated October 7, 1926, to Caroline MacIlvaine of the Chicago Historical Society. Her deeds during the ordeal were also acclaimed in a note to readers, *Chicago Legal News*, vol. 4, (1871) p. 2. Helmer's remarks as valedictorian of her law school graduating class are printed in *Chicago Legal News*, vol. 15, (1882) p. 337. Helmer's letter to Marion Talbot discussing Phi Beta Kappa, dated October 15, 1896; and her letter discussing her undergraduate experience at Northwestern, dated January 2, 1925 are kept in the Marion Talbot Collection, Department of Special Collections, The Joseph Regenstein Library, University of Chicago. Bessie Bradwell's marriage to Frank Ambrose Helmer was described in the *Chicago Legal News*, vol. 28, (Dec. 26, 1885) p. 253. Details of Helmer's involvement with the Western Association of Collegiate Alumnae (WACA), known today as the American Association of University Women (AAUW), and the Committee on Fellowships are discussed in: Marion Talbot, "History of the Chicago Association of Collegiate Alumnae: 1888-1917," Chicago Historical Society Archives; Marion Talbot and Lois Kimball Mathews Rosenberry, "The History of the American Association of University Women 1881-1931," pp. 45, 107 (footnoted), 108, 147-48, and Chapter XI (1931); Publications of the Association of Collegiate Alumnae, series III, number 17, p. 141-42 (1908); address given by Grace Elliott, 'Chicago Branch AAUW,' Chicago Historical Society Archives; and minutes of the Chicago Chapter of WACA, Chicago Historical Society Archives. Helmer's lead role in establishing the fellowship program and in hosting the first author's reading are discussed in the minutes of the Chicago Chapter of WACA, Chicago Historical Society Archives (June 21, 1890; March 7, 1891; and March 1, 1927). A history of the Chicago Chapter of the AAUW is given in the paper "The American Association of University Women Chicago Branch 1889-1949", Chicago Historical Society Archives. Helmer's role in the decision of the Western Association of Collegiate Alumnae (WACA) to join the national organization is chronicled in the minutes of the Chicago Chapter of WACA, Chicago Historical Society Archives (1889-1910). Bessie Helmer is also discussed in: the *Album of Genealogy and Biography*, 4th edition, (1896) pp. 215-16; James Bradwell, "Women Lawyers of Illinois," *Chicago Legal News*, vol. 32, (1900) p. 340; Entries from Myra Bradwell's Centennial Scrap Book, including

citations to the *Women's Journal*, (Boston: July 1, 1882 and October 17, 1891), *Chicago Daily News* (December 1890), *Inter-Ocean* and *Chicago Tribune* (October 30, 1895), comments by Lucy Stone, the *Green Bag*, and *Who's Who in America* (1926-1927), which are found in the AAUW clippings file, Washington D.C. office; *Dictionary of American Biography volume IV*, p. 514, edited by Allen Johnson and Dumas Malone (1931-32); and the Annual Report of the Illinois State Bar Association, p. 357 (1927). Upon Helmer's death, an obituary was written in the *Battle Creek Enquirer News*, (January 11, 1927). This obituary is part of the AAUW clippings file, Washington, D.C. office. Additional obituaries are included in the clippings file, however, sources are not listed. The *Winnetka Talk* published an obituary for Helmer on January 15, 1927.

Helmer's husband, Frank Ambrose Helmer, is discussed in Frederic B. Crossly, *Courts and Lawyers of Illinois*, vol. II, (1916) p. 495-96. Helmer and her daughter, Myra, are mentioned in the article. Helmer, her husband, and her brother, Thomas, are included in *The Book of Chicagoans - A Biographical Dictionary of Leading Living Men and Women of the City of Chicago*, (1917) pp. 80 and 317. Myra Bradwell and Judge James B. Bradwell are both discussed in Pierce, *A History of Chicago, vols. 2 and 3* (New York: A.A. Knopf, 1940); *Historical Encyclopedia of Illinois, volume I*, p. 58, edited by Newton Bateman and Paul Selby (Chicago: Munsell Publishing Co., 1914); *America's First Woman Lawyer: The Biography of Myra Bradwell*, by Jane M. Friedman, (Buffalo, N.Y.: Prometheus Books, 1993). During a conversation with Ms. Friedman in 1996, the authors of this article learned that the Bradwell documents discussed in her book did not contain Bessie Helmer documents. Further information about Judge James B. Bradwell, his life during the Civil War, and the founding of the Union League Club came from the following documents obtained from Mr. Everett Barlow, archivist of the Union League Club: a biography of James Bradwell compiled by Roger Henn, Director of Public Affairs of the Union League Club, 1959-1989, and *The First 100 Years*, Gerald E. Kellman, 1984; and from the *Chicago Legal News*, vol. 60, Nos. 16-18, (November 30, 1907), (December 7, 1907), and (December 14, 1907).

HELEN HONOR TUNNICLIFF CATTERALL

Titus M. Karlowicz, "Helen Honor Tunnicliff Catterall," an unpublished biography (August 19, 1996) was the main source of information for this article. Titus Karlowicz, in an unpublished article dated September 1995, also provided the information on St. George's Episcopal Church of Macomb. Several articles about Catterall appeared in the Macomb Daily Journal including the following dates: "Their New Church," (April 19, 1895), "St. Agnes School," (December 17, 1895), "Untitled" (March 9, 1896), "Catterall-Tunnicliff," (June 25, 1896). Biographical information also appears in J. Franklin Jameson, "Preface," in *Judicial Cases Concerning American Slavery and the Negro* Helen Tunnicliff Catterall, ed., volume IV (New York: Octagon Books, Inc., 1968, originally published by the Carnegie Institution of Washington, 1936). Obituaries for "Mrs. Helen H. Catterall," *New York Times* (November 12, 1933) and "Professor R. C. H. Catterall," *New York Times* (August 4, 1914). Information on Ruth Tunnicliff appears in *History of Medicine and Surgery and Physicians and Surgeons of Chicago* (Chicago: Biographical Publishing Corp., 1922); *Who's Who in Chicago* A. N. Marquis, ed., (Chicago: A. N. Marquis & Co, 1926); and "Dr. Ruth Tunnicliff" *New York Times* (September 23, 1946) p. 23. The Review of Ralph C. H. Catterall's book appeared in the *New York Times* (January 31, 1903) p. 80.

125 YEARS AND BEYOND

Acceptance Speech by Delores Hanna at the Chicago Bar Association Alliance for Women Founders Day Award (1997).

ABOUT THE EDITOR

Gwen Hoerr McNamee, a Ph.D. candidate in history at the University of Illinois at Chicago, also holds a J. D. from the University of Denver College of Law and a masters degree in criminal justice from the University of Illinois at Chicago. She has practiced law as a deputy district attorney in Colorado and is the mother of two children, as well as a member of the Chicago Bar Association Alliance for Women.

INDEX

Corboy & Demetrio, P.C.
Salutes
The First 125 Years Of
Women Lawyers
In Illinois

Susan J. Schwartz
Partner

Renee Blahuta

Mary E. Doherty

Michelle E. Meklir

Margaret M. Power

CORBOY & DEMETRIO
A PROFESSIONAL CORPORATION

The female attorneys of

SEYFARTH, SHAW, FAIRWEATHER & GERALDSON

honor the achievement of Alta Hulett,
who, 125 years ago,
became the first woman admitted to the Bar in Illinois

Chicago

Staci S. Beck
Janice L. Block
Danielle M. Calucchia
Rose Marie J. Chidichimo
Kelli L. Christenson
Carrie H. Clark
Stacey Loftus Cohen
Cassandra L. Curry
Pamela A. Davidson
Hillary A. Ebach
Marcy S. Edwards
Brenda H. Feis
Kathryn Hamilton Fink
Ana M. Flynn
Joan E. Gale
Susan F. Gallagher

Katharine E. Goldberg
Keri B. Goldstein
Patricia L. Gruber
Tonya R. Hanson
Amy Hartman
Yvette A. Heintzelman
Janet C. Hershman
Valerie J. Hoffman
Hallie G. Hohner
Patricia L. Hubbard
Liane J. Jackson
S. Leigh Jeter
Megan Kelly-Harris
Mary K. Klimesh
Deborah A. Kop
Michelle L. Kraft

Dixie Lee Laswell
Jill D. Leka
Laura A. Lindner
Barbara K. Lundergan
Marcia A. Mahoney
Marilyn H. Marchetti
Stephanie L. Marks
Lisa L. Marre
Ellen E. McLaughlin
Kristin E. Michaels
Cynthia C. Mooney
Jill S. Mulderink
Camille A. Olson
Jeryl L. Olson
Dianne M. Onichimowski
Kristin Jones Pierre

Allegra R. Rich
Theresa A. Robbins
Marya H. Savich
Kathleen R. Schwappach
Ann M. Scruggs
Dawn E. Sellstrom
Joy Sellstrom
Margaret A. Sewell
Kimberly A. Sipes-Early
Susannah A. Smetana
Eugenia Roig Sockel
Elizabeth P. Strand
Michele S. Suggs
Elaine M. Taussig
Debra A. Winiarski
Sandra P. Zemm

Atlanta

Denice S. Burch
Lisa T. Hale
Brenda D. Page
Ashley Watson

Houston

Kay L. Burkhalter
Renee M. Dominigue
Kristina M. Kerwin
Gloria M. Portela

Washington, D.C.

Anita Barondes
Grace Bateman
Sara M. Beiro Farabow
Adria Benner
Susan C. Benner
Shane J. Brennan
Lesa L. Carter
Karla Grossenbacher
Elizabeth L. (Betsy) Lewis
Rachel Sens
Trisa J. Thompson
Erica A. Watkins
Beth C. Wolffe

San Francisco

Elizabeth Blomberg
Kathleen G. Cahill
Kari J. Erickson
Michele D. Floyd
Amy R. Gustafson
Denise R. Hannan
Michelle Lemley
Kathryn K. Morrison
Ann M. O'Regan
Suzanne L. Page
Kimberly Papillon
Helen Posnansky
Claudia Renert
Luanne Sacks
Marthe C. Stanek
Sue J. Stott
Victoria Walter

New York

Laurie E. Almon
Mara-Louise Anzalone
Ellen Baumann
Lisa Bernstein
Tracy Missett
Lisa Reisman
Joyce Sun
Michelle Toll

Sacramento

Patricia K. Almon
Michelle M. Casey
Martha Michael Gates
Kristin White Maxwell

Los Angeles

Corrine Chandler
Barbara A. Fitzgerald
Georgeanne Henshaw
Gaye E. Hertan
Patricia A. Kinaga
Barbara T. Lindemann
Philecia L. Moore
Lorraine H. O'Hara
Laura Wilson Shelby
Diana Tabacopoulos
Vivian L. Williams
Michelle L. Youtz

First Woman Admitted to Illinois Bar
1873-1998
125th Anniversary

55 E. Monroe St. ◆ Suite 4200 ◆ Chicago, IL 60603 ◆ (312) 346-8000

The Past and Present Chairs of
The CBA's Alliance for Women

Salute the First 125 Years of Women Lawyers in Illinois and the First 100 Illinois Women Lawyers

The Determination, Confidence, Commitment and Achievement of these First Women are an Inspiration and Challenge to the CBA's Alliance for Women

Laurel G. Bellows
Elaine S. Fox • Dixie Lee Laswell
Judge Joan B. Gottschall • Bridget M. O'Keefe
Jennifer T. Nijman • Kaarina Salovaara
Janet M. Koran • Elizabeth Turley

"If I have seen further than you, it is by standing upon the shoulders of Giants."

CELEBRATING 125 YEARS OF WOMEN PRACTICING LAW IN ILLINOIS

OFFICES WORLDWIDE
CHICAGO HOUSTON LOS ANGELES NEW YORK WASHINGTON, D.C.
BERLIN COLOGNE LONDON

INDEPENDENT MEXICO CITY CORRESPONDENT
JAUREGUI, NAVARRETE, NADER Y ROJAS

INDEPENDENT PARIS CORRESPONDENT:
LAMBERT ARMENIADES & LEE

WWW.MAYERBROWN.COM

LORD, BISSELL & BROOK

A Journey of a Thousand Miles Begins with One Step.
Chinese Proverb

We salute Alta Hulett, the first woman admitted to the Illinois Bar, and the 82 women at Lord, Bissell & Brook who have made the journey after her. To the following women, our partners, we especially recognize the intelligence, diligence and passion they bring to the practice of law:

Margaret M. Anderson
M. Elizabeth Bennett
Marilee Clausing
Patricia J. Foltz
Laura J. Ginett
Leisa J. Hamm
W. Muzette Hill
Bobbe Hirsh
Diane I. Jennings
Celeste M. King

Karen J. Kowal
Janet Otsuka Love
Kay W. McCurdy
Kathryn Montgomery Moran
Judy Platt Perlman
Catalina J. Sugayan
Jane H. Veldman
Ann Marie Walsh
M. J. Yardley

Chicago • Los Angeles • Atlanta • New York
Oak Brook • Rockford • London

We Salute
The First 125 Years Of
Women Lawyers
In Illinois

Robert A. Clifford

Clifford Law Offices, P.C.
120 North LaSalle Street
Chicago, Illinois 60602
(312) 899-9090

HELEN W. NIES
1925-1996

In tribute to our first woman partner in 1966, a truly
pioneering woman and genuine friend who became
Chief Judge of the United States Court of Appeals for
the Federal Circuit in 1990.

The women of Foley & Lardner's Chicago office salute *"The First 100 Women Lawyers in Illinois,"* on this significant anniversary.

FOLEY & LARDNER

ATTORNEYS AT LAW

One IBM Plaza
330 North Wabash Avenue, Suite 3300
Chicago, IL 60611-3608

312-755-1900

CHICAGO   JACKSONVILLE   LOS ANGELES   MADISON   MILWAUKEE   ORLANDO   SACRAMENTO
SAN DIEGO   SAN FRANCISCO   TALLAHASSEE   TAMPA   WASHINGTON, D.C.   WEST PALM BEACH

GLOBALEX ALLIANCE MEMBER OFFICES WORLDWIDE

The Law Firm of
RUDNICK & WOLFE

We are proud to recognize
the women of the firm and their
many valuable contributions.

At Rudnick & Wolfe we recognize
that individual contributions
strengthen the firm.
Committed to diversity,
we value people
as our greatest asset.

RUDNICK & WOLFE
Chicago • Tampa • Washington, DC

JENNER & BLOCK IS PROUD TO CARRY ON THE TRADITION STARTED BY ALTA HULETT 125 YEARS AGO.

We have long lived by the principal that talent, commitment and the capacity to work hard, to excell, and to flourish professionally are in no way tied to gender, race or religion. We would like to take this opportunity to celebrate the invaluable contributions that women have made to the Bar and to salute the many women of Jenner & Block.

Cathryn Albrecht	Catherine Steege	Heidi Kitrosser
Jacqueline Bares	Barbara Steiner	Kristin Kruska
Debbie Berman	Maryann Waryjas	Ileana Kutler
Patricia Bronte	Catherine Wassberg	Christina Landgraf
Susan Carlson	Jessica Aspen	Deanne Maynard
Julie Carpenter	Kathleen Banar	Julie Montz
Theresa Chmara	Julie Bentz	Susan Moore
Cecelia Comito	Liz Appel Blue	Nadia Nagib
Deirdre Connell	Katherine Boychuk	Deborah Neal
Maureen Del Duca	Celiza Braganca	Rachelle Niedzwiecki
Natalia Delgado	Traci Braun	Jennifer Oosterbaan
Nicole Finitzo	Kara Novaco Brockmeyer	Julia Perkins
Paula Goedert	Elena Broder	Christine Picker
Lynn Grayson	Melissa Brown	Megan Poetzel
Joan Hall	Karen Bruntrager	Joyce Pollack
Ann Kappler	Jennifer Burke	Suzanne Prysak
Katherine Levy	Christy Campbell	Sherry Reading
Susan Levy	Elizabeth Abbene Coleman	Meg Reynolds
Teri Lindquist	Andrea Despotes	Jennifer Salvatore
Linda Listrom	Pamela Dicarlantonio	Shilpa Satoskar
Gretchen Livingston	Cynthia Drew	Ruth Schoenmeyer
Shelley Malinowski	Kristina Entner	Annemarie Schuller
Terri Mascherin	Felicia Franco-Feinberg	Christine Silverglade
Nory Miller	Gabriel Fuentes	Jodi Simala
Gail Morse	Johna Gaffke	Margaret Simpson
Kit Pierson	Erika George	Amy Skaggs
Susan Podolsky	Holly Georgell	Caroline Soodek
Rebecca Raftery	Heather Gerken	Katherine Strandburg
Carla Rozycki	Michelle Goodman	Mary Talarico
Stephanie Scharf	Valerie Grissom	Laura Tenbroeck
Gabrielle Sigel	Sarah Hardgrove	Aylice Toohey
Rochelle Slater	Laurel Haskell	Charlotte Wager
Lise Spacapan	Jodie Kelley	Kial Young
	Christine Kessler	

JENNER & BLOCK
CHICAGO · LAKE FOREST · WASHINGTON, D.C.

SIDLEY & AUSTIN

is Pleased to Honor

Alice M. Bright

We are pleased to honor the memory of our first woman partner, Alice M. Bright.

For 25 years following her admission to the firm in 1956, Alice, President of the Women's Bar Association of Illinois 1955-1956, brought to our firm intelligence, thoroughness and deep concern for her clients, and paved the way for the more than 70 women partners who have followed her.

— *The Partners of Sidley & Austin.*

ONE FIRST NATIONAL PLAZA • CHICAGO, ILLINOIS 60603
(312) 853-7000 • WWW.SIDLEY.COM

CHICAGO DALLAS LOS ANGELES NEW YORK WASHINGTON, D.C.
LONDON SINGAPORE TOKYO

THE BROWN ENVIRONMENTAL LAW GROUP, P.C.

35 EAST WACKER DRIVE, SUITE 1356
CHICAGO, ILLINOIS 60601-2102

312/236-1450

CHANGING THE WORLD
ONE BRIEF AT A TIME

ALL LAW – ALL WOMEN

JOHNINE J. BROWN   MARY BURKE

JULIE D. MELVIN   BARBARA A. FITZGERALD

SHEILA H. DEELY   TRACEY I. HOOKER

Certified women-owned business enterprise

BEIJING
BOSTON
BRUSSELS
CHICAGO
FRANKFURT
HONG KONG
HOUSTON
LONDON
LOS ANGELES
MOSCOW
NEWARK
NEW YORK
PALO ALTO
PARIS
PRAGUE
SAN FRANCISCO
SINGAPORE
SYDNEY
TOKYO
TORONTO
WASHINGTON, D.C.
WILMINGTON

SKADDEN ARPS SLATE MEAGHER & FLOM LLP & AFFILIATES

Skadden, Arps congratulates the Chicago Bar Association's Alliance For Women on the 125th anniversary of women lawyers in Illinois.

ALTHEIMER &GRAY

salutes the 125th anniversary
of women lawyers in Illinois and
pays special tribute to those
who are partners in our firm

Marlene R. Abrams
Cathleen H. Albrecht
Rita M. Alliss
Alena Bányaiová
Melanie Rovner Cohen
Alexandra R. Cole
Susan J. Daley
Faye B. Feinstein
Judith A. Gold

Donna M. Guerin
Jaroslawa Z. Johnson
Nancy L. Kasko
Carol S. Lepman
Bridget M. O'Keefe
Jeanine M. Pisoni
Anita J. Ponder
Audrey E. Selin
Julie A. Swanson

We also honor our 41 women associates
and all women in the firm who have
supported our service to clients since 1915.

ALTHEIMER & GRAY
10 South Wacker Drive
Chicago, Illinois 60606
Tel: (312) 715-4000
Fax: (312) 715-4800
http://www.altheimer.com

Chicago • Washington, D.C. • Warsaw • Prague
Kyiv • Bratislava • Istanbul • Shanghai • Bucharest

WINSTON & STRAWN

In 1873, Alta M. Hulett began
practice as the first woman attorney
in Illinois. Gradually others followed,
including Lizetta Strawn, cousin to
Winston & Strawn name partner Silas Strawn.

The ranks of women joining the legal
profession have continued to grow over the years,
and today there are more than 13,700 women
attorneys registered in the state of Illinois.

Winston & Strawn salutes the achievements
of women lawyers in Illinois

125 years
1873 - 1998

CHICAGO • NEW YORK • WASHINGTON, D.C. • GENEVA • PARIS

Tressler,
Soderstrom,
Maloney & Priess
is proud to acknowledge
and congratulate its
women lawyers

Landau, Omahana & Kopka
Acknowledges its Appreciation for our Extraordinary Women

PARTNERS: Byron L. Landau, **Gail Allyn Omahana**, Robert J. Kopka, Timothy M. Palumbo, Andrew D. Ellbogen, Gene A. Pinkus, **Mary E. Rosen**, Creed T. Tucker, **Susan Abbott Schwartz**, Lawrence M. Hansen, Mark L. Dolin, Joseph M. Forte, **Beth C. Boggs**, Robert A. Bower, John S. Kenefick, **Anne M. Shaw**, Glenn L. Silverii, Lancaster Smith, Jr., Gregory M. Bokota, James H. Milstone, Michael A. Aspy, Paul E. Garfinkel, **Pamela K. Harman**, J. Kevin Kindred, John J. Pawloski, Michael K. Siebenhaar

ASSOCIATES: **Pamela J. Anselmo**, Michael R. Baggot, Mark R. Bates, **Tricia G. Bellich**, Robert L. Belmonte, Brian C. Berger, Paul A. Bezney, Brian W. Bishop, W. Alan Bradley, **Sheryl A. Bradtke**, Garrett V. Conover, Todd M. Conover, Christopher H. Cross, Andrew D. Dillon, J Alexander Dillon, Thomas S. Ehrhardt, Paul J. Evans, Daniel E. Falb, Thomas B. Felix, Michael B. Gerstle, **Cynthia J. Grah**, Wayne A. Harris, Kevon V. Howald, **Barbara Kalobratsos**, **Victoria Parent-Karasik**, Stephen M. Koers, Scott K. Kubis, **Brenda J. Marcus**, Timothy G. Merker, Eric E. Meyer, Warren G. Michaelis, Timothy W. Mizerowski, James D. Nations, **Cris L. Nelson**, James E. O'Gallagher, Thomas M. Pavelko, Robert G. Pennell, Christopher J. Petersen, Michael J. Progar, Radford R. Raines, III, Michael J. Ripes, Barry A. Robin, Thomas E. Rosta, David F. Ryan, Robert P. Sass, Randall E. Server, **Angela J. Sorrell**, Leon N. Stiles, Jr., **Elizabeth Felt Wakeman**, Brian S. Weinstock, David J. Yates, Alan S. Zelkowitz

OFFICES:

500 North State College Boulevard, Suite 1260 ● Orange, CA 92868-1638
(714) 978-9630 ● Fax (714) 978-9690

23 South First Street ● Belleville, IL 62220-2029
(618) 746-9540 ● Fax (618) 746-9541

222 North LaSalle Street, Suite 200 ● Chicago, IL 60601-1005
(312) 630-9630 ● Fax (312) 630-9001

1001 Warrenville Road, Suite 255 ● Lisle, IL 60532-1393
(630) 434-9630 ● Fax (630) 434-9644

50 Lakeview Parkway, Suite 134 ● Vernon Hills, IL 60061-1527
(847) 918-4700 ● Fax (847) 918-4780

11611 North Meridian Street, Suite 706 ● Carmel, IN 46032-4542
(317) 846-6700 ● Fax (317) 846-6701

8585 Broadway Street, Suite 480 ● Merrillville, IN 46410-7001
(219) 769-9630 ● Fax (219) 769-9675

100 East Wayne Street, Suite 455 ● South Bend, IN 46601-2353
(219) 288-3270 ● Fax (219) 288-3280

26877 Northwestern Highway, Suite 408 ● Southfield, MI 48034-8418
(248) 208-8400 ● Fax (248) 208-8410

7912 Bonhomme Avenue, Suite 400 ● St. Louis, MO 63105-1912
(314) 726-2310 ● Fax (314) 726-2360

5430 LBJ Freeway, Suite 980 ● Dallas, TX 75240-6248
(972) 503-0100 ● (972) 503-0110

Congratulations

on the

125th Anniversary of

Women Lawyers in Illinois

KIRKLAND & ELLIS

Chicago
200 East Randolph Drive
Chicago, IL 60601
Tel. 312-861-2000

Los Angeles
300 South Grand Avenue
Suite 3000
Los Angeles, CA 90071
Tel. 213-680-8400

Washington
655 Fifteenth Street, N.W.
Washington, D.C. 20005-5793
Tel. 202-879-5000

New York
Citicorp Center
153 East 53rd Street
New York, NY 10022-4675
Tel. 212-446-4800

London
Kirkland & Ellis International
International Financial Centre
Old Broad Street
London, EC2N 1HQ
England
Tel. +44-171-816-8700

Wildman, Harrold, Allen & Dixon

salutes

The First 100 Women Lawyers in Illinois

and proudly acknowledges
the contributions of its women attorneys

Laura K. Bancroft	*Robin R. Lake*
Kathryn S. Bedward	*Gracelyn A. Leon*
Erin L. Bishop	*Susan J. Magar*
Kristin M. Buchholz	*Heather H. Martin*
Karen Buschardt-Pisarczyk	*Patricia L. McCarthy*
Kathie M. Contois	*Stephanie B. Miller*
Helen Contos	*Kelly L. Murray*
Jill A. Cuba	*Lily R. Nazerian*
Elisa L. Davis	*Sarah L. Olson*
Anne-Marie M. Dega	*Martha D. Owens*
Maria F. DiLorenzo	*Barbara M. Prohaska*
Vilia M. Drazdys	*Beth S. Rubin*
Karen Ecanow	*Lisa S. Simmons*
Diane G. Elder	*Linda E. Spring*
Kathy Pinkstaff Fox	*Jill Sulzberg*
Nancy J. Fuller	*Marlo Trocchio-Serritella*
Helaine Heydemann	*Jeanne E. Walker*
Dara J. Keidan	*Jennifer K. Walter*
Elizabeth M. Keiley	*Susan W. Wiles*
Anne G. Kimball	*Joleen S. Willis*
Michone J. Kuhlman	

WILDMAN, HARROLD, ALLEN & DIXON
225 WEST WACKER DRIVE
CHICAGO, ILLINOIS 60606-1229
312/201-2000   FAX: 312/201-2555

1961 Downer Place	4300 Commerce Court	404 West Water, P. O. Box 890
Aurora, Illinois 60506	Lisle, Illinois 60532	Waukegan, Illinois 60079
630/892-7021	630/955-0555	847/625-5550
Fax: 630/892-7158	Fax: 630/955-0662	Fax: 847/625-5555

http://www.whad.com

The Illinois women lawyers of

Gardner, Carton & Douglas salute

Alta Hulett

for her extraordinary will

and remarkable achievements

Kathleen M. Allen • Susan W. Ausman • Mona L. Bentz • Maja A. Berlin • Gail J. Berritt • Deborah F. Birndorf • Nancy M. Borders • Deborah H. Bornstein • M. Suzanne Bosch • Jennifer R. Breuer • Bernadette M. Broccolo • Tara Burke • Roxane C. Busey • Crystal Pruess Bush • Natalie M. Cadavid • Barbara A. Cronin • Mary Beth Cyze • Peggy A. Davis • Mary M. Donners • Ann M. Donohue • Noelle C. Dye • Karen A. Erikson • Karin J. Flynn • Angela Foster-Rice • Susan M. Franzetti • Wendy Freyer • Linda A. Green • Heidemarie Gregoriev • Carol M. Hines • Sally Doubet King • Nancy Laethem • Frances P. LaFleur • Marielle V. Lifshitz • Katherine K. Lobo • Lisa A. Martin • Joan McCarthy • Helen J. McSweeney • Joyce L. Meyer • Tracey L. Mihelic • Maureen A. Miller • Kathleen Mulligan • Deena Newlander • Katherine N. O'Connell • Mildred V. Palmer • Paulita Pike-Bokhari • Tracy L. Prosser • Lindsay N. Purcell • Sarah F. Rivera • Katherine O. Robinson • Kimberly K. Rubel • Roberta Saielli • Debra J. Schnebel • Lori Shannon • Eileen L. Strang • Andrea Stulgies-Clauss • Connie M. Tameling • Stacy L. Thomas • Catherine M. Thomson • Sherrie Travis • Linn M. Visscher • Susan M. Wagner • Priscilla A. Walter • Donna S. Wetzler • Mary G. Wilson • Elaine C. Zacharakis

GARDNER, CARTON & DOUGLAS

321 North Clark Street
Suite 3400
Chicago, Illinois 60610
(312) 644-3000

1301 K Street, N.W.
Suite 900, East Tower
Washington, D.C. 20005
(202) 408-7100

A Salute To The Three Women Presidents Of The Chicago Bar Association

PATRICIA C. BOBB
Current President
(1997-98)

ESTHER R. ROTHSTEIN
First Woman President
(1977-78)

LAUREL G. BELLOWS
Second Woman President
(1991-92)

You Are An Inspiration To All Lawyers!

THE CHICAGO BAR ASSOCIATION
FOUNDED 1874

Brittain Sledz Morris & Slovak

We celebrate those who went first and those who enrich our firm today

PATRICIA COSTELLO SLOVAK   MARY AILEEN O'CALLAGHAN

JANE M. MCFETRIDGE   CHRISTINE G. UHLIG

MAYA K. EWING   WENDY L. NUTT

KEARNEY W. KILENS

140 SOUTH DEARBORN STREET   CHICAGO, ILLINOIS 60603   312.346.4515

ON THE 125TH ANNIVERSARY
OF WOMEN LAWYERS IN ILLINOIS

WE PROUDLY AND GRATEFULLY ACKNOWLEDGE
THE ACCOMPLISHMENTS OF OUR WOMEN LAWYERS

Cynthia A. Homan, Doris Loew, Mary M. Squyres,
Barbara A. Larsen, Natalie D. Kadievitch, Alice O. Martin,
Colleen C. Butler, Stephanie S. Conis, Nanette M. Norton,
Laura Beth Miller, Karen L. Shannon, Emilia F. Cannella,
LaTonya T. Washington, Carmen T. Matos, Donna S. Hennessy

BRINKS
HOFER
GILSON
&LIONE

A Professional Corporation
Intellectual Property Attorneys

www.brinkshofer.com

BAKER & McKENZIE
ATTORNEYS AT LAW

We congratulate the Chicago Bar Foundation's Alliance for Women on the occasion of the 125th Anniversary of Women Lawyers in Illinois. We also take this opportunity to acknowledge our Chicago office women partners and associates for their many contributions and achievements:

Ellenore Angelidis	Regina Atkins	Lynn Baker
Karin Bensinger	Leslie Bertagnolli	Andrea Bertone
Suzanne Bish	Barrie Brejcha	Lisa Brogan
Andrea Camargo	Sarah Rudolph Cole	Regine Corrado
Jennifer DeLisle	Simone Dias	Carrie DiSanto
Christina Edson	Cintya Everett	Sarah Fandell
Tamara Frantzen	Patricia Gallagher	Amy Gray
Ashley Hall	Karen Kuenster	Ingrid Lenhardt
Elizabeth Lewis	Maura Ann McBreen	Mary Jo Naples Miller
Pamela Mills	Elizabeth Mitchell	Betsy Stelle Morgan
Susan Devendorf Newman	Patricia O'Brien	Joan Richman
Suzanne Russell	Mary Samsa	Erika Schechter
Julie Sherman	Cheryl Slusarchuk	Maureen Smith
Barbara Spudis	Tanya Witt	Mary Buck Young
Jia Zhao		

THE PARTNERS OF

ARONBERG GOLDGEHN DAVIS & GARMISA

RECOGNIZE THE CONTRIBUTION OF WOMEN IN LAW AND SALUTE

OUR PARTNER

DEBORAH G. COLE

AND OUR ASSOCIATES

LISA J. BRODSKY
JACQUELINE SHIM BRYANT
CAROL A. MARTIN
SUSAN H. MENDELSOHN
KELLI A. TORONYI
DAWN C. WRONA

MILLER SHAKMAN HAMILTON KURTZON & SCHLIFKE
is pleased to have the opportunity to honor

Ruth Goldman, Partner

Graduate, University of Chicago Law School, 1947
Associate, 1968 to 1977
Partner, 1977 to present
Member and President, Highland Park
        Board of Education, 1963 to 1969
Member, Lake County Building Comm., 1977 to 1980
Board Member and Vice President, Citizen's
        Information Service of Illinois, 1978 to 1994
Frequent lecturer on estate planning for women

Hon. Elaine E. Bucklo, Former Partner

Graduate, Northwestern University
        School of Law, 1972
Associate, 1974 to 1977
Partner, 1977 to 1979 [Miller Shakman
        predecessor firm Devoe, Shadur & Krupp]

U.S. Magistrate Judge, 1985 to 1994
U.S. District Judge, 1994 to present
Northern District of Illinois

Miller Shakman Women Partners: Ruth Goldman, Geraldine Soat Brown, Diane F. Klotnia
Women Associates: Julie H. Friedman, Sharon Zaban Letchinger, Jennifer A. Sachs

Schuyler, Roche, & Zwirner

a Professional Corporation

Shareholder
Alison Barkley

Partners
Dominique M. Frigo
Catherine C. Gryczan
Cheryl A. Kettler
Carol A. McGuire

Associates
Dolores Ayala
Emily C. Balfe
Sara E. Elder
Laurie A. Hybl

SRZ celebrates the contributions to the legal profession made by all our women attorneys and all women attorneys

130 E. Randolph, Suite 3800, Chicago
312.565.2400   www.srzlaw.com

BELL, BOYD & LLOYD

Joins the

Chicago Bar Association
Alliance for Women

in honoring
the 125th anniversary of
Women Lawyers in Illinois

Bell, Boyd & Lloyd
Serving the business community since 1888

Three First National Plaza, Suite 3300
Chicago, Illinois 60602

KIESLER & BERMAN

Congratulates and salutes
the women lawyers of Illinois
with special recognition to
the women lawyers of K&B:

Patti M. Deuel
Donna D. Ciancio
Mary E. Haeger
Shari J. Kalik
Cynthia A. Meister
Shannon F. O'Shea
Jeanne M. Zeiger

KIESLER & BERMAN
Attorneys at Law
188 West Randolph Street
Chicago, IL 60601-2970
Telephone: (312) 332-2840
Fax: (312) 332-4547

THE FIRST GENERATION OF women lawyers shared not only a collective dream but a righteous journey hard-earned, hard-fought, hard-pressed. Their tenacity of purpose and steady courage reach across the years to proclaim the oneness of women and men in the practice of law.

Much Shelist Freed Denenberg Ament Bell & Rubenstein, P.C.
ATTORNEYS AT LAW

THE LAW OFFICES OF
GWEN VERONICA CARROLL, LTD.

125 years of Women in the Law... Bravo!

445 West Erie Street
Suite 205
Chicago, Illinois 60610

(p) 312.202.0800
(f) 312.202.0805

gvcarroll@counsel.com
http://www.gvc-law.com